BEST OF
Country Cooking

Cranberry Bog Bars (p. 163)

© 2020 RDA Enthusiast Brands, LLC.
1610 N. 2nd St., Suite 102, Milwaukee WI 53212-3906
All rights reserved. Taste of Home is a registered trademark of RDA Enthusiast Brands, LLC.
Visit us at tasteofhome.com for other Taste of Home books and products.

International Standard Book Number: 978-1-61765-959-1
International Standard Series Number: 2166-0522
Component Number: 117000062H

Executive Editor: Mark Hagen
Senior Art Director: Raeann Thompson
Editor: Hazel Wheaton
Designer: Jazmin Delgado
Senior Editor, Copy Desk: Dulcie Shoener

Front Cover
Photographer: Mark Derse
Senior Set Stylist: Melissa Franco
Food Stylist: Josh Rink

Pictured on front cover:
The Best Beef Stew, p. 89

Pictured on title page:
Cherry Tomato Salad, p. 52

Pictured on back cover:
Fontina Rolled Chicken, p. 87; 7UP Pound Cake, p. 177; Spiced Pickled Beets, p. 31

Printed in China
1 3 5 7 9 10 8 6 4 2

Come Home to Country Cooking!

GREAT FAMILY MEALS MAKE GREAT FAMILY MEMORIES!

Quality ingredients, lovingly prepared, make for good food and warm memories. Treat your family to the best in home cooking with satisfying, comforting dishes—from snacks to stews, appetizers to side dishes, casseroles to angel food cake, and everything between!

Home cooks from across the nation (and beyond!) have shared their favorite recipes with us, and now we're sharing them with you in this newest edition of *Best of Country Cooking*. Fresh-baked breads, hearty soups, tempting pies and cookies, tasty vegetables, and savory roasts and casseroles—everything you remember from your grandmother's kitchen is here, ready for you to share with your family. And every recipe has been approved by the experts in the *Taste of Home* Test Kitchen, so you know they'll work right the first time.

LOOK INSIDE FOR:

Contest Winner

Blue-Ribbon Recipes

The special blue-ribbon icon calls out recipes that were chosen by our tasting experts as a *Taste of Home* contest winner. One bite and you'll know why they were winners!

Freeze It!

If you're looking for recipes you can have ready at short notice, check for the ❄ icon—with these in the freezer, you'll always have something delicious to serve family and guests.

The standout recipes in *Best of Country Cooking* deliver everything you need for family dinners, potluck parties, weekend cookouts, holiday feasts and more. Make sure your kitchen is the heart of your home by serving up delicious down-home meals that your family will always remember!

CONTENTS

Snacks & Beverages

When you're looking for the perfect recipe to start the party off right, take a look at the 30 recipes in this chapter! For party appetizers, light meals or snacks, these small bites are exactly what you need. A selection of delectable drinks, both hot and cold, help you entertain guests any time of year without opening a soda bottle!

SESAME-GARLIC PUMPKIN SEEDS

This "everything" mix of pumpkin seeds with other seeds and seasoning is a fun treat— a lively way to use the seeds left over from your Halloween jack-o'-lantern!
—*Danielle Lee, Sewickley, PA*

- -

Prep: 10 min. • **Bake:** 35 min. • **Makes:** 2 cups

1	large egg white
1	Tbsp. canola oil
2	cups fresh pumpkin seeds
1	tsp. sesame seeds
1	tsp. poppy seeds
1	tsp. dried minced onion
1	tsp. dried minced garlic
¾	tsp. kosher salt
½	tsp. caraway seeds

Preheat oven to 325°. In a small bowl, whisk egg white and oil until frothy. Add the pumpkin seeds; toss to coat. Stir in sesame seeds, poppy seeds, onion, garlic, salt and caraway seeds. Spread in a single layer in a parchment-lined 15x10x1-in. baking pan. Bake 35-40 minutes or until dry and golden brown, stirring every 10 minutes.

¼ cup: 95 cal., 5g fat (1g sat. fat), 0 chol., 190mg sod., 9g carb. (0 sugars, 3g fiber), 4g pro. **Diabetic exchanges:** 1 fat, ½ starch.

SMOOTH SWEET TEA

Baking soda eliminates bitterness in this smooth and easy-to-sip tea. It has just the right amount of sugar so it's not too sweet.
—*kelseylouise, tasteofhome.com*

- -

Takes: 15 min. + chilling • **Makes:** 7 servings

2	cups water
6	black tea bags
⅛	tsp. baking soda
⅔	cup sugar
6	cups cold water

In a small saucepan, bring 2 cups of water to a boil. Remove from the heat; add tea bags. Cover and steep for 10 minutes. Discard tea bags. Sprinkle baking soda into a 2-qt. pitcher. Transfer tea to pitcher; stir in sugar. Add cold water. Refrigerate until chilled.

1 cup: 76 cal., 0 fat (0 sat.fat), 0 chol., 29mg sod., 20g carb. (19g sugars, 0 fiber), 0 pro.

STRAWBERRY SALSA

This deliciously different salsa is versatile, fresh-tasting and colorful. People are usually surprised to see a salsa made with strawberries, but it's excellent over grilled chicken and pork and as a dip with corn chips.
—*Jean Giroux, Belchertown, MA*

Takes: 15 min. + chilling • **Makes:** 4 cups

- 1 pint fresh strawberries, chopped
- 4 plum tomatoes, seeded and chopped
- 1 small red onion, finely chopped
- 1 to 2 medium jalapeno peppers, minced
- 2 Tbsp. lime juice
- 1 Tbsp. olive oil
- 2 garlic cloves, minced

In a large bowl, combine strawberries, tomatoes, onion and jalapenos. Stir in the lime juice, oil and garlic. Cover and refrigerate for 2 hours. Serve with cooked poultry or pork, or as a dip for tortilla chips.

Note: Wear disposable gloves when cutting hot peppers; the oils can burn skin. Avoid touching your face.

¼ cup: 19 cal., 1g fat (0 sat. fat), 0 chol., 1mg sod., 3g carb. (2g sugars, 1g fiber), 0 pro.
Diabetic exchanges: Free food.

RHUBARB CITRUS PUNCH

Rhubarb grows abundantly in our large farm garden, so I have a lot of tried-and-true rhubarb recipes! I make this punch for summertime gatherings or for special occasions with our extended family.
—*Ina Frey, St. Clemens, ON*

Takes: 30 min. + chilling
Makes: about 12 cups

- 8 cups diced fresh or frozen rhubarb
- 5 cups water
- 1⅓ cups sugar
- 2 cups orange juice
- ¾ cup lemon juice
- 1 qt. ginger ale, chilled
- 1 qt. fresh or frozen strawberries, optional
  Ice cubes

1. In a Dutch oven or large saucepan, simmer rhubarb and water until rhubarb is soft, about 10 minutes. Cool; strain through several layers of cheesecloth, reserving the juice. Return 4 cups of juice to kettle with the sugar. Heat until the sugar is dissolved. Chill. Refrigerate or freeze any remaining juice for a future batch.

2. Combine orange and lemon juices and rhubarb juice mixture. Refrigerate until ready to serve. Just before serving, stir in the ginger ale and, if desired, strawberries. Serve over ice in chilled glasses.

Note: If using frozen rhubarb, measure while still frozen. Thaw completely and drain in a colander, but do not press out the liquid; follow recipe as directed.

1 cup: 153 cal., 0 fat (0 sat. fat), 0 chol., 9mg sod., 39g carb. (35g sugars, 2g fiber), 1g pro.

BLUE CHEESE GARLIC BREAD

This is an irresistible way to dress up an ordinary loaf of bread. Serve these cheesy, garlic-rich slices as appetizers or with a meal.
—*Kevalyn Henderson, Hayward, WI*

- -

Takes: 30 min. • **Makes:** 10 servings

½	cup butter, softened
4	oz. crumbled blue cheese
2	Tbsp. grated Parmesan cheese
1	Tbsp. minced chives
1	tsp. garlic powder
1	loaf (1 lb.) unsliced French bread

1. Preheat oven to 350°. In a small bowl, combine the first 5 ingredients. Cut into the bread to make 1-in.-thick slices, but don't cut all the way through; leave the slices attached at the bottom. Spread the cheese mixture between slices.
2. Wrap loaf in a large piece of heavy-duty foil (about 28x18 in.). Fold foil around bread and seal tightly. Bake until heated through, about 20 minutes. Serve warm.
1 slice: 250 cal., 14g fat (8g sat. fat), 34mg chol., 546mg sod., 24g carb. (1g sugars, 1g fiber), 7g pro.

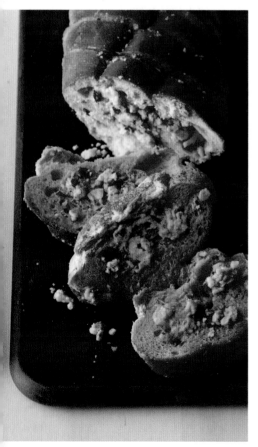

BACON-WRAPPED SWEET POTATO BITES

After making little bacon-wrapped sausages for years, I needed a change. I had an extra sweet potato and half a package of bacon on hand, so I put on my thinking cap and came up with this treat.
—*Kelly Williams, Forked River, NJ*

- -

Prep: 25 min. • **Bake:** 40 min.
Makes: about 2½ dozen

2	Tbsp. butter, melted
½	tsp. salt
½	tsp. cayenne pepper
¼	tsp. ground cinnamon
2	large sweet potatoes (about 1¾ lbs.), peeled and cut into 1-in. cubes
¼	cup packed brown sugar
1	lb. bacon strips, halved
	Maple syrup, warmed

1. Preheat oven to 350°. In a large bowl, mix butter and seasonings. Add sweet potatoes and toss to coat.
2. Wrap 1 piece bacon around each sweet potato cube; secure with a toothpick. Sprinkle with brown sugar. Place on a parchment-lined 15x10x1-in. baking pan.
3. Bake until the bacon is crisp and the sweet potato is tender, 40-45 minutes. Serve with maple syrup.
1 appetizer: 60 cal., 3g fat (1g sat. fat), 7mg chol., 136mg sod., 7g carb. (4g sugars, 1g fiber), 2g pro.

TO PEEL OR NOT?
If you prefer, you don't have to peel sweet potatoes. Simply scrub them to get rid of any dirt and pat them dry.

HEIRLOOM TOMATO GALETTE WITH PECORINO

I found beautiful heirloom tomatoes and had to show them off. In this easy galette, the tomatoes are tangy and the crust is beyond buttery.
—*Jessica Chang, Playa Vista, CA*

- -

Prep: 10 min. + chilling
Bake: 25 min. + cooling • **Makes:** 6 servings

- 1 **cup all-purpose flour**
- 1 **tsp. baking powder**
- ¾ **tsp. kosher salt, divided**
- ½ **cup cold unsalted butter, cubed**
- ½ **cup sour cream**
- 2 **cups cherry tomatoes, halved**
- 3 **oz. Pecorino Romano cheese, thinly sliced**

1. Whisk flour, baking powder and ½ tsp. salt; cut in butter until mixture resembles coarse crumbs. Stir in sour cream until the dough forms a ball. Shape dough into a disk; wrap and refrigerate until firm enough to roll, about 2 hours.
2. Place tomatoes in a colander; toss with the remaining salt. Let stand 15 minutes.
3. Preheat oven to 425°. On a floured sheet of parchment, roll dough into a 12-in. circle. Transfer to a baking sheet.
4. Place cheese slices over the crust to within 2 in. of edge; arrange tomatoes over the cheese. Fold the crust edges over the filling, pleating as you go and leaving the center uncovered. Bake until the crust is golden brown and the cheese is bubbly, about 25 minutes. Cool for 10 minutes before slicing.
1 piece: 317 cal., 23g fat (15g sat. fat), 68mg chol., 559mg sod., 19g carb. (2g sugars, 1g fiber), 9g pro.

HARVEST APPLE CIDER

Fall is apple cider season! I make this comforting cider every year. It smells delicious as it simmers away in my slow cooker!
—*Lesley Geisel, Severna Park, MD*

- -

Prep: 5 min. • **Cook:** 2 hours
Makes: about 2 qt.

- 8 **whole cloves**
- 4 **cups apple cider or juice**
- 4 **cups pineapple juice**
- ½ **cup water**
- 1 **cinnamon stick (3 in.)**
- 1 **tea bag**

1. Place cloves on a double thickness of cheesecloth; bring up the corners of the cloth and tie with kitchen string to form a bag. Place the remaining ingredients in a 3-qt. slow cooker; add the spice bag.
2. Cover and cook on low for 2 hours or until cider reaches desired temperature. Discard the spice bag, cinnamon stick and tea bag before serving.
1 cup: 130 cal., 0 fat (0 sat. fat), 0 chol., 14mg sod., 32g carb. (30g sugars, 0 fiber), 0 pro.

Contest Winner

SIMPLE GUACAMOLE

Because avocados can brown quickly, it's best to make this guacamole just before serving. If you do have to make it a little in advance, place the avocado pit in the guacamole until you're ready to serve.

—*Heidi Main, Anchorage, AK*

- -

Takes: 10 min. • **Makes:** 1½ cups

- 2 **medium ripe avocados**
- 1 **Tbsp. lemon juice**
- ¼ **cup chunky salsa**
- ⅛ **to ¼ tsp. salt**

Peel and chop avocados; place in a small bowl. Sprinkle with lemon juice. Add the salsa and salt; mash coarsely with a fork. Refrigerate until serving.

2 Tbsp.: 53 cal., 5g fat (1g sat. fat), 0 chol., 51mg sod., 3g carb. (0 sugars, 2g fiber), 1g pro.

CARAMELIZED HAM & SWISS BUNS

My next-door neighbor shared this recipe with me, and I simply cannot improve it! You can assemble it ahead of time and then cook it quickly when company arrives. The combo of poppy seeds, ham and cheese, horseradish and brown sugar is so delicious.

—*Iris Weihemuller, Baxter, MN*

- -

Prep: 25 min. + chilling • **Bake:** 30 min.
Makes: 1 dozen

- 1 **pkg. (18 oz.) Hawaiian sweet rolls**
- ½ **cup horseradish sauce**
- ¾ **lb. sliced deli ham**
- 6 **slices Swiss cheese, halved**
- ½ **cup butter, cubed**
- 2 **Tbsp. finely chopped onion**
- 2 **Tbsp. brown sugar**
- 1 **Tbsp. spicy brown mustard**
- 2 **tsp. poppy seeds**
- 1½ **tsp. Worcestershire sauce**
- ¼ **tsp. garlic powder**

1. Spread cut side of roll bottoms with horseradish sauce. Layer with ham and cheese; replace tops. Arrange in a single layer in a greased 13x9-in. baking pan.
2. In a small skillet, heat butter over medium-high heat. Add the chopped onion; cook and stir for 1-2 minutes or until tender. Stir in remaining ingredients. Pour over rolls. Refrigerate, covered, several hours or overnight.
3. Preheat oven to 350°. Bake, covered, 25 minutes. Bake, uncovered, until golden brown, 5-10 minutes longer.

1 sandwich: 315 cal., 17g fat (9g sat. fat), 61mg chol., 555mg sod., 29g carb. (13g sugars, 2g fiber), 13g pro.

═══════════════════════

TWO GREAT VARIATIONS

Swap in corned beef or pastrami for the ham, add a layer of sauerkraut and substitute caraway seeds for poppy seeds, and you have a Reuben version. Or, If you have vegetarians coming for dinner, omit the ham and double the cheese; we like Swiss and cheddar.

BARBECUED MEATBALLS

Grape jelly and chili sauce are the secret ingredients that make these meatballs so fantastic. If I'm serving them at a party, I prepare the meatballs and sauce in advance and reheat them right before guests arrive.
—*Irma Schnuelle, Manitowoc, WI*

- -

Prep: 20 min. • **Cook:** 15 min.
Makes: about 3 dozen

- ½ cup dry bread crumbs
- ⅓ cup finely chopped onion
- ¼ cup whole milk
- 1 large egg, lightly beaten
- 1 Tbsp. minced fresh parsley
- 1 tsp. salt
- 1 tsp. Worcestershire sauce
- ½ tsp. pepper
- 1 lb. lean ground beef (90% lean)
- ¼ cup canola oil
- 1 bottle (12 oz.) chili sauce
- 1 jar (10 oz.) grape jelly

1. In a large bowl, combine the first 8 ingredients. Crumble beef over the mixture and mix well. Shape into 1-in. balls. In a large skillet, brown meatballs in oil on all sides.

2. Remove meatballs from the skillet and drain. In the same pan, combine chili sauce and jelly; cook and stir over medium heat until jelly has melted. Return meatballs to pan; heat through.

1 meatball: 71 cal., 3g fat (1g sat. fat), 13mg chol., 215mg sod., 9g carb. (7g sugars, 0 fiber), 3g pro.

BEER DIP

Ranch dressing mix flavors this fast-to-fix mixture packed with shredded cheese. It pairs perfectly with pretzels. Be careful—once you start eating it, you simply can't stop!
—*Michelle Long, New Castle, CO*

- -

Takes: 5 min. • **Makes:** 3½ cups

- 2 pkg. (8 oz. each) cream cheese, softened
- ⅓ cup beer or nonalcoholic beer
- 1 envelope ranch salad dressing mix
- 2 cups shredded cheddar cheese
  Pretzels

In a large bowl, beat the cream cheese, beer and dressing mix until smooth. Stir in cheddar cheese. Serve with pretzels.

2 Tbsp.: 89 cal., 8g fat (5g sat. fat), 26mg chol., 177mg sod., 1g carb. (0 sugars, 0 fiber), 3g pro.

HAZELNUT HOT CHOCOLATE

Vanilla beans and a hazelnut liqueur like Frangelico lend a sophisticated flavor to this hot chocolate. With such a rich taste, it could be served as a dessert.
—*Michael Compean, Fountain Hills, AZ*

- -

Takes: 25 min. • **Makes:** 22 servings

- 3   **vanilla beans**
- 16   **oz. bittersweet chocolate, divided**
- ½   **cup Nutella**
- 2   **Tbsp. dark brown sugar**
- 1   **Tbsp. sugar**
- ¼   **tsp. salt**
- 9   **cups whole milk**
- 2¾   **cups heavy whipping cream, divided**
- ¾   **cup hazelnut liqueur**
- ¼   **cup chopped hazelnuts, toasted**
     Cinnamon sticks, optional

1. Split vanilla beans in half lengthwise. With a sharp knife, scrape the beans to remove the seeds. Set seeds aside; discard the beans. Chop 15 oz. chocolate. In a large heat-proof bowl, combine the chopped chocolate, Nutella, sugars, salt and vanilla seeds.

2. In a large saucepan, heat the milk and ¾ cup cream over medium heat just until mixture comes to a simmer. Pour the warm milk mixture over the chocolate mixture. Let stand for 1 minute.

3. Meanwhile, whip the remaining cream and shave the remaining chocolate. Whisk the chocolate mixture until smooth; stir in liqueur. Serve with whipped cream, shaved chocolate and chopped hazelnuts. Garnish with a cinnamon stick if desired.

½ cup: 299 cal., 20g fat (10g sat. fat), 29mg chol., 88mg sod., 26g carb. (22g sugars, 2g fiber), 6g pro.

DEVILED EGGS WITH BACON

These yummy deviled eggs went over so well at our summer cookouts, I started making them for holiday dinners as well. The addition of crumbled bacon is a big hit—because who doesn't love bacon?
—*Barbara Reid, Mounds, OK*

- -

Takes: 30 min. • **Makes:** 2 dozen

- 12   **hard-boiled large eggs**
- ⅓   **cup mayonnaise**
- 3   **bacon strips, cooked and crumbled**
- 3   **Tbsp. finely chopped red onion**
- 3   **Tbsp. sweet pickle relish**
- ¼   **tsp. smoked paprika**

Cut eggs in half lengthwise. Remove the yolks; set whites aside. In a small bowl, mash yolks. Add mayonnaise, bacon, onion and relish; mix well. Stuff into egg whites. Refrigerate until serving. Sprinkle with paprika.

1 stuffed egg half: 68 cal., 5g fat (1g sat. fat), 108mg chol., 82mg sod., 1g carb. (1g sugars, 0 fiber), 3g pro.

SESAME CHICKEN DIP

I can't tell you how many times I'm asked to bring this easy dip to holidays, birthday parties or girls' weekend getaways. It's fresh and light, and the Asian flavors make it stand out. The rice crackers are a must!
—Dawn Schutte, Sheboygan, WI

Takes: 30 min. + chilling
Makes: 36 servings

- 2 Tbsp. reduced-sodium soy sauce
- 4 tsp. sesame oil
- 2 garlic cloves, minced
- 4 cups shredded cooked chicken breast
- 3 pkg. (8 oz. each) reduced-fat cream cheese
- 1 jar (10 oz.) sweet-and-sour sauce
- 2 cups chopped fresh baby spinach
- 1 cup thinly sliced green onions (about 8)
- ½ cup chopped salted peanuts
  Sesame rice crackers

1. Mix soy sauce, sesame oil and garlic; toss with chicken. Refrigerate, covered, for at least 1 hour.
2. Spread cream cheese onto a large serving plate; top with sweet-and-sour-sauce, spinach and chicken. Sprinkle with green onions and peanuts. Refrigerate, covered, at least 2 hours. Serve with rice crackers.
¼ cup: 97 cal., 6g fat (3g sat. fat), 25mg chol., 176mg sod., 4g carb. (2g sugars, 0 fiber), 7g pro.

Contest Winner

SPICY ALMONDS

We like to adventure out into the Selkirk mountain range, which surrounds our family cabin. These nuts never tasted better than when we enjoyed them together at the end of an amazing hike. Almonds are extremely nutritious, and when dressed up with a wonderful blend of spices, they go from ordinary to awesome!

—*Gina Myers, Spokane, WA*

Prep: 10 min. • **Bake:** 30 min. + cooling
Makes: 2½ cups

1 Tbsp. sugar
1½ tsp. kosher salt
1 tsp. paprika
½ tsp. ground cinnamon
½ tsp. ground cumin
½ tsp. ground coriander
¼ tsp. cayenne pepper
1 large egg white, room temperature
2½ cups unblanched almonds

1. Preheat oven to 325°. In a small bowl, combine the first 7 ingredients. In another small bowl, whisk egg white until foamy. Add almonds; toss to coat. Sprinkle with the spice mixture; toss to coat.
2. Spread almonds in a single layer in a greased 15x10x1-in. baking pan. Bake for 30 minutes; stir every 10 minutes. Spread on waxed paper to cool completely. Store in an airtight container.

¼ cup: 230 cal., 20g fat (2g sat. fat), 0 chol., 293mg sod., 9g carb. (3g sugars, 4g fiber), 8g pro.

HOT SPINACH SPREAD WITH PITA CHIPS

Warm and cheesy, this spread is absolutely scrumptious served on toasted pita wedges. Its colorful appearance makes a stunning addition to any buffet.

—*Teresa Emanuel, Smithville, MO*

Prep: 30 min. • **Bake:** 20 min.
Makes: 16 servings (4 cups spread)

2 cups shredded Monterey Jack cheese
1 pkg. (10 oz.) frozen chopped spinach, thawed and squeezed dry
1 pkg. (8 oz.) cream cheese, cubed
2 plum tomatoes, seeded and chopped
¾ cup chopped onion
⅓ cup half-and-half cream
1 Tbsp. finely chopped seeded jalapeno pepper
6 pita breads (6 in.)
½ cup butter, melted
2 tsp. lemon-pepper seasoning
2 tsp. ground cumin
¼ tsp. garlic salt

1. Preheat oven to 375°. In a large bowl, combine the first 7 ingredients. Transfer to a greased 1½-qt. baking dish. Bake, uncovered, 20-25 minutes or until bubbly.
2. Meanwhile, cut each pita bread into 8 wedges. Place in two 15x10x1-in. baking pans. Combine the butter, lemon pepper, cumin and garlic salt; brush over the pita wedges.
3. Bake for 7-9 minutes or until crisp. Serve with spinach spread.

Note: Wear disposable gloves when cutting hot peppers; the oils can burn skin. Avoid touching your face.

¼ cup spread with 3 pita wedges: 231 cal., 16g fat (10g sat. fat), 46mg chol., 381mg sod., 15g carb. (1g sugars, 1g fiber), 8g pro.

HAM & CHEESE QUICHES

When I need a festive finger food, this is the recipe I reach for. With cheese in both the crust and the filling, eating one quiche naturally leads to another.
—*Virginia Abraham, Oxford, MS*

- -

Prep: 15 min. + chilling • **Bake:** 30 min.
Makes: 2 dozen

- ½ cup butter
- 1 jar (5 oz.) process sharp cheese spread
- 1 cup all-purpose flour
- 2 Tbsp. water

FILLING

- 1 large egg
- ½ cup milk
- ¼ tsp. salt
- ½ cup finely chopped ham
- ½ cup shredded Monterey Jack cheese

1. In a small bowl, cut butter and cheese spread into flour until well blended. Add water and toss with a fork until a ball forms. Refrigerate for 1 hour.

2. Preheat oven to 350°. Press tablespoonfuls of the butter mixture onto the bottom and up the sides of greased miniature muffin cups.

3. In a bowl, beat the egg, milk and salt. Stir in ham and the Monterey Jack cheese. Spoon a rounded teaspoonful of the egg mixture into each shell. Bake for 30 minutes or until golden brown. Let stand for 5 minutes before serving.

3 mini quiches: 265 cal., 19g fat (12g sat. fat), 81mg chol., 645mg sod., 15g carb. (2g sugars, 0 fiber), 8g pro.

SIMPLE SALMON DIP

This is my go-to dip recipe for summer barbecues. The secret is the green chiles—they add enough heat to keep things lively without being too spicy!
—*Susan Jordan, Denver, CO*

- -

Takes: 15 min. + chilling • **Makes:** 1¼ cups

- 1 pkg. (8 oz.) reduced-fat cream cheese
- 2 Tbsp. canned chopped green chiles
- 1½ tsp. lemon juice
- 2 green onions, chopped, divided
- 2 oz. smoked salmon fillet Assorted crackers or toasted French bread baguette slices

1. In a small bowl, mix cream cheese, green chiles, lemon juice and half of the green onions. Flake salmon into small pieces; stir into the cream cheese mixture. Refrigerate, covered, for at least 2 hours before serving.

2. Top dip with the remaining green onion. Serve with crackers.

3 Tbsp.: 107 cal., 8g fat (5g sat. fat), 29mg chol., 246mg sod., 2g carb. (1g sugars, 0 fiber), 6g pro.

SWEET ONION SKILLET BREAD

Because there are only a few ingredients in this recipe, you'll get the best results if you use the finest-quality foods, like a fresh Vidalia onion and aged Parmesan cheese.

—Lisa Speer, Palm Beach, FL

- -

Prep: 25 min. • **Bake:** 10 min.
Makes: 4 servings

- 1 large sweet onion, thinly sliced
- 2 Tbsp. butter
- 2 Tbsp. olive oil, divided
- 1 can (13.8 oz.) refrigerated pizza crust
- ¼ cup grated Parmesan cheese

1. In a large cast-iron or other ovenproof skillet, saute the onion in butter and 1 Tbsp. oil until softened. Reduce heat to medium-low; cook, stirring occasionally, until golden brown, 15-20 minutes. Set aside.

2. Preheat oven to 450°. Brush the bottom and sides of skillet with the remaining oil. Unroll dough into skillet; flatten dough and build up edge slightly. Top with onion mixture and cheese. Bake until golden brown, 10-12 minutes. Cut into 4 wedges.

1 wedge: 415 cal., 17g fat (5g sat. fat), 19mg chol., 776mg sod., 53g carb. (9g sugars, 2g fiber), 11g pro.

OLD-FASHIONED EGGNOG

Celebrating the holidays with eggnog is an American tradition that dates to Colonial days. I toast the season with a smooth and creamy concoction that keeps family and friends coming back for more.

—Pat Waymire, Yellow Springs, OH

- -

Takes: 40 min. + chilling
Makes: 18 servings (about 3 qt.)

- 12 large eggs
- 1½ cups sugar
- ½ tsp. salt
- 2 qt. whole milk, divided
- 2 Tbsp. vanilla extract
- 1 tsp. ground nutmeg
- 2 cups heavy whipping cream
  Whipped cream, additional nutmeg and cinnamon sticks, optional

1. In a heavy saucepan, whisk together eggs, sugar and salt. Gradually add 1 qt. milk. Cook and stir over low heat until a thermometer reads 160°, about 25 minutes. Pour into a large bowl; stir in vanilla, nutmeg and the remaining milk. Place bowl in an ice-water bath; stir frequently until cool. If mixture separates, process in a blender until smooth. Cover and refrigerate for at least 3 hours.

2. When ready to serve, beat cream on high until soft peaks form; whisk gently into cooled mixture. Pour into a chilled 5-qt. punch bowl. If desired, top with dollops of whipped cream, sprinkle with nutmeg and serve with cinnamon sticks.

¾ cup: 274 cal., 16g fat (9g sat. fat), 165mg chol., 167mg sod., 23g carb. (23g sugars, 0 fiber), 8g pro.

SPICY BUTTERSCOTCH WINGS

We love big-time-spicy chicken wings. I do a caramel sauce to balance the heat, but you could also glaze the wings with melted brown sugar.

—*Aaron Salazar, Westminster, CO*

- -

Prep: 25 min. • **Bake:** 25 min.
Makes: 20 servings

- 2 **lbs. chicken wings**
- 2 **Tbsp. soy sauce**
- 2 **Tbsp. ketchup**
- 2 **Tbsp. Sriracha chili sauce**
- 1 **tsp. pepper**
- 1 **tsp. crushed red pepper flakes**
- 1 **tsp. onion powder**
- ½ **tsp. salt**

BUTTERSCOTCH SAUCE
- ½ **cup sugar**
- ½ **cup 2% milk, warmed**
- 2 **Tbsp. butter**

CRUMB TOPPING
- 1 **Tbsp. butter**
- ½ **cup panko bread crumbs**
- 2 **green onions, sliced diagonally, divided**
- 1 **garlic clove, minced**
- ½ **tsp. salt**
- ½ **tsp. pepper**
- 2 **red bird's eye chili peppers, sliced, optional**

1. Preheat oven to 400°. Using a sharp knife, cut through the 2 wing joints; discard the wing tips. Combine the next 7 ingredients; add wings and toss to coat.
2. Line a 15x10-in. pan with foil; grease with cooking spray. Bake wings in the prepared pan 10 minutes; reduce heat to 350° and bake until juices run clear, 12-15 minutes. Remove from oven; keep warm.
3. Meanwhile, in a small skillet, spread the sugar; cook, without stirring, over medium heat until sugar begins to melt. Gently drag the melted sugar to the center of the pan so it melts evenly. Cook, without stirring, until the melted sugar turns amber. Carefully stir in warm milk and butter. Simmer, stirring frequently, until thickened, 5-7 minutes. Keep warm.
4. For the crumb topping, in a large skillet over medium heat, melt butter; add the bread crumbs, 1 green onion, garlic, salt and pepper. Cook and stir until the bread crumbs are golden brown, about 2 minutes. Set aside.
5. To serve, toss wings in butterscotch sauce. Sprinkle with the crumb topping, the remaining green onion and, if desired, sliced peppers. Serve hot.

1 wing: 100 cal., 5g fat (2g sat. fat), 20mg chol., 312mg sod., 8g carb. (6g sugars, 0 fiber), 5g pro.

SOFT GIANT PRETZELS

My husband and our friends and family love these soft, chewy pretzels. Let your bread machine mix the dough, then all you have to do is shape and bake these fun snacks.

—*Sherry Peterson, Fort Collins, CO*

- -

Prep: 20 min. + rising • **Bake:** 10 min.
Makes: 8 pretzels

1	cup plus 2 Tbsp. water (70° to 80°)
3	cups all-purpose flour
3	Tbsp. brown sugar
1½	tsp. active dry yeast
2	qt. water
½	cup baking soda
	Coarse salt

1. In bread machine pan, place the first 4 ingredients in order suggested by the manufacturer. Select dough setting (check dough after 5 minutes of mixing; add 1 to 2 Tbsp. water or flour if needed).
2. When cycle is completed, turn dough onto a lightly floured surface. Divide into 8 balls. Roll each ball into a 20-in. rope; form each rope into a pretzel shape.
3. Preheat oven to 425°. In a large saucepan, bring water and baking soda to a boil. Drop pretzels into boiling water, 2 at a time; boil for 10-15 seconds. Remove with a slotted spoon; drain on paper towels.
4. Place pretzels on greased baking sheets. Bake until golden brown, 8-10 minutes. Spritz or lightly brush with water. Sprinkle with salt.
1 pretzel: 193 cal., 1g fat (0 sat. fat), 0 chol., 380mg sod., 41g carb. (5g sugars, 1g fiber), 5g pro.

SWEET RASPBERRY TEA

You need only a handful of ingredients to stir together this bright and refreshing sipper. It makes a lovely treat as the weather warms up.
—Taste of Home *Test Kitchen*

Prep: 10 min. • **Cook:** 15 min. + chilling
Makes: 15 servings

- 4 qt. water, divided
- 10 tea bags
- 1 pkg. (12 oz.) frozen unsweetened raspberries, thawed and undrained
- 1 cup sugar
- 3 Tbsp. lime juice

1. In a saucepan, bring 2 qt. water to a boil; remove from heat. Add tea bags; steep, covered, 5-8 minutes according to taste. Discard tea bags.

2. Place raspberries, sugar and the remaining water in a large saucepan; bring to a boil, stirring to dissolve the sugar. Reduce heat; simmer, uncovered, for 3 minutes. Press mixture through a fine-mesh strainer into a bowl; discard the pulp and seeds.

3. In a large pitcher, combine tea, raspberry syrup and lime juice. Refrigerate, covered, until cold.

1 cup: 63 cal., 0 fat (0 sat. fat), 0 chol., 0 sod., 16g carb. (15g sugars, 1g fiber), 0 pro.

CHEESY SAUSAGE STROMBOLI

I must have had a hundred requests for this recipe over the years. Perfect for brunch or as an evening snack, this sausage-filled bread is not tricky to make—and I never have to worry about storing leftovers!
—*Vada McRoberts, Silver Lake, KS*

Prep: 30 min. + rising • **Bake:** 20 min.
Makes: 2 loaves (16 slices each)

- 5 cups all-purpose flour
- 2 Tbsp. sugar
- 2 tsp. salt
- 2 pkg. (¼ oz. each) active dry yeast
- 1½ cups warm water (120° to 130°)
- ½ cup warm 2% milk (120° to 130°)
- 2 Tbsp. butter, melted
- 2 lbs. bulk pork sausage
- 4 cups shredded part-skim mozzarella cheese
- 3 large eggs, divided use
- 1 tsp. minced fresh basil or ¼ tsp. dried basil
- 2 Tbsp. grated Parmesan cheese

1. In a large bowl, combine the flour, sugar, salt and yeast. Add water, milk and butter; beat on low until well combined Turn onto a well-floured surface; knead until smooth and elastic, 6-8 minutes. Place in a greased bowl, turning once to grease top. Cover and let rise in a warm place until doubled, about 1 hour.

2. In a large skillet over medium-high heat, cook sausage until no longer pink; drain and cool. Stir in the mozzarella, 2 eggs and the basil; set aside.

3. Punch dough down; divide in half. Roll 1 half into a 15x10-in. rectangle on a greased baking sheet. Spoon half the sausage mixture lengthwise down 1 side of rectangle to within 1 in. of edges.

4. Fold dough over filling; pinch edges to seal. Cut 4 slits on top of stromboli. Repeat with remaining dough and filling. Beat remaining egg; brush over loaves. Sprinkle with Parmesan cheese. Cover; let rise until doubled, about 45 minutes.

5. Bake at 375° for 20-25 minutes or until golden brown. Slice; serve warm.

1 slice: 370 cal., 18g fat (8g sat. fat), 82mg chol., 702mg sod., 34g carb. (4g sugars, 1g fiber), 17g pro.

Refreshing Lemonades

There's nothing better in the heat of summer than savoring homemade lemonade.
Start with the classic sipper, then try some new ways to enjoy an old favorite!

OLD-FASHIONED LEMONADE

This sweet-tart lemonade is a traditional part of my Memorial Day and Fourth of July menus. Folks can't get enough of the classic fresh-squeezed flavor.

—*Tammi Simpson, Greensburg, KY*

- -

Prep: 10 min. • **Cook:** 5 min. + chilling
Makes: 7 servings

- 1⅓ cups sugar
- 5 cups water, divided
- 1 Tbsp. grated lemon zest
- 1¾ cups lemon juice (about 10 large lemons)

In a large saucepan, combine sugar, 1 cup water and lemon zest. Cook and stir over medium heat until the sugar is dissolved, about 4 minutes. Remove from heat. Stir in lemon juice and the remaining water; refrigerate until cold. Serve over ice.

1 cup: 142 cal., 0 fat (0 sat. fat), 0 chol., 1mg sod., 37g carb. (35g sugars, 0 fiber), 0 pro.

Limeade: Substitute lime zest for lemon zest and limes for lemons.

Lavender Lemonade: Add 2 Tbsp. dried lavender to the sugar and lemon zest mixture before simmering. If desired, strain before serving.

Ginger-Mint Lemonade: Add 1-2 Tbsp. grated fresh gingerroot and 1-2 mint sprigs to the sugar and lemon zest mixture before simmering. If desired, strain before serving.

RED, WHITE & BLUE FROZEN LEMONADE

This patriotic drink is as pretty as it is delicious. With raspberries, blueberries and lemon juice, we created a striped lemonade that is perfect for Fourth of July celebrations.

—*Shawn Carleton, San Diego, CA*

- -

Takes: 10 min. • **Makes:** 4 servings

- 1 cup lemon juice
- 1 cup sugar
- 4 cups ice cubes
- 1 cup fresh or frozen blueberries
  Maraschino cherries

Place lemon juice, sugar and ice in a blender; cover and process until slushy. Divide the blueberries among 4 chilled glasses; muddle slightly. Add lemon slush; top with cherries.

¾ cup: 229 cal., 0 fat (0 sat. fat), 0 chol., 1mg sod., 60g carb. (55g sugars, 1g fiber), 0 pro.

LEMONADE ICED TEA

I have always loved iced tea with lemon, and this irresistible thirst-quencher takes it one step further. Lemonade gives the drink a nice color, too. I dress up each glass with a slice of lemon on the rim.
—*Gail Buss, New Bern, NC*

- -

Takes: 15 min. + chilling
Makes: 12 servings (about 3 qt.)

- 3 qt. water
- 9 tea bags
- ¾ to 1¼ cups sugar
- 1 can (12 oz.) frozen lemonade concentrate, thawed
  Lemon slices, optional

In a Dutch oven, bring water to a boil. Remove from the heat; add tea bags. Cover and steep for 5 minutes. Discard tea bags. Stir in sugar and lemonade concentrate. Cover and refrigerate until chilled. Serve over ice. If desired, garnish with lemon slices.

1 cup: 100 cal., 0 fat (0 sat. fat), 0 chol., 1mg sod., 26g carb. (25g sugars, 0 fiber), 0 pro.

AUNT FRANCES' LEMONADE

When we were kids, my sister and I spent a week every summer with our Aunt Frances, who always had this lemonade in a stoneware crock in the refrigerator. It makes a refreshing drink after a hot day of running around.
—*Debbie Reinhart, New Cumberland, PA*

- -

Takes: 15 min. • **Makes:** 16 servings (1 gallon)

- 5 lemons
- 5 limes
- 5 oranges
- 3 qt. water
- 1½ to 2 cups sugar

1. Squeeze the juice from 4 each of the lemons, limes and oranges; pour into a gallon container.
2. Thinly slice the remaining fruit and set aside for garnish. Add water and sugar to juices; mix well. Store in the refrigerator. Serve over ice with fruit slices.

1 cup: 92 cal., 0 fat (0 sat. fat), 0 chol., 1mg sod., 24g carb. (21g sugars, 1g fiber), 0 pro.

SPIKED LEMONADE

A touch of rum gives a tropical twist to this fabulous homemade lemonade. For a variation, substitute vodka for the rum.
—*Taste of Home Test Kitchen*

- -

Takes: 15 min. + chilling
Makes: 8 servings (about 2 qt.)

- 2¼ cups sugar
- 5 cups water, divided
- 1 Tbsp. grated lemon zest
- 1¾ cups lemon juice
- 1 cup light rum or vodka
- 6 to 8 cups ice cubes

GARNISH

  Lemon slices

1. In a large saucepan, combine the sugar, 1 cup water and lemon zest. Cook and stir over medium heat until sugar is dissolved, about 4 minutes. Remove from the heat. Stir in lemon juice and remaining water. Pour into a 2-qt. pitcher; refrigerate until chilled.
2. Stir in rum. For each serving, place ¾-1 cup ice in a Collins or highball glass. Pour lemonade mixture into glass. Garnish with lemon slices as desired.

1 cup: 296 cal., 0 fat (0 sat. fat), 0 chol., 1mg sod., 61g carb. (56g sugars, 0 fiber), 0 pro.

Side Dishes & Condiments

Never underestimate the power of a first-rate side dish! Few foods are more appealing than fresh vegetables, beautifully prepared, and the rich textures of rice and grains are a lovely complement to any main course. Here are 26 delicious side dishes to round out your meal, plus sauces, salsas and relishes to take everything up a level!

ROSEMARY ROOT VEGETABLES

This heartwarming side dish is sure to get rave reviews! Although the ingredient list may look long, you'll see that this colorful fall medley is a snap to prepare.
—Taste of Home *Test Kitchen*

Prep: 20 min. • **Bake:** 20 min.
Makes: 10 servings

1   **small rutabaga, peeled and chopped**
1   **medium sweet potato, peeled and chopped**
2   **medium parsnips, peeled and chopped**
1   **medium turnip, peeled and chopped**
¼   **lb. fresh Brussels sprouts, halved**
2   **Tbsp. olive oil**
2   **Tbsp. minced fresh rosemary or 2 tsp. dried rosemary, crushed**
1   **tsp. minced garlic**
½   **tsp. salt**
½   **tsp. pepper**

Preheat oven to 425°. Place vegetables in a large bowl. In a small bowl, combine oil, rosemary, garlic, salt and pepper. Pour over vegetables; toss to coat. Arrange vegetables in a single layer in two 15x10x1-in. baking pans coated with cooking spray. Bake, uncovered, stirring once, until tender, 20-25 minutes.

¾ cup: 78 cal., 3g fat (0 sat. fat), 0 chol., 137mg sod., 13g carb. (5g sugars, 3g fiber), 1g pro. **Diabetic exchanges:** 1 starch, ½ fat.

===

VEGGIE-ROASTING SUCCESS

To ensure your vegetables cook evenly, cut them into roughly the same size pieces. Make sure they're spread out on the pan in a single layer, and that there's room between them. If they're packed too tightly, they'll absorb moisture from each other and turn out soft and soggy. Don't be tempted to add more oil than is called for, either; that'll make them greasy.

CREAMY POLENTA WITH BALSAMIC GLAZE

This easy side dish goes incredibly well with braised meat, elevating any meal!
—*Sarah Vasques, Milford, NH*

Prep: 15 min. • **Cook:** 2 hours
Makes: 4 servings

   4   **Tbsp. butter, divided**
   1½ **cups half-and-half cream, divided**
   1   **cup 2% milk**
   ¼   **tsp. salt**
   ⅓   **cup cornmeal**
   ½   **cup grated Parmesan cheese**
   1   **cup balsamic vinegar**
   1   **Tbsp. sugar**

1. In medium saucepan, melt 2 Tbsp. butter over medium heat. Add 1 cup cream, milk and salt. Bring to a low simmer. Gradually whisk in cornmeal. Cook and stir for 3 minutes.

2. Pour polenta into a 3-qt. slow cooker coated with cooking spray. Cook, covered, on low for 2 hours, stirring every 30 minutes.

3. In a small saucepan, bring vinegar and sugar to a boil. Reduce heat; simmer, uncovered, until reduced to ⅓ cup. Just before serving, stir cheese and the remaining cream and butter into polenta. To serve, drizzle with balsamic glaze.

½ cup polenta with 1 Tbsp. glaze: 415 cal., 25g fat (16g sat. fat), 89mg chol., 494mg sod., 37g carb. (25g sugars, 1g fiber), 9g pro.

SPRING ASPARAGUS

Served warm or cold, this fresh and colorful side really lets beautiful spring vegetables shine. I get lots of compliments on the homemade dressing.
—*Millie Vickery, Lena, IL*

Takes: 25 min. • **Makes:** 8 servings

   1½ **lbs. fresh asparagus, trimmed and cut into 2-in. pieces**
   2   **small tomatoes, cut into wedges**
   3   **Tbsp. cider vinegar**
   ¾   **tsp. Worcestershire sauce**
   ⅓   **cup sugar**
   1   **Tbsp. grated onion**
   ½   **tsp. salt**
   ½   **tsp. paprika**
   ⅓   **cup canola oil**
   ⅓   **cup sliced almonds, toasted**
   ⅓   **cup crumbled blue cheese, optional**

1. In a large saucepan, bring 1 cup water to a boil. Add asparagus; cook, covered, until crisp-tender, 3-5 minutes. Drain; place in a large bowl. Add tomatoes; cover and keep warm.

2. Place vinegar, Worcestershire sauce, sugar, onion, salt and paprika in a blender; cover and process until smooth. While processing, gradually add oil in a steady stream. Toss with the asparagus mixture. Top with almonds and, if desired, cheese.

Note: To toast nuts, bake in a shallow pan in a 350° oven for 5-10 minutes or cook in a skillet over low heat until lightly browned, stirring occasionally.

¾ cup: 154 cal., 11g fat (1g sat. fat), 0 chol., 159mg sod., 12g carb. (10g sugars, 1g fiber), 2g pro. **Diabetic exchanges:** 2 fat, 1 vegetable, ½ starch.

SOUTHERN GREEN BEANS WITH APRICOTS

Green beans and apricots have become a tradition in our family. Enhanced with balsamic vinegar, the flavors will make your taste buds pop.

—*Ashley Davis, Easley, SC*

Prep: 15 min. • **Cook:** 20 min.
Makes: 8 servings

- 2 lbs. fresh green beans, trimmed
- 1 can (14½ oz.) chicken broth
- ½ lb. bacon strips, chopped
- 1 cup dried apricots, chopped
- ¼ cup balsamic vinegar
- ¾ tsp. salt
- ¾ tsp. garlic powder
- ¾ tsp. pepper

1. In a large saucepan, bring the beans and broth to a boil. Cook, covered, until beans are crisp-tender, 4-7 minutes; drain.
2. In a large skillet, cook the bacon over medium heat until crisp, stirring occasionally. Remove with a slotted spoon; drain on paper towels. Discard drippings, reserving 1 Tbsp. drippings in the pan.
3. Add apricots to the drippings in the pan; cook and stir over medium heat until softened. Stir in vinegar, salt, garlic powder, pepper and beans; cook and stir until beans are coated, 2-3 minutes longer. Sprinkle with bacon.

¾ cup: 149 cal., 6g fat (2g sat. fat), 12mg chol., 464mg sod., 21g carb. (14g sugars, 5g fiber), 6g pro.

STUFFED ACORN SQUASH

Our Test Kitchen offers up this new and unusual way to present leftover stuffing. Serve this as a hearty side dish or as a meatless entree.

—*Taste of Home Test Kitchen*

Prep: 20 min. • **Bake:** 50 min.
Makes: 6 servings

- 3 small acorn squash
- 1 large egg, lightly beaten
- ¼ tsp. salt
- ⅛ tsp. pepper
- 1 tsp. chicken bouillon granules
- 2 Tbsp. boiling water
- 2 cups cooked stuffing
- ¼ cup grated Parmesan cheese, optional
- 1 tsp. paprika
   Chopped fresh parsley, optional

1. Preheat oven to 400°. Cut squash in half; discard seeds. Place cut side down in a 15x10x1-in. baking pan; add ½ in. of hot water. Bake, uncovered, until tender, about 30 minutes.
2. When cool enough to handle, scoop out squash flesh, leaving a ¼-in. shell (flesh will measure about 3 cups). Drain water from pan; place shells cut side up in the pan and set aside.
3. In a large bowl, combine the squash, egg, salt and pepper. Dissolve bouillon in boiling water; add to the squash mixture. Add stuffing; spoon into squash shells. If desired, top with cheese. Sprinkle with paprika. Bake, uncovered, until heated through, 20-25 minutes. If desired, top with chopped parsley.

1 stuffed squash half: 240 cal., 8g fat (2g sat. fat), 38mg chol., 680mg sod., 39g carb. (7g sugars, 5g fiber), 6g pro.

BUTTERY SWEET POTATO CASSEROLE

Whenever we get together as a family for holidays, my kids, nieces and nephews beg me to make this dish. It goes together in minutes with canned sweet potatoes, which is ideal for the busy holiday season.
—*Sue Miller, Mars, PA*

Prep: 15 min. • **Bake:** 20 min.
Makes: 8 servings

- 2 cans (15¾ oz. each) sweet potatoes, drained and mashed
- ½ cup sugar
- 1 large egg
- ¼ cup butter, melted
- ½ tsp. ground cinnamon
  Dash salt

TOPPING
- 1 cup coarsely crushed butter-flavored crackers (about 25 crackers)
- ½ cup packed brown sugar
- ¼ cup butter, melted

1. Preheat oven to 350°. In a large bowl, combine the first 6 ingredients. Transfer to a greased 8-in. square baking dish. Combine the topping ingredients; sprinkle over the sweet potato mixture.
2. Bake, uncovered, until a thermometer reads 160°, 20-25 minutes.

½ cup: 369 cal., 15g fat (8g sat. fat), 57mg chol., 255mg sod., 57g carb. (42g sugars, 3g fiber), 3g pro.

Contest Winner

QUINOA WITH PEAS & ONION

Even picky eaters will love this fresh dish. Frozen peas are fine for this, but in season, it's even better with fresh shelled peas!
—*Lori Panarella, Phoenixville, PA*

Prep: 30 min. • **Cook:** 10 min.
Makes: 6 servings

- 2 cups water
- 1 cup quinoa, rinsed
- 1 small onion, chopped
- 1 Tbsp. olive oil
- 1½ cups frozen peas
- ½ tsp. salt
- ¼ tsp. pepper
- 2 Tbsp. chopped walnuts

1. In a large saucepan, bring water to a boil. Add quinoa. Reduce heat; cover and simmer for 12-15 minutes or until water is absorbed. Remove from the heat; fluff with a fork.
2. Meanwhile, in a large skillet, saute onion in oil until tender. Add peas; cook and stir until heated through. Stir in the cooked quinoa, salt and pepper. Sprinkle with walnuts.

⅔ cup: 174 cal., 6g fat (1g sat. fat), 0 chol., 244mg sod., 26g carb. (2g sugars, 4g fiber), 6g pro. **Diabetic exchanges:** 1½ starch, 1 fat.

FRIED ONIONS & APPLES

Since a lot of delicious onions are grown in our state, they are always part of my menu. This tangy side dish is good with pork and beef. The inspiration for this unusual combination was a prolific apple tree!

—Janice Mitchell, Aurora, CO

- -

Takes: 30 min. • **Makes:** 12 servings

  3 large yellow onions, sliced
  3 Tbsp. butter
  6 large tart red apples, sliced
  ½ cup packed brown sugar
  1 tsp. salt
  ½ tsp. paprika
  ⅛ tsp. ground nutmeg

1. In a large, heavy skillet, saute onions in butter until tender. Place apples on top of onions. Combine the remaining ingredients; sprinkle over apples.
2. Cover and simmer for 10 minutes. Uncover and simmer until the apples are tender, 5 minutes longer. Serve with a slotted spoon.
1 cup: 137 cal., 3g fat (2g sat. fat), 8mg chol., 230mg sod., 28g carb. (24g sugars, 4g fiber), 1g pro.

ZESTY SUGAR SNAP PEAS

Lemon-pepper seasoning and garlic make these crisp-tender sugar snap peas flavorful and an ideal accompaniment to a variety of entrees. You'll come to rely on this six-ingredient dish.

—Taste of Home *Test Kitchen*

- -

Takes: 15 min. • **Makes:** 4 servings

  1 lb. fresh or frozen sugar snap peas
  ½ cup water
  1 Tbsp. butter
  1 garlic clove, minced
  ¾ tsp. lemon-pepper seasoning
  ¼ tsp. salt

In a skillet, bring peas and water to a boil. Reduce heat. Cover and cook until tender, 6-7 minutes. Drain. Add the remaining ingredients. Cook and stir until well-coated, 2-3 minutes.
¾ cup: 74 cal., 3g fat (2g sat. fat), 8mg chol., 267mg sod., 8g carb. (4g sugars, 3g fiber), 4g pro. **Diabetic exchanges:** 1 vegetable, ½ fat.

THREE-BEAN BAKED BEANS

I got this recipe from an aunt and made a couple of changes to suit our tastes. With ground beef and bacon mixed in, these satisfying beans are a big hit at backyard barbecues and church picnics. Whenever there's a party, I'm always asked to bring my special beans!

—Julie Currington, Gahanna, OH

- -

Prep: 20 min. • **Bake:** 1 hour
Makes: 12 servings

  ½ lb. ground beef
  5 bacon strips, diced
  ½ cup chopped onion
  ⅓ cup packed brown sugar
  ¼ cup sugar
  ¼ cup ketchup
  ¼ cup barbecue sauce
  2 Tbsp. molasses
  2 Tbsp. prepared mustard
  ½ tsp. chili powder
  ½ tsp. salt
  2 cans (16 oz. each) pork and beans, undrained
  1 can (16 oz.) butter beans, rinsed and drained
  1 can (16 oz.) kidney beans, rinsed and drained

1. Preheat oven to 350°. In a large skillet, cook and crumble beef with bacon and onion over medium heat until the beef is no longer pink; drain.
2. Stir in sugars, ketchup, barbecue sauce, molasses, mustard, chili powder and salt until blended. Stir in beans. Transfer to a greased 2½-qt. baking dish. Bake, covered, until beans reach desired thickness, about 1 hour.
Freeze option: Freeze cooled bean mixture in freezer containers. To use, partially thaw in refrigerator overnight. Heat through in a saucepan, stirring occasionally and adding a little water if necessary.
¾ cup: 269 cal., 8g fat (2g sat. fat), 19mg chol., 708mg sod., 42g carb. (21g sugars, 7g fiber), 13g pro.

AUTUMN PEPPER RELISH

This colorful relish is a favorite with friends and family because it tastes amazing on just about everything. I like to serve it over cream cheese or a block of sharp cheddar cheese along with crackers or French baguette slices. I also include a jar in gift baskets.
—*Barbara Pletzke, Herndon, VA*

- -

Prep: 1 hour 20 min. + standing
Process: 20 min./batch • **Makes:** 8 half-pints

- 8 **medium sweet red peppers (about 3 lbs.)**
- 6 **jalapeno peppers**
- 4 **medium Granny Smith apples (about 1¼ lbs.)**
- 2 **medium pears (about 1 lb.)**
- 1 **medium onion**
- 3 **Tbsp. canning salt**
- 2 **cups white vinegar**
- 2 **cups sugar**
- 1 **cup packed brown sugar**
- ¾ **tsp. fennel seed**

1. Seed and coarsely chop peppers. Peel and cut apples, pears and onion into 1-in. pieces. Pulse in batches in a food processor until finely chopped. Transfer to a large bowl; sprinkle with salt and toss. Let stand for 6 hours. Rinse and drain well; blot dry with paper towels.
2. In a Dutch oven, combine the drained pepper mixture, vinegar, sugars and fennel seed; bring to a boil. Reduce heat; simmer, uncovered, for 40-45 minutes or until slightly thickened.
3. Carefully ladle hot mixture into 8 hot half-pint jars, leaving ½-in. headspace. Remove air bubbles and adjust headspace, if necessary, by adding more of the hot mixture. Wipe rims. Center lids on jars; screw on bands until fingertip tight.
4. Place the jars into canner with simmering water, ensuring that they are completely covered with water. Bring to a boil; process for 20 minutes. Remove jars and cool.
Note: The processing time listed is for altitudes of 1,000 feet or less. For altitudes up to 3,000 feet, add 5 minutes; 6,000 feet, add 10 minutes; 8,000 feet, add 15 minutes; 10,000 feet, add 20 minutes. Wear disposable gloves when cutting hot peppers; the oils can burn skin. Avoid touching your face.
2 Tbsp.: 13 cal., 0 fat (0 sat. fat), 0 chol., 4mg sod., 3g carb. (2g sugars, 1g fiber), 0 pro.

BLACK-EYED PEAS WITH COLLARD GREENS

This is a worthy side dish any time of year but has special meaning on New Year's Day, when Southerners eat greens for future wealth and black-eyed peas for prosperity.
—*Athena Russell, Greenville, SC*

- -

Takes: 25 min. • **Makes:** 6 servings

- 2 **Tbsp. olive oil**
- 1 **garlic clove, minced**
- 8 **cups chopped collard greens**
- ½ **tsp. salt**
- ¼ **tsp. cayenne pepper**
- 2 **cans (15½ oz. each) black-eyed peas, rinsed and drained**
- 4 **plum tomatoes, seeded and chopped**
- ¼ **cup lemon juice**
- 2 **Tbsp. grated Parmesan cheese**

In a Dutch oven, heat oil over medium heat. Add garlic; cook and stir 1 minute. Add collard greens, salt and cayenne; cook and stir 6-8 minutes or until greens are tender. Add peas, tomatoes and lemon juice; heat through. Sprinkle servings with cheese.
¾ cup: 177 cal., 5g fat (1g sat. fat), 1mg chol., 412mg sod., 24g carb. (3g sugars, 6g fiber), 9g pro.

ULTIMATE SCALLOPED POTATOES

This tasty variation on traditional scalloped potatoes is dressed up with garlic, Swiss cheese and Parmesan cheese. It takes a family classic up to "ultimate" level!

—Glenda Malan, Lake Forest, CA

- -

Prep: 20 min. + cooling • **Bake:** 1 hour
Makes: 6 servings

  1 **tsp. butter, softened**
  1 **cup heavy whipping cream**
  ⅓ **cup whole milk**
  1 **tsp. salt**
  ½ **tsp. pepper**
  2 **garlic cloves, crushed**
  6 **medium potatoes**
  1 **cup shredded Swiss cheese**
  ¼ **cup shredded Parmesan cheese**

1. Preheat the oven to 350°. Grease a shallow 13x9 baking dish with butter; set aside. In a small saucepan, combine the cream, milk, salt, pepper and garlic. Cook just until bubbles begin to form around the sides of the pan. Remove from the heat; let cool for 10 minutes.

2. Peel and thinly slice the potatoes; pat dry with paper towels. Layer half the potatoes in the prepared dish; top with half the cream mixture and half the cheeses. Repeat layers.

3. Bake, covered, 40 minutes. Uncover and continue baking until the potatoes are tender, 20-25 minutes longer. Let stand 5-10 minutes before serving.

1 serving: 402 cal., 22g fat (14g sat. fat), 77mg chol., 538mg sod., 41g carb. (6g sugars, 3g fiber), 12g pro.

SPICED PICKLED BEETS

With sweet, tangy and spiced flavors, these pickled beets are so good that they'll win over just about everyone.

—*Edna Hoffman, Hebron, IN*

Prep: 1¼ hours • **Process:** 35 min.
Makes: 4 pints

- 3 lbs. small fresh beets
- 2 cups sugar
- 2 cups water
- 2 cups cider vinegar
- 2 cinnamon sticks (3 in.)
- 1 tsp. whole cloves
- 1 tsp. whole allspice

1. Scrub the beets and trim tops to 1 in. Place in a Dutch oven and cover with water. Bring to a boil. Reduce heat; cover and simmer until tender, 25-35 minutes. Remove from water; cool. Peel beets and cut into fourths.

2. Place beets in a Dutch oven. Add the sugar, water and vinegar. Place spices on a double thickness of cheesecloth; bring up corners of cloth and tie with string to form a bag. Add to beet mixture. Bring to a boil. Reduce heat; cover and simmer for 10 minutes. Discard spice bag.

3. Carefully pack beets into 4 hot 1-pint jars to within ½ in. of the top. Carefully ladle hot liquid over beets, leaving ½-in. headspace. Remove air bubbles and adjust headspace, if necessary, by adding more hot mixture. Wipe rims. Center lids on jars; screw on bands until fingertip tight.

4. Place jars into canner with simmering water, ensuring that they are completely covered with water. Bring to a boil and process for 35 minutes. Remove jars and let cool.

Note: The processing time listed is for altitudes of 1,000 feet or less. For altitudes up to 3,000 feet, add 5 minutes; 6,000 feet, add 10 minutes; 8,000 feet, add 15 minutes; 10,000 feet, add 20 minutes.

¼ cup: 53 cal., 0 fat (0 sat. fat), 0 chol., 44mg sod., 12g carb. (11g sugars, 1g fiber), 1g pro. **Diabetic exchanges:** 1 vegetable, ½ starch.

OVEN-DRIED TOMATOES

We owned an organic greenhouse and a business that included classes. I had 100 different tomato varieties to work with, so I started oven-drying them—I taught my students how to make these, too.

—*Sue Gronholz, Beaver Dam, WI*

Prep: 15 min. • **Bake:** 5 hours
Makes: 4 servings

- 8 plum tomatoes
    Ice water
- ¼ cup olive oil
- ¼ cup minced fresh basil
- 4 garlic cloves, minced
- ½ tsp. salt
- ¼ tsp. pepper

1. Preheat oven to 250°. Fill a large saucepan two-thirds with water bring to a boil. Cut a shallow X on the bottom of each tomato. Place tomatoes, a few at a time, in boiling water just until the skin at the X begins to loosen, about 30 seconds. Remove and immediately drop into ice water. Pull off and discard skins.

2. Cut tomatoes in half lengthwise. Combine olive oil, basil, cloves, and pepper. Add tomatoes; toss to coat. Transfer tomatoes, cut side up, to a greased 15x10x1-in. baking pan. Roast until tomatoes are soft and slightly shriveled, about 5 hours. Let cool completely; refrigerate.

4 tomato halves: 147 cal., 14g fat (2g sat. fat), 0 chol., 302mg sod., 6g carb. (3g sugars, 2g fiber), 1g pro. **Diabetic exchanges:** 3 fat, 1 vegetable.

FRIED ASPARAGUS

This battered asparagus is a favorite at events. It's fun to eat with a side of ranch dressing for dipping.

—*Lori Kimble, Montgomery, AL*

Takes: 30 min. • **Makes:** 2½ dozen

- 1 cup all-purpose flour
- ¾ cup cornstarch
- 1¼ tsp. salt
- 1¼ tsp. baking powder
- ¾ tsp. baking soda
- ¾ tsp. garlic salt
- ½ tsp. pepper
- 1 cup beer or nonalcoholic beer
- 3 large egg whites
- 2½ lbs. fresh asparagus, trimmed
  Oil for deep-fat frying
  Ranch salad dressing

1. In a large bowl, combine the first 7 ingredients. Combine beer and egg whites; stir into the dry ingredients just until moistened. Dip asparagus into the batter.

2. In a deep cast-iron or electric skillet, heat 1½ in. oil to 375°. Fry asparagus in batches until golden brown, 2-3 minutes on each side. Drain on paper towels. Serve immediately with ranch dressing.

1 asparagus stalk: 70 cal., 4g fat (0 sat. fat), 0 chol., 207mg sod., 7g carb. (1g sugars, 0 fiber), 1g pro.

FOUR-TOMATO SALSA

A variety of tomatoes, onions and peppers makes this colorful, chunky salsa so good. Whenever I make a batch for a get-together, it's hard to keep my family from finishing it off first! Serve it as a snack with tortilla chips or a relish with meat.

—*Connie Siese, Wayne, MI*

Takes: 30 min. • **Makes:** 56 servings (14 cups)

- 7 plum tomatoes, chopped
- 7 medium red tomatoes, chopped
- 3 medium yellow tomatoes, chopped
- 3 medium orange tomatoes, chopped
- 1 tsp. salt
- 2 Tbsp. lime juice
- 2 Tbsp. olive oil
- 1 medium white onion, chopped
- 1 medium red onion, chopped
- 2 green onions, chopped
- ½ cup each chopped green, sweet red, orange and yellow pepper
- 3 pepperoncini, chopped
- ⅓ cup mild pickled pepper rings, chopped
- ½ cup minced fresh parsley
- 2 Tbsp. minced fresh cilantro
- 1 Tbsp. dried chervil
  Tortilla chips

1. In a colander, combine tomatoes and salt. Let drain for 10 minutes.

2. Transfer to a large bowl. Stir in the lime juice, oil, onions, peppers, parsley, cilantro and chervil. Serve with tortilla chips. Refrigerate leftovers for up to 1 week.

¼ cup: 15 cal., 1g fat (0 sat. fat), 0 chol., 62mg sod., 2g carb. (1g sugars, 1g fiber), 0 pro. **Diabetic exchanges:** 1 free food.

PICKING PICKLED PEPPERS

Look for pepperoncinis (pickled peppers) and pickled banana peppers in the pickle and olive aisle of your grocery store.

SPICY GRILLED EGGPLANT

This grilled side goes well with pasta or with meats also made on the grill. Thanks to the Cajun seasoning, it gets more attention than an ordinary veggie.
—*Greg Fontenot, The Woodlands, TX*

- -

Takes: 20 min. • **Makes:** 8 servings

2 **small eggplants, cut into ½-in. slices**
¼ **cup olive oil**
2 **Tbsp. lime juice**
3 **tsp. Cajun seasoning**

1. Brush eggplant slices with olive oil. Drizzle with lime juice; sprinkle with Cajun seasoning. Let stand 5 minutes.
2. Grill eggplant, covered, over medium heat or broil 4 in. from heat until tender, 4-5 minutes per side.
1 serving: 88 cal., 7g fat (1g sat. fat), 0 chol., 152mg sod., 7g carb. (3g sugars, 4g fiber), 1g pro. **Diabetic exchanges:** 1½ fat, 1 vegetable

ASIAGO MASHED CAULIFLOWER

Asiago and fresh parsley help turn this healthier mashed potato alternative into a flavorful side dish that will leave you feeling satisfied but not guilty or overstuffed.
—*Colleen Delawder, Herndon, VA*

- -

Takes: 30 min. • **Makes:** 4 servings

1 **medium head cauliflower, cut into 1-in. pieces**
1 **tsp. sea salt, divided**
4 **oz. cream cheese, softened**
½ **cup shredded Asiago cheese**
2 **Tbsp. unsalted butter**
2 **Tbsp. coarsely chopped fresh parsley**
¼ **tsp. pepper**

1. Place cauliflower and ½ tsp. sea salt in a large saucepan; add water to cover. Bring to a boil. Cook, covered, until very tender, 12-15 minutes. Drain; cool slightly.
2. Transfer to a food processor. Add the cream cheese, Asiago cheese, butter, parsley, pepper and the remaining sea salt. Process until blended.
½ cup: 239 cal., 20g fat (12g sat. fat), 56mg chol., 530mg sod., 10g carb. (4g sugars, 3g fiber), 9g pro.

LEEKS IN MUSTARD SAUCE

Leeks have a deliciously delicate onion flavor, and they're so wonderful in this side dish. The mustard sauce complements the leeks, and goes well with many entrees.
—Taste of Home *Test Kitchen*

- -

Prep: 15 min. • **Cook:** 20 min.
Makes: 8 servings

10	medium leeks (white portion only)
2	green onions with tops, chopped
1	garlic clove, minced
1	Tbsp. olive oil

MUSTARD SAUCE

3	large egg yolks
¼	cup water
2	Tbsp. lemon juice
6	Tbsp. cold butter
1	Tbsp. Dijon mustard
	Dash white pepper

1. Cut leeks into 1½-in. slices, then julienne. In a large skillet, saute leeks, onions and garlic in oil until tender.
2. Meanwhile, in a small, heavy saucepan, whisk the egg yolks, water and lemon juice. Cook and stir over low heat until the mixture begins to thicken, bubbles around the edges and reaches 160°, about 20 minutes. Add butter, 1 Tbsp. at a time, whisking after each addition until melted. Remove from the heat; stir in mustard and pepper.
3. Transfer the leek mixture to a serving bowl; top with the mustard sauce.
½ cup with about 4 tsp. sauce: 185 cal., 13g fat (6g sat. fat), 103mg chol., 160mg sod., 17g carb. (5g sugars, 2g fiber), 3g pro.

MAPLE-GINGER GLAZED CARROTS

I first made this dish for my family and friends one Thanksgiving. Not only do the carrots look splendid on any table, but they taste terrific, too.
—Jeannette Sabo, Lexington Park, MD

- -

Prep: 15 min. • **Cook:** 25 min.
Makes: 16 servings

4	lbs. medium carrots, cut into ¼-in. slices
¼	cup water
3	Tbsp. butter, divided
1	Tbsp. minced fresh gingerroot
⅓	cup maple syrup
1	Tbsp. cider vinegar
½	tsp. salt
¼	tsp. pepper
	Minced fresh parsley, optional

1. In a Dutch oven, combine carrots, water, 2 Tbsp. butter and ginger. Cover and cook for 10 minutes. Continue cooking, uncovered, until carrots are crisp-tender, 6-8 minutes longer.
2. Stir in syrup, vinegar, salt and pepper. Cook, stirring frequently, or until the sauce is thickened, 5-6 minutes. Stir in the remaining butter. If desired, garnish with parsley.
¾ cup: 83 cal., 2g fat (1g sat. fat), 6mg chol., 168mg sod., 15g carb. (9g sugars, 3g fiber), 1g pro. **Diabetic exchanges:** 2 vegetable, ½ fat.

STORING GINGERROOT

Unpeeled gingerroot can be frozen for up to 1 year in an airtight freezer container. When needed, simply peel and grate.

CRANBERRY CONSERVE

I still remember my grandmother from Germany making this lovely, delectable conserve for the holidays. She'd give it to family members and friends. Serve as a relish alongside meat or spread on biscuits.
—*Mildred Marsh Banker, Austin, TX*

- -

Prep: 20 min. + chilling
Cook: 10 min. + cooling • **Makes:** 3 pints

- 4 **cups fresh or frozen cranberries, halved**
- 1 **Tbsp. grated orange zest**
- 2 **oranges, peeled, sliced and quartered**
- 1 **cup raisins**
- 1¼ **cup water**
- 1 **cup chopped pecans**
- 2½ **cups sugar**

In a large saucepan, combine cranberries, orange zest, oranges, raisins and water. Cover and simmer over medium heat until cranberries are soft. Add pecans and sugar; stir well. Simmer, uncovered, 10-15 minutes, stirring often. Cool. Spoon into covered containers and refrigerate. Serve as a relish with poultry or pork, or spread on biscuits or rolls.
2 Tbsp.: 72 cal., 2g fat (0 sat. fat), 0 chol., 1mg sod., 15g carb. (13g sugars, 1g fiber), 0 pro.

BRUSSELS SPROUTS BROWN BETTY

I had the idea to make a savory version of the family-favorite brown betty using vegetables in place of fruit, while keeping the classic crunchy bread crumb topping. The result is a creamy, decadent side that is a surefire way to turn anyone into a Brussels sprouts fan.
—*Shauna Havey, Roy, UT*

- -

Prep: 30 min. • **Bake:** 40 min.
Makes: 8 servings

- 1½ **lbs. fresh Brussels sprouts, sliced**
- 1 **small onion, chopped**
- 4 **garlic cloves, minced**
- 2 **Tbsp. olive oil**
- 1 **tsp. salt**
- ½ **tsp. pepper**
- 1½ **cups shredded Swiss cheese**
- 1 **cup heavy whipping cream**
- 8 **bacon strips, cooked and crumbled**
- 3 **slices whole wheat bread, torn**
- 2 **Tbsp. butter, melted**
  Minced fresh thyme, optional

1. Preheat oven to 425°. In a large bowl, combine the first 6 ingredients; toss to coat. Transfer to a greased 13x9-in. baking dish. Bake, uncovered, 20 minutes. Stir in the cheese, cream and bacon. Bake until the casserole is bubbly and starting to brown, 12-15 minutes longer.
2. Meanwhile, place bread in a food processor or blender. Cover and pulse until crumbs form. Transfer to a small bowl and stir in butter. Sprinkle over casserole. Bake until topping is golden brown, 8-10 minutes longer. If desired, top with thyme just before serving.
¾ cup: 301 cal., 25g fat (13g sat. fat), 62mg chol., 554mg sod., 9g carb. (3g sugars, 3g fiber), 12g pro.

CREAMY CHIVE MASHED POTATOES

Buttermilk and cream cheese lend rich flavor—rather like sour cream—to these wonderful whipped potatoes.
—*Bonnie Thompson, Rathdrum, ID*

Prep: 15 min. • **Cook:** 25 min.
Makes: 4 servings

- 5 medium potatoes, peeled
- 1½ tsp. salt, divided
- 4 oz. cream cheese, softened
- 2 Tbsp. butter, softened
- 2 Tbsp. minced fresh chives
- ¼ tsp. pepper
- ¼ to ½ cup buttermilk

1. Place potatoes in a large saucepan and cover with water; add 1 tsp. salt. Bring to a boil. Reduce heat; cover and cook until tender, 15-20 minutes. Drain.
2. In a large bowl, mash the potatoes with the cream cheese, butter, chives, pepper and remaining salt; gradually beat in enough buttermilk to achieve the desired consistency.

¾ cup: 249 cal., 13g fat (8g sat. fat), 38mg chol., 838mg sod., 30g carb. (3g sugars, 2g fiber), 5g pro.

Contest Winner

ROASTED ASPARAGUS RISOTTO

This recipe's wow factor makes it perfect for special occasions. To save time, the asparagus and prosciutto can be roasting while the rice cooks on the stovetop. They'll be ready to stir into the risotto by the time the rice is done.

—Deonna Mazur, Buffalo, NY

Prep: 35 min. • **Cook:** 30 min.
Makes: 8 servings

- 12 thin slices prosciutto
- 2 lbs. fresh asparagus, cut into 1-in. pieces
- 5½ to 6 cups reduced-sodium chicken broth
- 1 shallot, chopped
- 2 garlic cloves, minced
- 2 tsp. olive oil
- 2 cups uncooked arborio rice
- ½ cup white wine
- ½ tsp. pepper
- 1 cup grated Parmesan cheese

1. Preheat oven to 400°. Place asparagus in an ungreased 15x10x1-in. baking sheet. Bake, uncovered, until crisp-tender, 20-25 minutes; stir occasionally.
2. Meanwhile, place prosciutto in another ungreased baking pan. Bake until crisp, 10-12 minutes. Crumble prosciutto; set aside prosciutto and asparagus.
3. In a large saucepan, heat broth and keep warm. In a large skillet, saute shallot and garlic in oil until tender. Add rice; cook and stir for 2-3 minutes. Reduce heat; stir in wine, pepper and salt. Cook and stir until all the liquid is absorbed.
4. Add heated broth, ½ cup at a time, stirring constantly. Allow the liquid to absorb between additions. Cook until risotto is creamy and the rice is almost tender, 20 minutes.
5. Add the asparagus, prosciutto and cheese; cook and stir until heated through. Serve immediately.

¾ cup: 311 cal., 7g fat (3g sat. fat), 28mg chol., 962mg sod., 44g carb. (2g sugars, 2g fiber), 16g pro.

FRENCH MUSTARD

Have grill masters on your Christmas list? Consider giving them a special homemade mustard flavored with maple syrup, allspice and turmeric. Everyone just loves it.

—Lorraine Caland, Shuniah, ON

Prep: 15 min. • **Cook:** 30 min. + chilling
Makes: 1 cup

- 1 tsp. whole allspice
- ¾ cup plus 3 Tbsp. water, divided
- ½ cup white vinegar
- ¼ cup maple syrup
- 1 Tbsp. all-purpose flour
- 1 Tbsp. cornstarch
- 2 tsp. ground mustard
- 1 tsp. ground turmeric
- ¾ tsp. salt

1. Place allspice on a double thickness of cheesecloth. Gather corners of cloth to enclose seasonings; tie securely with string. In a small bowl, mix ¾ cup water, vinegar and maple syrup; set aside.
2. In a small saucepan, mix the flour, cornstarch, mustard, turmeric, salt and remaining water until smooth. Gradually whisk in the vinegar mixture. Add the spice bag. Simmer over medium heat until thickened, 5-10 minutes, stirring occasionally.
3. Discard spice bag. Transfer mustard to a covered container and cool slightly. Refrigerate until cold. Store in refrigerator up to 1 month.

1 Tbsp.: 19 cal., 0 fat (0 sat. fat), 0 chol., 111mg sod., 4g carb. (3g sugars, 0 fiber), 0 pro.

Homemade Barbecue Sauce

When it comes to barbecue sauce, everyone has their own preference—sweet or spicy, mild or hot. Family recipes are guarded secrets, and everyone's mom's is the best. One thing's for sure, though: When homemade is this good, you'll never settle for bottled sauce again!

CHERRY BARBECUE SAUCE

You can use fresh or frozen cherries to make this flavorful barbecue sauce. It tastes phenomenal on ribs and chicken!
—*Ilene Harrington, Nipomo, CA*

- -

Takes: 30 min. • **Makes:** about 3½ cups

- 1 medium onion, chopped
- 2 Tbsp. butter
- 2 garlic cloves, minced
- 2 cups fresh or frozen dark sweet cherries, pitted and coarsely chopped
- 1 cup ketchup
- ⅔ cup packed brown sugar
- ¼ cup cider vinegar
- 1 Tbsp. Worcestershire sauce
- 2 tsp. ground mustard
- ½ tsp. pepper
- ⅛ tsp. Liquid Smoke, optional

In a large saucepan, saute onion in butter until tender. Add garlic; cook 1 minute longer. Stir in the remaining ingredients. Cook, uncovered, over medium-low heat for 20 minutes or until the cherries are tender and sauce is thickened, stirring occasionally.

3 Tbsp.: 74 cal., 2g fat (1g sat. fat), 3mg chol., 184mg sod., 16g carb. (12g sugars, 1g fiber), 1g pro.

GRILLING WITH SAUCE

For best results when grilling with a barbecue sauce, be sure your grill is at the proper temperature before placing the food on the rack. Wait to brush on thick or sweet sauces until the last 10-15 minutes of cooking. Baste and turn every few minutes to prevent burning.

BARBECUED CHICKEN MARINADE

When the family comes together, I pull out the chili powder, Worcestershire and garlic for this marinade that makes my chicken a home run.
—*Barbara Blickens Derfer, Edgewater, FL*

- -

Takes: 10 min. • **Makes:** about 1⅓ cups

- 1 large onion, chopped
- ⅔ cup butter, melted
- ⅓ cup cider vinegar
- 4 tsp. sugar
- 1 Tbsp. chili powder
- 2 tsp. salt
- 2 tsp. Worcestershire sauce
- 1½ tsp. pepper
- 1½ tsp. ground mustard
- 2 garlic cloves, minced
- ½ tsp. hot pepper sauce

In a small bowl, mix all ingredients. Use to marinate chicken.

BARBECUE GRILLING SAUCE

This slightly sweet basting sauce was made for chicken, but don't stop there. Try it on pork or grilled veggies, too.
—*Kathryn Dunn, Axton, VA*

- -

Takes: 5 min. • **Makes:** 2½ cups

- 1 bottle (12 oz.) chili sauce
- 1 jar (10 oz.) orange marmalade
- ¼ cup cider vinegar
- 1 Tbsp. Worcestershire sauce
- 1½ tsp. celery seed

In a small bowl, combine all ingredients. Store sauce in an airtight container in the refrigerator for up to 1 month. Use as a basting sauce for grilled meats.

2 Tbsp.: 55 cal., 0 fat (0 sat. fat), 0 chol., 293mg sod., 14g carb. (12g sugars, 0 fiber), 0 pro.

SWEET & SPICY BARBECUE SAUCE

I've never cared for store-bought barbecue sauce. I like to make things from scratch—including this spicy, deep red-brown sauce. It clings really well when you slather it on grilled meat.

—*Helena Mann, Sacramento, CA*

Prep: 30 min. • **Cook:** 35 min.
Makes: 1½ cups

- 1 medium onion, chopped
- 1 Tbsp. canola oil
- 1 garlic clove, minced
- 1 to 3 tsp. chili powder
- ¼ tsp. cayenne pepper
- ¼ tsp. coarsely ground pepper
- 1 cup ketchup
- ⅓ cup molasses
- 2 Tbsp. cider vinegar
- 2 Tbsp. Worcestershire sauce
- 2 Tbsp. spicy brown mustard
- ½ tsp. hot pepper sauce

1. In a large saucepan, saute onion in oil until tender. Add garlic; cook 1 minute. Stir in chili powder, cayenne and pepper; cook 1 minute longer.
2. Stir in ketchup, molasses, vinegar, Worcestershire sauce, mustard and pepper sauce. Bring to a boil. Reduce heat; simmer, uncovered, 30-40 minutes or until the sauce reaches the desired consistency. Cool for 15 minutes.
3. Strain through a fine mesh strainer over a large bowl, discarding vegetables and seasonings. Store in an airtight container in the refrigerator up to 1 month. Use as a basting sauce for grilled meats.

2 Tbsp.: 68 cal., 1g fat (0 sat. fat), 0 chol., 325mg sod., 14g carb. (11g sugars, 1g fiber), 0 pro.

RED-EYE BARBECUE SAUCE

I made this recipe for an assignment in culinary school—my first time making barbecue sauce. I have to say, it was the best barbecue sauce I'd had in a long time! The hint of coffee livens up the sweet sauce perfectly.

—*Evan Haut, Canton, OH*

Prep: 30 min. • **Cook:** 1 hour • **Makes:** 4 cups

- ¼ cup butter
- 4 garlic cloves, minced
- 1 shallot, finely chopped
- 1½ cups packed brown sugar
- 12 plum tomatoes, peeled, chopped and drained
- ½ cup cider vinegar
- 3 Tbsp. instant coffee granules
- 1 Tbsp. salt
- 1 tsp. pepper
- 1 tsp. adobo seasoning
- 1 tsp. harissa chili paste
- 1 tsp. cayenne pepper

1. In a Dutch oven, heat butter over medium heat. Add garlic and shallot; cook and stir until softened, 5-7 minutes. Add the brown sugar. Reduce heat to medium-low; cook, stirring occasionally, until deep golden brown, 15-17 minutes.
2. Add remaining ingredients; simmer 10 minutes. Remove from heat. Puree sauce using an immersion blender, or cool slightly and puree in batches in a blender. Strain through a fine-mesh strainer. Return to pan; cook and stir until liquid is reduced by a third, 30-40 minutes.
3. Refrigerate, covered, until serving. Serve with grilled meats.

2 Tbsp.: 60 cal., 2g fat (1g sat. fat), 4mg chol., 281mg sod., 12g carb. (11g sugars, 0 fiber), 0 pro.

Soups, Salads & Sandwiches

Many classic meals are built around soups, salads and sandwiches. Here you can choose one, two or all three of these greats to create a satisfying spread that folks will love. Mix and match these dishes to suit your tastes—or make a meal of one hearty option by adding the sides of your choice.

❄

SPINACH & SAUSAGE LENTIL SOUP

During the cooler months of the year, this soup makes regular appearances on our dinner table. It is approved by all, including my picky 6-year-old.
—*Kalyn Gensic, Ardmore, OK*

Prep: 5 min. • **Cook:** 45 min.
Makes: 6 servings (2 qt.)

Contest Winner

1   lb. bulk spicy pork sausage
1   cup dried brown lentils, rinsed
1   can (15 oz.) cannellini beans, rinsed and drained
1   carton (32 oz.) reduced-sodium chicken broth
1   cup water
1   can (14½ oz.) fire-roasted diced tomatoes, undrained
6   cups fresh spinach (about 4 oz.)
    Crumbled goat cheese, optional

1. In a Dutch oven, cook and crumble sausage over medium heat until no longer pink, 5-7 minutes; drain.
2. Stir in lentils, beans, broth and water; bring to a boil. Reduce heat; simmer, covered, until the lentils are tender, about 30 minutes. Stir in the tomatoes; heat through.
3. Remove from heat; stir in spinach until wilted. If desired, serve with goat cheese.
Freeze option: Freeze cooled soup in freezer containers. To use, partially thaw in refrigerator overnight. Heat through in a saucepan, stirring occasionally.
1⅓ cups: 390 cal., 17g fat (5g sat. fat), 41mg chol., 1242mg sod., 37g carb. (3g sugars, 8g fiber), 22g pro.

❄️
GREEK TOMATO SOUP WITH ORZO

My recipe for *manestra*, which means "orzo" in Greek, is straightforward and easy to make. It takes only a few steps— and about 30 minutes—to transform simple ingredients into a creamy and tomatoey one-pot-wonder.

—*Kiki Vagianos, Melrose, MA*

- -

Prep: 10 min. • **Cook:** 25 min.
Makes: 4 servings

    2   Tbsp. olive oil
    1   medium onion, chopped
    1¼ cups uncooked whole wheat
        orzo pasta
    2   cans (14½ oz. each) whole tomatoes,
        undrained, coarsely chopped
    3   cups reduced-sodium chicken broth
    2   tsp. dried oregano
    ¼   tsp. salt
    ¼   tsp. pepper
        Crumbled feta cheese and minced
        fresh basil, optional

1. In large saucepan, heat oil over medium heat; saute onion until tender, 3-5 minutes. Add orzo; cook and stir until lightly toasted.
2. Stir in the tomatoes, broth and seasonings; bring to a boil. Reduce heat; simmer, covered, until the orzo is tender, 15-20 minutes, stirring occasionally. If desired, top with feta and basil.
Freeze option: Freeze cooled soup in freezer containers. To use, partially thaw in refrigerator overnight. Heat through in a saucepan, stirring occasionally and adding a little broth or water if necessary.
1 cup: 299 cal., 8g fat (1g sat. fat), 0 chol., 882mg sod., 47g carb. (7g sugars, 12g fiber), 11g pro.

CRUNCHY LEMON-PESTO GARDEN SALAD

I love using fresh vegetables straight from the garden to prepare this salad. If I pick the squash and cucumbers early enough, their skins are so tender that there's no need to remove them! Best of all, it's very easily adaptable—any fresh veggie from the garden can be swapped in with delicious results.
—*Carmell Childs, Clawson, UT*

- -

Takes: 25 min. • **Makes:** 6 servings

    5   Tbsp. prepared pesto
    1   Tbsp. lemon juice
    2   tsp. grated lemon zest
    1½ tsp. Dijon mustard
    ¼   tsp. garlic salt
    ¼   tsp. pepper
    2½ cups thinly sliced yellow
        summer squash
    1¾ cups thinly sliced mini cucumbers
    ¾   cup fresh peas
    ½   cup shredded Parmesan cheese
    ¼   cup thinly sliced green onions
    5   thick-sliced bacon strips,
        cooked and crumbled

In a bowl, whisk together the first 6 ingredients until blended. In another bowl, combine squash, cucumbers, peas, Parmesan and green onions. Pour the dressing over the salad; toss to coat. Top with bacon to serve.
¾ cup: 159 cal., 11g fat (3g sat. fat), 13mg chol., 586mg sod., 8g carb. (4g sugars, 2g fiber), 8g pro. **Diabetic exchanges:** 2 fat, 1 vegetable.

KANSAS CUCUMBER SALAD

Cucumbers are my favorite garden vegetable, so I use this recipe often. I got it from a friend many years ago. I've heard this refreshing dish keeps very well in the refrigerator, but it goes so fast around our house, I've never found out for myself!
—Karen Ann Bland, Gove,KS

- -

Takes: 10 min. + chilling • **Makes:** 8 servings

- 1 cup Miracle Whip
- ¼ cup sugar
- 4 tsp. cider vinegar
- ½ tsp. dill weed
- ½ tsp. salt, optional
- 4 medium cucumbers, peeled and thinly sliced
- 3 green onions, chopped

In a large bowl, combine Miracle Whip, sugar, vinegar, dill and, if desired, salt; mix well. Add cucumbers and onions; toss. Cover and chill for at least 1 hour.
⅔ cup: 122 cal., 7g fat (1g sat. fat), 2mg chol., 201mg sod., 12g carb. (10g sugars, 2g fiber), 2g pro.

SLOW-COOKED LASAGNA SOUP

I have modified one of my favorite soup recipes so I can prep it the night before and put it in the slow cooker in the morning. It makes a welcome contribution to work parties—my colleagues love it!
—Sharon Gerst, North Liberty, IA

- -

Prep: 35 min. • **Cook:** 5 hours + standing
Makes: 8 servings (2½ qt.)

- 1 pkg. (19½ oz.) Italian turkey sausage links, casings removed
- 1 large onion, chopped
- 2 medium carrots, chopped
- 2 cups sliced fresh mushrooms
- 3 garlic cloves, minced
- 1 carton (32 oz.) reduced-sodium chicken broth
- 2 cans (14½ oz. each) no-salt-added stewed tomatoes
- 2 cans (8 oz. each) no-salt-added tomato sauce
- 2 tsp. Italian seasoning
- 6 lasagna noodles, broken into 1-in. pieces
- 2 cups coarsely chopped fresh spinach
- 1 cup cubed or shredded part-skim mozzarella cheese
  Optional: Shredded Parmesan cheese and minced fresh basil

1. In a large skillet, cook sausage over medium-high heat, breaking into crumbles, until no longer pink, 8-10 minutes; drain. Transfer to a 5- or 6-qt. slow cooker.
2. Add onion and carrots to same pan; cook and stir until softened, 2-4 minutes. Stir in mushrooms and garlic; cook and stir until the mushrooms are softened, 2-4 minutes. Transfer to slow cooker. Stir in broth, tomatoes, tomato sauce and Italian seasoning. Cook, covered, on low until the vegetables are tender, 4-6 hours.
3. Add noodles; cook until tender, 1 hour longer. Stir in spinach. Remove insert; let stand 10 minutes. Divide mozzarella cheese among serving bowls; ladle soup over cheese. If desired, sprinkle with Parmesan cheese and basil.
1⅓ cups: 266 cal., 8g fat (3g sat. fat), 36mg chol., 725mg sod., 30g carb. (11g sugars, 5g fiber), 18g pro. **Diabetic exchanges:** 2 lean meat, 2 vegetable, 1½ starch.

TERRIFIC TERIYAKI BURGERS

Golden flecks of pineapple give these burgers a touch of sweetness, while the gingerroot adds spice. Ground chicken works well in this recipe, too.

—*Margaret Wilson, San Bernardino, CA*

Prep: 20 min. • **Grill:** 15 min.
Makes: 6 servings

- ¼ cup ketchup
- 2 Tbsp. reduced-sodium soy sauce
- 1 Tbsp. brown sugar
- 1 Tbsp. unsweetened crushed pineapple
- 1½ tsp. minced fresh gingerroot
- 1 garlic clove, minced
- ½ tsp. sesame oil

BURGERS
- 1 large egg white, lightly beaten
- ⅓ cup dry bread crumbs
- 3 green onions, chopped
- 2 Tbsp. unsweetened crushed pineapple
- ¾ lb. ground beef
- ¾ lb. lean ground turkey
- 6 slices unsweetened pineapple
- 6 hamburger buns, split and toasted
- 6 lettuce leaves
- 6 slices tomato

Contest Winner

1. In a small bowl, combine the ketchup, soy sauce, brown sugar, pineapple, ginger, garlic and sesame oil; set aside.

2. In a large bowl, combine the egg white, bread crumbs, onions, crushed pineapple and 3 Tbsp. of the ketchup mixture. Crumble beef and turkey over the mixture and mix well. Shape into 6 burgers.

3. Grill burgers, covered, on a lightly oiled grill rack over medium heat or broil 4 in. from the heat for 5-7 minutes on each side or until a thermometer reads 165° and the juices run clear. Brush occasionally with what remains of the ketchup mixture.

4. Grill or broil pineapple slices for 2-3 minutes on each side or until heated through. Serve burgers and pineapple on buns with lettuce and tomato.

1 burger: 386 cal., 12g fat (4g sat. fat), 79mg chol., 677mg sod., 41g carb. (16g sugars, 2g fiber), 27g pro. **Diabetic exchanges:** 3 lean meat, 2 starch, ½ fruit.

BEEF STROGANOFF SANDWICHES

For an American take on classic Russian comfort food, we turn beef Stroganoff into a sandwich. It comes together quickly, and our family devours it.
—*Alison Garcia, Beatrice, NE*

- -

Takes: 25 min. • **Makes:** 6 servings

- 1 **lb. ground beef**
- 1 **cup sliced fresh mushrooms**
- 1 **small green pepper, finely chopped**
- 1 **small onion, finely chopped**
- 1 **envelope ranch dip mix**
- ¾ **cup sour cream**
- 1 **loaf (about 8 oz.) French bread**
- 2 **cups shredded part-skim mozzarella cheese**

1. Preheat broiler. In a large skillet, cook beef, mushrooms, pepper and onion over medium-high heat until beef is no longer pink, breaking up beef into crumbles, 8-10 minutes; drain. Stir in dip mix and sour cream.
2. Split French bread horizontally; place halves on a baking sheet, cut side up. Broil 3-4 in. from heat until lightly toasted, 1-2 minutes. Remove from broiler.

3. Spoon beef mixture over bread. Sprinkle with cheese. Broil until cheese is lightly browned, 1-2 minutes longer. To serve, cut each into 3 pieces.
1 piece: 434 cal., 23g fat (11g sat. fat), 78mg chol., 1163mg sod., 27g carb. (4g sugars, 1g fiber), 28g pro.

POTATO-BEAN SALAD WITH HERB DRESSING

My garden inspired this combo of green beans, potatoes and herbs. I toss the salad with a lightly spiced ranch-style dressing.
—*Christopher Cummer, Rincon, GA*

- -

Prep: 15 min. • **Cook:** 20 min. + chilling
Makes: 6 servings

- 1 **lb. potatoes (about 2 medium), peeled and cubed**
- ½ **lb. fresh green beans, trimmed and cut into 2-in. pieces**

DRESSING
- ⅓ **cup buttermilk**
- 2 **Tbsp. mayonnaise**
- 2 **Tbsp. sour cream**
- 1 **Tbsp. Creole mustard**
- 1 **Tbsp. minced chives**
- 1 **Tbsp. minced fresh parsley or 1 tsp. dried parsley flakes**
- 1½ **tsp. snipped fresh dill or ½ tsp. dill weed**
- 1½ **tsp. cider vinegar**
- 1 **garlic clove, minced**
- ½ **tsp. salt**
- ⅛ **tsp. celery seed**
- ⅛ **tsp. pepper**

1. Place potatoes in a large saucepan; add water to cover. Bring to a boil. Reduce heat; cook, uncovered, 10-15 minutes or until tender, adding green beans during the last 4 minutes of cooking. Drain; cool completely.
2. In a small bowl, mix the dressing ingredients. Pour over potato mixture; toss to coat. Refrigerate salad, covered, until cold.
⅔ cup: 109 cal., 5g fat (1g sat. fat), 6mg chol., 305mg sod., 14g carb. (3g sugars, 2g fiber), 2g pro. **Diabetic exchanges:** 1 starch, 1 fat.

NO CREOLE MUSTARD ON HAND?

Then fake it by adding a little Tabasco or other hot sauce to Dijon or spicy brown mustard. Add a drop or two of Worcestershire sauce if desired.

BEET SALAD WITH LEMON DRESSING

I was looking for a recipe for pickled beets and saw one with lemon instead of vinegar. I immediately thought of making a tabbouleh-inspired salad with beets instead of tomatoes.
—*Ann Sheehy, Lawrence, MA*

- -

Prep: 15 min. • **Bake:** 1¼ hours
Makes: 6 servings

- 3 medium fresh beets (about 1 lb.)
- 1 cup finely chopped English cucumber
- 6 green onions, thinly sliced
- ½ cup shredded carrot
- ½ cup chopped sweet yellow or red pepper
- ¼ cup finely chopped red onion
- ¼ cup finely chopped radish
- ¾ cup minced fresh parsley

DRESSING

- 3 Tbsp. olive oil
- 2 tsp. grated lemon zest
- 3 Tbsp. lemon juice
- 1 garlic clove, minced
- ¼ tsp. salt
- ¼ tsp. pepper

1. Preheat oven to 400°. Scrub beets and trim tops. Wrap beets in foil; place on a baking sheet. Bake until tender, 1¼-1½ hours. Cool slightly. Peel beets and cut into cubes.

2. Place remaining vegetables and parsley in a large bowl. Whisk together dressing ingredients; toss with cucumber mixture. Gently stir in beets.

⅔ cup: 116 cal., 7g fat (1g sat. fat), 0 chol., 173mg sod., 13g carb. (8g sugars, 3g fiber), 2g pro. **Diabetic exchanges:** 1½ fat, 1 vegetable.

CHICKEN WILD RICE SOUP

I'm originally from Minnesota, where wild rice grows in abundance and is popular in recipes. This soup has been part of our Christmas Eve menu for years. To save time, I cook the chicken and wild rice and cut up the vegetables the day before.
—*Virginia Montmarquet, Riverside, CA*

- -

Prep: 20 min. • **Cook:** 40 min.
Makes: 14 servings (3½ qt.)

- 2 qt. chicken broth
- ½ lb. fresh mushrooms, chopped
- 1 cup finely chopped celery
- 1 cup shredded carrots
- ½ cup finely chopped onion
- 1 tsp. chicken bouillon granules
- 1 tsp. dried parsley flakes
- ¼ tsp. garlic powder
- ¼ tsp. dried thyme
- ¼ cup butter, cubed
- ¼ cup all-purpose flour
- 1 can (10¾ oz.) condensed cream of mushroom soup, undiluted
- ½ cup dry white wine or additional chicken broth
- 3 cups cooked wild rice
- 2 cups cubed cooked chicken

1. In a large saucepan, combine the first 9 ingredients. Bring to a boil. Reduce heat; cover and simmer for 30 minutes.

2. In Dutch oven, melt butter; stir in flour until smooth. Gradually whisk in broth mixture. Bring to a boil; cook and stir for 2 minutes or until thickened. Whisk in soup and wine. Add rice and chicken; heat through.

1 cup: 154 cal., 6g fat (3g sat. fat), 27mg chol., 807mg sod., 14g carb. (2g sugars, 2g fiber), 10g pro.

CORNED BEEF & COLESLAW SANDWICHES

These open-faced sandwiches with layers of savory beef, creamy slaw and melty Swiss take only 15 minutes to create.
—*Marilou Robinson, Portland, OR*

Takes: 15 min. • **Makes:** 4 servings

- 2 cups coleslaw mix
- 3 Tbsp. sour cream
- 4 tsp. mayonnaise
- 1 Tbsp. horseradish sauce
- 1 tsp. prepared mustard
- ⅛ tsp. salt
- 4 slices rye bread
- ½ lb. thinly sliced corned beef
- 8 slices Swiss cheese

1. Place coleslaw mix in a small bowl. Combine the sour cream, mayonnaise, horseradish sauce, mustard and salt. Pour over coleslaw mix and toss to coat.

2. Place bread slices on an ungreased baking sheet. Broil 4 in. from the heat until toasted, 2-3 minutes on each side. Layer with corned beef, coleslaw mixture and cheese. Broil 2-3 minutes longer or until cheese is melted.

1 sandwich: 423 cal., 26g fat (14g sat. fat), 100mg chol., 1203mg sod., 19g carb. (3g sugars, 3g fiber), 26g pro.

COUNTRY FISH CHOWDER

You'll think you're on Cape Cod when you taste this thick, wholesome chowder made from a recipe I've treasured for many years. It's one of my husband's favorites. He likes it more and more because over the years I've customized the basic recipe by including ingredients he enjoys.
—*Linda Lazaroff, Hebron, CT*

Prep: 15 min. • **Cook:** 25 min.
Makes: 10 servings (2½ qt.)

- 1 cup chopped onion
- 4 bacon strips, chopped
- 3 cans (12 oz. each) evaporated milk
- 1 can (15¼ oz.) whole kernel corn, undrained
- 1 can (6½ oz.) chopped clams, undrained
- 3 medium potatoes, peeled and cubed
- 3 Tbsp. butter
- 1 tsp. salt
- ¾ tsp. pepper
- 1 lb. fish fillets (haddock, cod or flounder), cooked and broken into pieces
  Crumbled cooked bacon, optional
  Minced chives, optional

In a large saucepan, cook onion and bacon over medium heat until bacon is crisp; drain. Add milk, corn, clams, potatoes, butter, salt and pepper. Cover and cook over medium heat, stirring occasionally, until potatoes are tender, about 20 minutes. Stir in fish and heat through. Ladle into bowls. If desired, top with bacon and chives.

1 cup: 250 cal., 12g fat (6g sat. fat), 57mg chol., 598mg sod., 19g carb. (7g sugars, 2g fiber), 15g pro.

TOMATO, AVOCADO & GRILLED CORN SALAD

With ripe tomatoes, fresh basil and grilled corn off the cob, this sunny salad tastes just like summertime!
—*Angela Spengler, Niceville, FL*

- -

Prep: 20 min. • **Grill:** 10 min. + cooling
Makes: 8 servings

- 1 medium ear sweet corn, husks removed
- 3 large red tomatoes, sliced
- 3 large yellow tomatoes, sliced
- ¾ tsp. kosher salt, divided
- ½ tsp. pepper, divided
- 2 medium ripe avocados, peeled and sliced
- ¼ cup olive oil
- 2 Tbsp. red wine vinegar
- 1 Tbsp. minced fresh basil, plus more for garnish
- ⅓ cup crumbled feta cheese

1. Grill corn, covered, over medium heat 10-12 minutes or until lightly browned and tender, turning occasionally. Cool slightly. Cut corn from cob.

2. Arrange tomato slices on a large serving platter. Sprinkle with ½ tsp. salt and ¼ tsp. pepper. Top with avocado slices. Whisk together the oil, vinegar, basil and remaining salt and pepper; drizzle half over the tomatoes and avocado. Top with grilled corn and feta; drizzle remaining dressing over top. Garnish with additional chopped basil.

1 serving: 164 cal., 13g fat (2g sat. fat), 3mg chol., 237mg sod., 11g carb. (4g sugars, 4g fiber), 3g pro. **Diabetic exchanges:** 2 fat, 1 vegetable, ½ starch.

TASTES OF SUMMER
This dish is spectacular with fresh heirloom tomatoes, and all that flavor means you can use less salt. For a quick, healthy dinner, serve the salad with grilled chicken.

Contest Winner

CHEDDAR POTATO CHOWDER

I made this soup only occasionally because the original recipe was quite high in fat. I doctored it up a bit using healthier ingredients, and now we eat this flavorful chowder more often.

—Ellie Rausch, Goodsoil, SK

Prep: 20 min. • **Cook:** 20 min.
Makes: 7 servings

- 2 cups water
- 2 cups diced unpeeled red potatoes
- 1 cup diced carrot
- ½ cup diced celery
- ¼ cup chopped onion
- 1 tsp. salt
- ¼ tsp. pepper
- ¼ cup all-purpose flour
- 2 cups 2% milk
- 2 cups shredded reduced-fat cheddar cheese
- 1 cup cubed fully cooked ham

1. In a Dutch oven, combine the first 7 ingredients. Bring to a boil. Reduce heat; cover and simmer for 10-12 minutes or until tender.

2. Meanwhile, place flour in a large saucepan; gradually whisk in milk. Bring to a boil over medium heat; cook and stir for 2 minutes or until thickened. Remove from the heat. Add cheese; stir until melted. Stir the ham and the cheese sauce into undrained vegetables; stir until combined.

1 cup: 212 cal., 9g fat (5g sat. fat), 29mg chol., 847mg sod., 18g carb. (0 sugars, 2g fiber), 16g pro.

Contest Winner

HOT PEPPER-BEEF SANDWICHES

If you like your shredded beef with a little kick of heat, then this recipe is for you. For an even zestier version, add a second jar of jalapenos or use hot peppers instead of the pepperoncini.

—Kristen Langmeier, Faribault, MN

Prep: 15 min. • **Cook:** 8 hours
Makes: 12 servings

- 1 boneless beef chuck roast (4 to 5 lbs.)
- 2 medium onions, coarsely chopped
- 1 jar (16 oz.) sliced pepperoncini, undrained
- 1 jar (8 oz.) pickled jalapeno slices, drained
- 1 bottle (12 oz.) beer or nonalcoholic beer
- 1 envelope onion soup mix
- 5 garlic cloves, minced
- ½ tsp. pepper
- 12 kaiser rolls, split
- 12 slices provolone cheese

1. Place roast in a 4- or 5-qt. slow cooker. Add the onions, pepperoncini, jalapenos, beer, soup mix, garlic and pepper.

2. Cover and cook on low until meat is tender, 8-10 hours.

3. Remove meat. Skim fat from cooking liquid. When cool enough to handle, shred meat with 2 forks and return to slow cooker; heat through. Serve ½ cup meat mixture on each roll with a slice of cheese.

Note: Look for pepperoncini (pickled peppers) in the pickle and olive section of your grocery store.

1 sandwich: 534 cal., 23g fat (9g sat. fat), 113mg chol., 1187mg sod., 38g carb. (3g sugars, 3g fiber), 41g pro.

FARMER'S MARKET ORZO SALAD

Orzo is a tiny pasta shaped like rice. We like to use it as a base for veggies, lemony vinaigrette and cheeses like mozzarella, feta or smoked Gouda.
—*Heather Dezzutto, Raleigh, NC*

Prep: 25 min. • **Grill:** 10 min.
Makes: 8 servings

- 1 pkg. (16 oz.) orzo pasta
- 2 small yellow summer squash, halved lengthwise
- 1 medium zucchini, halved lengthwise
- 1 medium red onion, quartered
- 8 Tbsp. olive oil, divided
- ½ tsp. salt, divided
- ¼ tsp. pepper, divided
- 3 Tbsp. lemon juice
- 8 oz. smoked mozzarella cheese, cut into ¼-in. cubes
- 1½ cups grape tomatoes, halved lengthwise
- ½ cup chopped fresh basil
- ½ cup pine nuts, toasted

1. Cook orzo according to package directions; drain. Brush yellow squash, zucchini and onion with 2 Tbsp. oil; sprinkle with ¼ tsp. salt and ⅛ tsp. pepper. Grill vegetables, covered, over medium heat or broil 4 in. from heat 10-12 minutes or until lightly charred and tender, turning once. Cool slightly. Cut into 1-in. pieces.
2. In a small bowl, whisk lemon juice and remaining oil until blended. In a large bowl, combine orzo, grilled vegetables, mozzarella, tomatoes, basil and remaining salt and pepper. Add dressing; toss to coat. Sprinkle with pine nuts.

1¼ cups: 291 cal., 27g fat (7g sat. fat), 25mg chol., 274mg sod., 7g carb. (4g sugars, 2g fiber), 9g pro.

BAKED HAM & COLBY SANDWICHES

This yummy recipe is a winner with our friends and family. Not only are the warm sandwiches a snap to prepare, but they also smell so good when they're baking that no one has been able to resist them. They're a staple at our get-togethers.
—*Sherry Crenshaw, Fort Worth, TX*

Takes: 30 min. • **Makes:** 8 servings

- ½ cup butter, melted
- 2 Tbsp. prepared mustard
- 1 Tbsp. dried minced onion
- 1 Tbsp. poppy seeds
- 2 to 3 tsp. sugar
- 8 hamburger buns, split
- 8 slices Colby cheese
- 16 thin slices deli ham (about 1 lb.)
- 1½ cups shredded part-skim mozzarella cheese

1. In a small bowl, combine the butter, mustard, onion, poppy seeds and sugar. Place bun bottoms, cut side up, in an ungreased 15x10x1-in. baking pan. Top each with Colby cheese, ham and mozzarella. Brush with half of the butter mixture.
2. Replace bun tops. Brush with the remaining butter mixture. Bake, uncovered, at 350° until cheese is melted, 10-15 minutes.

1 sandwich: 504 cal., 32g fat (18g sat. fat), 102mg chol., 1444mg sod., 27g carb. (5g sugars, 1g fiber), 27g pro.

GRILLED PEACH, RICE & ARUGULA SALAD

This hearty salad was created when I needed to clear out some leftovers from the fridge—and it became an instant hit! The grilled peaches are the ultimate "tastes like summer" salad booster.

—*Lauren Wyler, Dripping Springs, TX*

Takes: 30 min. • **Makes:** 6 servings

- 3 Tbsp. cider vinegar
- 2 Tbsp. Dijon mustard
- 2 Tbsp. canola oil
- 2 Tbsp. maple syrup
- 1 Tbsp. finely chopped shallot
- ¼ tsp. cayenne pepper

SALAD

- 1 pkg. (8.8 oz.) ready-to-serve long grain and wild rice
- 2 medium peaches, quartered
- 6 cups fresh arugula (about 4 oz.)
- 6 bacon strips, cooked and crumbled
- ½ cup crumbled goat cheese

1. For dressing, whisk together first 6 ingredients.

2. Prepare rice according to package directions; cool slightly. Place the peaches on an oiled grill rack over medium heat. Grill, covered, until lightly browned, 6-8 minutes, turning occasionally.

3. To serve, add bacon and ¼ cup dressing to the rice. Line a platter with arugula; top with rice mixture and peaches. Drizzle with the remaining dressing; top with cheese.

1 serving: 218 cal., 11g fat (3g sat. fat), 20mg chol., 530mg sod., 23g carb. (9g sugars, 2g fiber), 7g pro. **Diabetic exchanges:** 1 starch, 1 vegetable, 2 fat.

CHERRY TOMATO SALAD

This recipe evolved from a need to use the bumper crops of cherry tomatoes that we regularly grow. It has become a summer favorite, especially at cookouts.

—*Sally Sibley, St. Augustine, FL*

Takes: 15 min. + marinating
Makes: 6 servings

- 1 qt. cherry tomatoes, halved
- ¼ cup canola oil
- 3 Tbsp. white vinegar
- ½ tsp. salt
- ½ tsp. sugar
- ¼ cup minced fresh parsley
- 1 to 2 tsp. minced fresh basil
- 1 to 2 tsp. minced fresh oregano

Place tomatoes in a shallow bowl. In a small bowl, whisk oil, vinegar, salt and sugar until blended; stir in herbs. Pour over tomatoes; gently toss to coat. Refrigerate, covered, overnight.

¾ cup: 103 cal., 10g fat (1g sat. fat), 0 chol., 203mg sod., 4g carb. (3g sugars, 1g fiber), 1g pro. **Diabetic exchanges:** 2 fat, 1 vegetable.

Contest Winner

ITALIAN GRILLED STEAK SANDWICH

If you need to feed a hungry crowd, you can't go wrong with steak sandwiches. They're easy to make and everyone loves them.

—*Gilda Lester, Millsboro, DE*

- -

Prep: 35 min. + marinating
Grill: 15 min. + chilling • **Makes:** 8 servings

- ½   cup reduced-sodium teriyaki sauce
- 2   Tbsp. lemon juice
- 2   Tbsp. olive oil
- 2   Tbsp. Worcestershire sauce
- 1   beef flank steak (1 lb.)
- 1   round loaf Italian bread (about 2 lbs.), unsliced
- 4   plum tomatoes, chopped
- 4   green onions, thinly sliced
- ¼   cup Greek olives, coarsely chopped
- ¼   cup sliced pepperoni
- 1   Tbsp. thinly sliced fresh basil leaves
- 2   Tbsp. plus ¼ cup prepared Italian salad dressing, divided
- 2   cups fresh arugula

1. Place first 4 ingredients in a large bowl or shallow dish. Add steak and turn to coat. Refrigerate, covered, 8 hours or overnight.

2. Remove steak, discarding marinade. Grill steak, covered, over medium heat or broil 4 in. from heat until meat reaches desired doneness (for medium-rare, a thermometer should read 135°; medium, 140°), 6-8 minutes per side. Cool.

3. Cut bread loaf horizontally in half. Hollow out both halves, leaving a ½-in. shell (save removed bread for another use). Cut steak across the grain into thin slices. In a bowl, toss tomatoes with green onions, olives, pepperoni, basil and 2 Tbsp. dressing. In another bowl, toss arugula with remaining dressing.

4. Place half the arugula in bread bottom. Layer with steak, tomato mixture and remaining arugula; replace top. Wrap in foil; refrigerate at least 1 hour. Cut into wedges to serve.

1 wedge: 260 cal., 10g fat (3g sat. fat), 30mg chol., 567mg sod., 24g carb. (4g sugars, 2g fiber), 16g pro. **Diabetic exchanges:** 2 lean meat, 1½ starch, 1 fat.

WHITE CHILI WITH A KICK

Rotisserie chicken makes this spicy chili easy, but you could also cook your own chicken or use leftovers if you prefer. We like to top our bowls with sour cream, green onions, cheese and salsa.

—*Emmajean Anderson, Mendota Heights, MN*

- -

Prep: 20 min. • **Cook:** 15 min.
Makes: 9 servings (2¼ qt.)

- 1 **large onion, chopped**
- 6 **Tbsp. butter, cubed**
- 2 **Tbsp. all-purpose flour**
- 2 **cups chicken broth**
- ¾ **cup half-and-half cream**
- 1 **rotisserie chicken, cut up**
- 2 **cans (15 oz. each) cannellini beans, rinsed and drained**
- 1 **can (11 oz.) white corn, drained**
- 2 **cans (4 oz. each) chopped green chiles**
- 2 **tsp. ground cumin**
- 1 **tsp. chili powder**
- ½ **tsp. salt**
- ½ **tsp. white pepper**
- ½ **tsp. hot pepper sauce**
- 1½ **cups shredded pepper jack cheese**
  Optional: Salsa and chopped green onions

1. In a Dutch oven, saute onion in butter. Stir in flour until blended; cook and stir until golden brown, 3 minutes. Gradually add broth and cream. Bring to a boil; cook and stir until thickened, 2 minutes.
2. Add the chicken, beans, corn, chiles, cumin, chili powder, salt, pepper and pepper sauce; heat through. Stir in cheese until melted.
3. If desired, garnish each serving with salsa and green onions.
1 cup: 424 cal., 21g fat (11g sat. fat), 113mg chol., 896mg sod., 26g carb. (3g sugars, 5g fiber), 31g pro.

═══════════════════════════

PILE IT ON

This chili is so rich and creamy, you can pile on the crisp, crunchy toppings. Besides salsa and green onions, consider black olives, shredded lettuce, and even crushed tortilla chips or oyster crackers.

BLUE PLATE OPEN-FACED TURKEY SANDWICH

Turkey with gravy makes divine comfort food that reminds me of old-time diners on the East Coast.

—*Christine Schwester, Divide, CO*

Takes: 25 min. • **Makes:** 6 servings

- ⅓ cup butter, cubed
- 1 small onion, chopped
- ⅓ cup all-purpose flour
- 2 tsp. minced fresh parsley
- ¼ tsp. pepper
- ⅛ tsp. garlic powder
- ⅛ tsp. dried thyme
- 3 cups reduced-sodium chicken broth
- 1¼ lbs. sliced deli turkey
- 12 slices white bread

1. In a large cast-iron or other heavy skillet, heat butter over medium heat. Add onion; cook and stir until tender, 4-5 minutes. Stir in flour, parsley and seasonings until blended; gradually whisk in broth. Bring to a boil, stirring constantly; cook and stir until slightly thickened, 1-2 minutes.
2. Add turkey, 1 slice at a time; heat through. Serve over bread.

2 open-faced sandwiches: 361 cal., 14g fat (7g sat. fat), 60mg chol., 1462mg sod., 33g carb. (4g sugars, 2g fiber), 25g pro.

BACON-BLUE CHEESE STUFFED BURGERS

These loaded burgers are a hearty meal in a bun. They're sure to satisfy even the biggest appetites.

—*Christine Keating, Norwalk, CA*

Prep: 30 min. • **Grill:** 10 min.
Makes: 4 servings

- 1½ lbs. lean ground beef (90% lean)
- 3 oz. cream cheese, softened
- ⅓ cup crumbled blue cheese
- ⅓ cup bacon bits
- ½ tsp. salt
- ½ tsp. garlic powder
- ¼ tsp. pepper
- 1 lb. sliced fresh mushrooms
- 1 Tbsp. olive oil
- 1 Tbsp. water
- 1 Tbsp. Dijon mustard
- 4 whole wheat hamburger buns, split
- ¼ cup mayonnaise
- 4 romaine leaves
- 1 medium tomato, sliced

1. Shape ground beef into 8 thin patties. Combine the cream cheese, blue cheese and bacon bits; spoon onto the center of 4 patties. Top with remaining patties and press edges firmly to seal. Combine the salt, garlic powder and pepper; sprinkle over patties.
2. Grill burgers, covered, over medium heat or broil 4 in. from the heat on each side until a thermometer reads 160° and juices run clear, for 5-7 minutes.
3. Meanwhile, in a large skillet, saute mushrooms in oil until tender. Stir in water and mustard.
4. Serve burgers on buns with mayonnaise, romaine, tomato and mushroom mixture.

1 burger: 701 cal., 43g fat (15g sat. fat), 149mg chol., 1280mg sod., 31g carb. (7g sugars, 5g fiber), 48g pro.

Herb & Cheese-Stuffed Burgers: Omit blue cheese and bacon bits. Mix cream cheese with ¼ cup shredded cheddar cheese, 2 Tbsp. minced fresh parsley and 1 tsp. Dijon mustard. Season meat with ¾ tsp. crushed dried rosemary and ¼ dried sage leaves. Proceed as recipe directs.

Greek-Stuffed Burgers: Omit cream cheese, blue cheese and bacon bits. Mix ⅓ cup feta cheese, ⅓ cup chopped tomato, 2 Tbsp. chopped red onion, 4 tsp. chopped ripe olives, 2 tsp. olive oil and ¼ tsp. dried oregano. Stuff burgers with feta mixture and proceed as recipe directs.

That's a Wrap!

Need a quick meal that's satisfying but not too heavy? These simple roll-ups are ready in 30 minutes or less...and tortillas instead of bread help keep things light. For breakfast or lunch at home or on the move, these self-contained sandwiches are just the thing!

HAM & EGG WRAPS

This kid-friendly recipe takes only 20 minutes to prepare and cook.
—*Sharon Haswell, Cheshire, MA*

Takes: 20 min. • **Makes:** 4 servings

    8   large eggs, room
    2   green onions, sliced
    1   Tbsp. Dijon mustard
    ½   tsp. salt
    ¼   tsp. pepper
    2   tsp. butter
    4   oz. sliced deli ham, cut into strips
    4   flour tortillas (8 in.), warmed

1. In a large bowl, whisk the first 5 ingredients. In a large skillet, heat butter over medium heat. Add ham; cook and stir 1-2 minutes or until lightly browned. Pour in egg mixture; cook and stir until eggs are thickened and no liquid egg remains. Remove from heat.
2. Spoon a fourth of the egg mixture down center of each tortilla. Fold bottom of tortilla over filling; fold both sides to close.
1 wrap: 341 cal., 16g fat (5g sat. fat), 441mg chol., 1053mg sod., 28g carb. (2g sugars, 0 fiber), 22g pro.

MOZZARELLA BEEF ROLL-UPS

Kids will love these pepperoni and beef wraps. They're easy to assemble because each tortilla is simply wrapped around a portion of hearty meat filling with a piece of string cheese.
—Taste of Home *Test Kitchen*

Takes: 30 min. • **Makes:** 6 servings

    1   lb. ground beef
    1   medium green pepper, chopped
    ⅓   cup chopped onion
    1   can (8 oz.) pizza sauce
    2   oz. sliced pepperoni (about ⅔ cup)
    ½   tsp. dried oregano
    6   flour tortillas (10 in.), warmed
    6   pieces string cheese (about 6 oz.)

1. Preheat oven to 350°. In a large skillet, cook and crumble beef with pepper and onion over medium-high heat until no longer pink, 5-7 minutes; drain. Stir in pizza sauce, pepperoni and oregano.
2. Spoon ½ cup mixture across center of each tortilla; top with a string cheese. Fold bottom and sides of tortilla over filling and roll up.
3. Place on an ungreased baking sheet, seam side down. Bake until heated through, about 10 minutes.
Freeze option: Cool beef mixture before assembly. Individually wrap roll-ups in foil and freeze in a freezer container. To use, partially thaw overnight in refrigerator. Reheat foil-wrapped roll-ups on a baking sheet in a preheated 350° oven until heated through. To reheat individually, remove foil and rewrap in paper towel; place on a microwave-safe plate. Microwave on high until heated through, turning once. Let stand 15 seconds.
1 roll-up: 513 cal., 25g fat (11g sat. fat), 71mg chol., 1064mg sod., 41g carb. (5g sugars, 4g fiber), 30g pro.

SPICY BUFFALO CHICKEN WRAPS

This recipe has a real kick and is one of my husband's favorites. It is ready in a flash, is easily doubled and is the closest thing to restaurant Buffalo wings I've ever tasted in a light version.
—*Jennifer Beck, Meridian, ID*

Takes: 25 min. • **Makes:** 2 servings

- ½ lb. boneless skinless chicken breast, cubed
- ½ tsp. canola oil
- 2 Tbsp. Louisiana-style hot sauce
- 1 cup shredded lettuce
- 2 flour tortillas (6 in.), warmed
- 2 tsp. reduced-fat ranch salad dressing
- 2 Tbsp. crumbled blue cheese

1. In a large nonstick skillet, cook chicken in oil over medium heat for 6 minutes; drain. Stir in hot sauce. Bring to a boil. Reduce heat; simmer, uncovered, until sauce is thickened and chicken is no longer pink, 3-5 minutes.

2. Place lettuce on tortillas; drizzle with ranch dressing. Top with chicken mixture and blue cheese; roll up.

1 wrap: 273 cal., 11g fat (3g sat. fat), 70mg chol., 453mg sod., 15g carb. (1g sugars, 1g fiber), 28g pro. **Diabetic exchanges:** 3 lean meat, 1½ fat, 1 starch.

WARM TURKEY & TOMATO WRAPS

When my wife was out and about one day, I invented these wraps to surprise her when she came home. Sometimes I substitute cranberry sauce for the chutney, or I use mascarpone cheese instead of cream cheese.
—*Alfred Lester, Millsboro, DE*

Takes: 30 min. • **Makes:** 4 servings

- 3 plum tomatoes, thinly sliced
- ½ cup julienned roasted sweet red peppers
- 4 green onions, thinly sliced
- ½ cup olive oil vinaigrette
- 1 pkg. (8 oz.) cream cheese, softened
- ¼ cup chutney
- ½ tsp. curry powder
- 1¼ lbs. turkey breast cutlets, cut into ½-in. strips
- 1 Tbsp. olive oil
- ½ tsp. salt
- ½ tsp. ground cumin
- ½ tsp. pepper
- 4 flour tortillas (10 in.), warmed
- 4 lettuce leaves

1. In a small bowl, combine tomatoes, red peppers and green onions; add vinaigrette and toss to coat. In another bowl, beat cream cheese, chutney and curry powder until blended.

2. In a small bowl, combine turkey, oil and seasonings; toss to coat. In a large skillet, add turkey mixture in batches; cook and stir 1-2 minutes or until no longer pink. Remove from heat; keep warm.

3. Spread ¼ cup cream cheese mixture over each tortilla. Near center of tortilla, layer lettuce, tomato mixture and turkey. Fold bottom and sides of tortilla over filling and roll up. Serve immediately.

1 wrap: 711 cal., 33g fat (15g sat. fat), 150mg chol., 1298mg sod., 48g carb. (12g sugars, 8g fiber), 46g pro.

BLT WRAPS

My mom used to make these delicious wraps for all of the kids and grandkids on summer days at the lake. Nowadays, we love to pack them along for picnics and days in the park.
—*Shelly Burks, Brighton, MO*

Takes: 15 min. • **Makes:** 8 servings

- 16 ready-to-serve fully cooked bacon strips, warmed if desired
- 8 flour tortillas (8 in.), room temperature
- 4 cups chopped lettuce
- 2 cups chopped tomatoes (3 small tomatoes)
- 2 cups shredded cheddar cheese
- ½ cup ranch salad dressing

Place 2 bacon strips across the center of each tortilla. Top with lettuce, tomatoes and cheese; drizzle with salad dressing. Fold bottom and sides of tortilla over filling and roll up.

1 wrap: 409 cal., 25g fat (9g sat. fat), 31mg chol., 689mg sod., 31g carb. (2g sugars, 3g fiber), 15g pro.

Breads, Rolls & More

When it comes to great country cooking, nothing beats warm home-baked bread. It comforts, satisfies, and turns even humble fare into a special meal. Let the inviting aroma of these selections welcome your loved ones to the table for breakfast, dinner and any time.

CINNAMON SWIRL BREAD

Your family will be impressed with the soft texture and appealing swirls of cinnamon in these lovely breakfast loaves.
—*Diane Armstrong, Elm Grove, WI*

Prep: 25 min. + rising • **Bake:** 30 min.
Makes: 2 loaves (16 slices each)

- 2 pkg. (¼ oz. each) active dry yeast
- ⅓ cup warm water (110° to 115°)
- 1 cup warm milk (110° to 115°)
- 1 cup sugar, divided
- 2 large eggs, room temperature
- 6 Tbsp. butter, softened
- 1½ tsp. salt
- 5½ to 6 cups all-purpose flour
- 2 Tbsp. ground cinnamon

1. In a large bowl, dissolve yeast in warm water. Add milk, ½ cup sugar, eggs, butter, salt and 3 cups flour; beat on medium speed until smooth. Stir in enough of the remaining flour to form a soft dough.
2. Turn dough onto a floured surface; knead until smooth and elastic, about 6-8 minutes. Place in a greased bowl, turning once to grease the top. Cover; let rise in a warm place until doubled, about 1 hour.
3. Mix cinnamon and remaining sugar. Punch down dough. Turn onto a lightly floured surface; divide in half. Roll each dough portion into an 18x8-in. rectangle; sprinkle each with about ¼ cup cinnamon sugar to within ½ in. of edges. Roll up jelly-roll style, starting with a short side; pinch seam to seal. Place in 2 greased 9x5-in. loaf pans, seam side down.
4. Cover with kitchen towels; let rise in a warm place until doubled, about 1½ hours. Preheat oven to 350°.
5. Bake bread until golden brown, about 30-35 minutes. Remove from the pans to wire racks to cool.
1 slice: 133 cal., 3g fat (2g sat. fat), 18mg chol., 136mg sod., 24g carb. (7g sugars, 1g fiber), 3g pro.

HUSH PUPPIES

Mom is well-known for her wonderful hush puppies. Her recipe is easy to prepare, and the chopped onion adds to the tasty results.
—*Mary McGuire, Graham, NC*

- -

Takes: 25 min. • **Makes:** 2 dozen

- 1   cup yellow cornmeal
- ¼   cup all-purpose flour
- 1½ tsp. baking powder
- ½   tsp. salt
- 1   large egg, room temperature, lightly beaten
- ¾   cup 2% milk
- 1   small onion, finely chopped
  Oil for deep-fat frying

1. In a large bowl, combine the cornmeal, flour, baking powder and salt. Whisk the egg, milk and onion; add the mixture to the dry ingredients just until combined.
2. In cast-iron Dutch oven or electric skillet, heat oil to 365°. Drop batter by tablespoonfuls into oil. Fry until golden brown, 2-2½ minutes. Drain on paper towels. Serve warm.
1 hush puppy: 55 cal., 3g fat (0 sat. fat), 9mg chol., 86mg sod., 7g carb. (1g sugars, 0 fiber), 1g pro.

HUSH PUPPY HISTORY
Hush puppies are said to have originated in New Orleans in 1727. They are a traditional accompaniment to fried catfish.

SAVORY COCKTAIL SCONES

Scones are my comfort food, and I wanted to make a savory version with roasted garlic butter. The addition of bacon seemed natural. Their cocktail size makes them fun; they also work great for a brunch buffet.
—*Donna-Marie Ryan, Topsfield, MA*

- -

Prep: 55 min. • **Bake:** 15 min.
Makes: 16 servings

- 1   whole garlic bulb
- 2   tsp. olive oil
- ½   cup butter, softened

SCONES

- 2   bacon strips, chopped
- ⅓   cup chopped onion
- 2   cups all-purpose flour
- 3   tsp. baking powder
- ½   tsp. baking soda
- ½   tsp. salt
- ½   cup cold butter
- 1   large egg, room temperature
- ½   cup sherry
- ⅓   cup heavy whipping cream
- ¼   cup 2% milk

1. Remove papery outer skin from garlic (do not peel or separate cloves). Cut top off of garlic bulb. Brush with oil. Wrap bulb in heavy-duty foil. Bake at 400° for

40-45 minutes or until softened. Cool for 10-15 minutes. Squeeze softened garlic into a small bowl; mash with fork. Stir in butter; set aside.
2. In a small skillet, cook the bacon over medium heat until crisp. Remove bacon to paper towels with a slotted spoon; drain, reserving 1 Tbsp. drippings. In the same skillet, cook and stir onion in the drippings until softened. Reduce heat to medium-low; cook, stirring onion occasionally, for 30 minutes or until deep golden brown. Set aside.
3. In a large bowl, combine the flour, baking powder, baking soda and salt. Cut in butter until mixture resembles coarse crumbs. Whisk the egg, sherry and cream; stir into crumb mixture just until moistened. Fold in onion and bacon.
4. Turn onto a floured surface; knead 10 times. Pat into a 10x5-in. rectangle. Using a floured knife, cut the dough into eight 2½-in. squares; cut each square diagonally in half.
5. Place scones on a parchment-lined baking sheet; brush with milk. Bake at 400° for 12-15 minutes or until golden brown. Serve warm with butter.
1 scone: 204 cal., 15g fat (9g sat. fat), 52mg chol., 297mg sod., 13g carb. (1g sugars, 1g fiber), 3g pro.

YORKSHIRE PUDDING WITH BACON & SAGE

Individual Yorkshire puddings are a nice change from traditional dinner rolls. These savory popovers are topped with crumbled bacon and fresh sage.
—*Melissa Jelinek, Apple Valley, MN*

Prep: 15 min. • **Bake:** 20 min. • **Makes:** 1 dozen

- 5   bacon strips, chopped
- 2   Tbsp. butter, melted
- 1½ cups all-purpose flour
- 3   Tbsp. minced fresh sage, divided
- ½   tsp. salt
- 1½ cups 2% milk
- 3   large eggs, room temperature

1. In a large skillet, cook the bacon over medium heat until crisp. Remove to paper towels with a slotted spoon; drain bacon, reserving drippings.
2. Transfer drippings to a measuring cup; add enough melted butter to measure ¼ cup. Pour into 12 ungreased muffin cups. Place in a 450° oven until hot.
3. Meanwhile, in a small bowl, combine the flour, 2 Tbsp. sage and salt; beat in the milk and eggs until smooth. Fold in two-thirds of the bacon. Divide batter among prepared muffin cups.
4. Bake at 450° for 10 minutes. Reduce heat to 350° (do not open oven door). Bake 10-12 minutes longer or until puffed and golden brown. Sprinkle popovers with remaining bacon and sage.
1 pudding: 150 cal., 8g fat (3g sat. fat), 67mg chol., 224mg sod., 14g carb. (2g sugars, 0 fiber), 5g pro.

ROASTED RED PEPPER BREAD

These pretty loaves are loaded with flavor from grated Parmesan cheese and roasted sweet red peppers. You can't ever go wrong serving them at dinner or as an appetizer.
—*Cheryl Perry, Hertford, NC*

Prep: 45 min. + rising • **Bake:** 20 min. + cooling
Makes: 2 loaves (12 slices each)

- 1½ cups roasted sweet red peppers, drained
- 1   pkg. (¼ oz.) active dry yeast
- 2   Tbsp. warm water (110° to 115°)
- 1¼ cups grated Parmesan cheese, divided
- ⅓   cup warm 2% milk (110° to 115°)
- 2   Tbsp. butter, softened
- 1¼ tsp. salt
- 3¼ to 3¾ cups all-purpose flour
- 1   large egg, room temperature
- 1   Tbsp. water
- 1½ tsp. coarsely ground pepper

1. Place red peppers in a food processor; cover and process until pureed. In a large bowl, dissolve yeast in warm water. Add red peppers, 1 cup cheese, milk, butter, salt and 1½ cups flour. Beat until smooth. Stir in enough remaining flour to form a firm dough.
2. Turn onto a floured surface; knead dough until smooth and elastic, about 6-8 minutes. Place in a greased bowl, turning once to grease the top. Cover; let dough rise in a warm place until doubled, about 1 hour.
3. Punch dough down. Turn onto a lightly floured surface; divide the dough into 6 pieces. Shape each into a 18-in. rope. Place 3 ropes on a greased baking sheet and braid; pinch ends to seal and tuck under. Repeat with remaining dough. Cover and let loaves rise until doubled, about 1 hour.
4. In a small bowl, combine egg and water; brush over braids. Sprinkle with pepper and remaining cheese. Bake bread at 350° for 18-22 minutes or until golden brown.
1 slice: 99 cal., 3g fat (1g sat. fat), 15mg chol., 254mg sod., 14g carb. (1g sugars, 1g fiber), 4g pro. **Diabetic exchanges:** 1 starch.

RUSTIC PUMPKIN BREAD

I got this pumpkin bread recipe from a co-worker at an office party. It is so yummy and moist that I now make it every year at the holidays for friends and family.
—*Sandy Sandaval, Sandy Valley, NV*

Prep: 25 min. • **Bake:** 1 hour + cooling
Makes: 2 loaves (16 slices each)

- 3 cups sugar
- 1 can (15 oz.) pumpkin
- 1 cup canola oil
- 4 large eggs, room temperature
- ⅔ cup water
- 3½ cups all-purpose flour
- 2 tsp. baking soda
- 1 tsp. salt
- 1 tsp. ground cinnamon
- 1 tsp. ground nutmeg
- ½ tsp. ground cloves
- ½ cup chopped pecans

TOPPING
- ⅓ cup all-purpose flour
- ¼ cup packed brown sugar
- ½ tsp. ground cinnamon
- 2 Tbsp. cold butter
- ¼ cup chopped pecans

1. In a large bowl, beat the sugar, pumpkin, oil, eggs and water until blended. In a large bowl, combine the flour, baking soda, salt, cinnamon, nutmeg and cloves; gradually beat into pumpkin mixture until blended. Stir in pecans.
2. Pour into 2 greased 9x5-in. loaf pans. For topping, in a small bowl, combine the flour, brown sugar and cinnamon; cut in the butter until mixture resembles coarse crumbs. Stir in pecans. Sprinkle topping over batter.
3. Bake at 350° for 60-65 minutes or until a toothpick inserted in center comes out clean. Cool loaves for 10 minutes before removing from pans to wire racks.
1 slice: 233 cal., 10g fat (2g sat. fat), 28mg chol., 168mg sod., 33g carb. (21g sugars, 1g fiber), 3g pro.

ROLLED BUTTERMILK BISCUITS

I scribbled down this recipe on a trip our family made to The Farmers' Museum in Cooperstown, New York, many years ago. I must have gotten it right, because these biscuits turn out great every time.
—*Patricia Kile, Elizabethtown, PA*

Prep: 20 min. • **Bake:** 15 min.
Makes: 8 biscuits

- 2 cups all-purpose flour
- 3 tsp. baking powder
- ½ tsp. baking soda
- ¼ tsp. salt
- 3 Tbsp. cold butter
- ¾ to 1 cup buttermilk
- 1 Tbsp. fat-free milk

1. In a large bowl, combine the flour, baking powder, baking soda and salt; cut in butter until mixture resembles coarse crumbs. Stir in enough buttermilk just to moisten dough.
2. Turn onto a lightly floured surface; knead 3-4 times. Pat or roll the dough to ¾-in. thickness. Cut with a floured 2½-in. biscuit cutter. Place in a large ungreased cast-iron or other ovenproof skillet.
3. Brush with milk. Bake at 450° until golden brown, 12-15 minutes.
1 biscuit: 162 cal., 5g fat (3g sat. fat), 12mg chol., 412mg sod., 25g carb. (1g sugars, 1g fiber), 4g pro. **Diabetic exchanges:** 1½ starch, 1 fat.

BLUEBERRY STREUSEL COFFEE CAKE

Filled with juicy berries and crunchy pecans, this family-favorite smells so wonderful as it bakes.

—*Lori Snedden, Sherman, TX*

- -

Prep: 20 min. • **Bake:** 35 min. + cooling
Makes: 9 servings

- 2   **cups all-purpose flour**
- 2   **tsp. baking powder**
- ¼   **tsp. salt**
- ¾   **cup sugar**
- ½   **cup butter, softened**
- 1   **large egg, room temperature**
- ½   **cup whole milk**
- 1   **cup fresh or frozen blueberries**
- 1   **cup chopped pecans**

STREUSEL TOPPING

- ½   **cup sugar**
- ⅓   **cup all-purpose flour**
- ¼   **cup cold butter**

1. Preheat oven to 375°. Whisk flour, baking powder and salt. In another bowl, cream sugar and butter until light and fluffy. Add egg and milk; stir into the dry ingredients. Fold in the blueberries and pecans. Spread the batter into a greased 9-in. square baking pan.

2. For topping, combine sugar and flour; cut in butter until crumbly. Sprinkle over the batter. Bake until a toothpick inserted in the center comes out clean, for about 35-40 minutes. Cool on a wire rack.

Note: If using frozen blueberries, use without thawing to avoid discoloring the batter.

1 slice: 476 cal., 26g fat (11g sat. fat), 66mg chol., 323mg sod., 57g carb. (30g sugars, 3g fiber), 6g pro.

Raspberry Streusel Coffee Cake: Substitute raspberries for the blueberries.

CONFETTI CORNBREAD

My grandmother Virginia always served us Southwest cornbread. To honor her, I created a recipe that cuts down on the chopping but never skimps on flavor.
—*Angie Price, Bradford, TN*

Prep: 20 min. • **Bake:** 50 min.
Makes: 12 servings

- 2 pkg. (8½ oz. each) cornbread/muffin mix
- ¼ tsp. cayenne pepper
- 2 large eggs, room temperature
- 1 can (14¾ oz.) cream-style corn
- ½ cup buttermilk
- ¼ cup plus 1½ tsp. canola oil, divided
- 1 cup shredded cheddar cheese
- 1 small onion, chopped
- 1 can (4 oz.) chopped green chiles
- 1 jar (2 oz.) pimiento strips, drained
- 1 jalapeno pepper, seeded and chopped

1. Preheat oven to 350°. In large bowl, combine the muffin mixes and cayenne pepper. In another bowl, mix eggs, corn, buttermilk and ¼ cup oil until blended. Add to the dry ingredients; stir just until moistened. Fold in cheese, onion, chiles, pimiento strips and jalapeno.
2. Brush remaining oil onto bottom of a 13x9-in. baking pan; place in oven until hot, 4-5 minutes. Pour batter into hot pan. Bake until edges are golden brown and a toothpick inserted in center comes out clean, 50-60 minutes. Cool in pan on a wire rack. Serve warm.
1 piece: 299 cal., 14g fat (4g sat. fat), 42mg chol., 547mg sod., 36g carb. (10g sugars, 3g fiber), 7g pro.

Contest Winner

SPECIAL BANANA NUT BREAD

This extra special banana bread makes a wonderful gift for friends and neighbors. The recipe makes two loaves, so I can serve one and keep the other one in the freezer to use as a last-minute gift.
—*Beverly Sprague, Baltimore, MD*

Prep: 25 min. • **Bake:** 1 hour + cooling
Makes: 2 loaves (12 slices each)

- ¾ cup butter, softened
- 1 pkg. (8 oz.) cream cheese, softened
- 2 cups sugar
- 2 large eggs, room temperature
- 1½ cups mashed ripe bananas (about 4 medium)
- ½ tsp. vanilla extract
- 3 cups all-purpose flour
- ½ tsp. baking powder
- ½ tsp. baking soda
- ½ tsp. salt
- 2 cups chopped pecans, divided

ORANGE GLAZE
- 1 cup confectioners' sugar
- 3 Tbsp. orange juice
- 1 tsp. grated orange zest

1. Preheat oven to 350°. Cream butter, cream cheese and sugar until light and fluffy. Add eggs, one at a time, beating well after each addition. Beat in bananas and vanilla. In another bowl, combine flour, baking powder, baking soda and salt; gradually add to creamed mixture. Fold in 1 cup pecans.
2. Transfer to 2 greased 8x4-in. loaf pans. Sprinkle with remaining pecans. Bake loaves, covering with foil if they darken too rapidly, until a toothpick inserted in center comes out clean, 1-1¼ hours. Cool 10 minutes before removing the loaves to wire racks.
3. While the loaves are still slightly warm, whisk glaze ingredients. Drizzle over the loaves, using a baking pan or parchment paper under racks to catch excess. Cool bread completely.
1 slice: 234 cal., 13g fat (5g sat. fat), 32mg chol., 119mg sod., 29g carb. (18g sugars, 1g fiber), 3g pro.

CHEDDAR CORN BISCUITS

Biscuits with cheddar and corn are especially good with soup. If you have leftovers, rewarm them and pass the butter and jam.
—*Susan Braun, Swift Current, SK*

- -

Prep: 20 min. • **Bake:** 20 min.
Makes: 16 biscuits

4¼ cups all-purpose flour
  2 Tbsp. baking powder
  1 tsp. ground mustard
  ¾ tsp. salt
  ¾ cup cold butter, cubed
  1 can (14¾ oz.) cream-style corn
1½ cups shredded cheddar cheese
  2 large eggs, room temperature, lightly beaten
  2 Tbsp. 2% milk

1. Preheat oven to 425°. In a large bowl, whisk flour, baking powder, mustard and salt. Cut in butter until mixture resembles coarse crumbs. Add the corn, cheese and eggs; stir just until moistened.
2. Turn onto a lightly floured surface; knead gently 8-10 times. Pat or roll dough to 1-in. thickness; cut with a floured 2½-in. biscuit cutter. Place 2 in. apart on ungreased baking sheets; brush with milk. Bake biscuits for 18-22 minutes or until golden brown. Serve warm.
1 biscuit: 270 cal., 13g fat (8g sat. fat), 57mg chol., 476mg sod., 30g carb. (1g sugars, 1g fiber), 7g pro.

DUTCH APPLE LOAF

Being of Dutch descent, I knew I had to try this recipe for a moist, fruity quick bread. It freezes well, so I often keep a loaf on hand.
—*Gladys Meyer, Ottumwa, IA*

- -

Prep: 15 min. • **Bake:** 55 min. + cooling
Makes: 1 loaf (16 slices)

  ½ cup butter, softened
  1 cup sugar
  2 large eggs, room temperature
  ¼ cup buttermilk
  1 tsp. vanilla extract
  2 cups all-purpose flour
1½ tsp. baking powder
  ½ tsp. salt
  ¼ tsp. baking soda
  2 cups diced peeled tart apples
  ½ cup chopped walnuts
TOPPING
  ¼ cup sugar
  ¼ cup all-purpose flour
  2 tsp. ground cinnamon
  ¼ cup cold butter, cubed

1. In a large bowl, cream butter and sugar until light and fluffy. Add eggs, one at a time, beating well after each addition. Beat in buttermilk and vanilla. Combine the flour, baking powder, salt and baking soda; gradually add to creamed mixture. Fold in apples and walnuts. Pour into a greased 9x5-in. loaf pan.
2. For topping, combine the sugar, flour and cinnamon. Cut in butter until mixture resembles coarse crumbs. Sprinkle over the batter.
3. Bake at 350° for 55-60 minutes or until a toothpick inserted in the center comes out clean. Cool the bread for 10 minutes before removing from pan to a wire rack.
1 slice: 243 cal., 12g fat (6g sat. fat), 50mg chol., 252mg sod., 32g carb. (17g sugars, 1g fiber), 4g pro.

FOCACCIA BARESE

This focaccia has been in my mom's family for several generations. It's one of my most requested recipes. In fact, some hosts tell me I can't attend their parties unless I make sure to bring this with me!

—*Dora Travaglio, Mount Prospect, IL*

- -

Prep: 30 min. + rising • **Bake:** 30 min.
Makes: 8 servings

- 1⅛ tsp. active dry yeast
- ¾ cup warm water (110° to 115°), divided
- ½ tsp. sugar
- ⅓ cup mashed potato flakes
- 1½ tsp. plus 2 Tbsp. olive oil, divided
- ¼ tsp. salt
- 1¾ cups bread flour

TOPPING

- 2 medium tomatoes, thinly sliced
- ¼ cup pitted Greek olives, halved
- 1½ tsp. minced fresh or dried oregano
- ½ tsp. coarse salt

1. In a large bowl, dissolve yeast in ½ cup warm water. Add sugar; let stand for 5 minutes. Add the potato flakes, 1½ tsp. oil, salt, 1 cup flour and remaining water. Beat until smooth. Stir in enough of the remaining flour to form a soft dough.

2. Turn onto a floured surface; knead until smooth and elastic, 6-8 minutes. Place in a greased bowl, turning once to grease the top. Cover and let rise in a warm place until doubled, about 1 hour. Punch dough down. Cover and let rest for 10 minutes.

3. Place 1 Tbsp. olive oil in a 10-in. cast-iron or other ovenproof skillet; tilt pan to evenly coat. Add dough; shape to fit pan. Cover and let rise until doubled, about 30 minutes.

4. With fingertips, make several dimples over top of dough. Brush with remaining Tbsp. of oil. Blot tomato slices with paper towels. Arrange tomato slices and olives over the dough; sprinkle the focaccia with oregano and salt.

5. Bake at 375° for 30-35 minutes or until golden brown.

1 slice: 142 cal., 4g fat (0 sat. fat), 0 chol., 269mg sod., 24g carb. (1g sugars, 1g fiber), 4g pro. **Diabetic exchanges:** 1½ starch, ½ fat.

MARINA'S GOLDEN CORN FRITTERS

Just one bite of these fritters takes me back to when my kids were young. They're all grown up now, but the tradition lives on at get-togethers, when I sometimes even triple the recipe. Serve fritters with maple syrup or agave nectar.
—*Marina Castle Kelley, Canyon Country, CA*

Takes: 30 min. • **Makes:** 32 fritters

- 2½ cups all-purpose flour
- 3 tsp. baking powder
- 2 tsp. dried parsley flakes
- 1 tsp. salt
- 2 large eggs
- ¾ cup 2% milk
- 2 Tbsp. butter, melted
- 2 tsp. grated onion
- 1 can (15¼ oz.) whole kernel corn, drained
- Oil for deep-fat frying

1. In a large bowl, whisk the flour, baking powder, parsley and salt. In another bowl, whisk eggs, milk, melted butter and onion until blended. Add to the dry ingredients, stirring just until moistened. Fold in corn.
2. In an electric skillet or deep fryer, heat oil to 375°. Drop batter by tablespoonfuls, several at a time, into hot oil. Fry fritters for 2-3 minutes on each side or until golden brown. Drain on paper towels.

2 fritters: 162 cal., 8g fat (2g sat. fat), 28mg chol., 327mg sod., 18g carb. (2g sugars, 1g fiber), 4g pro.

Contest Winner

CONTEST-WINNING POTATO PAN ROLLS

Beautiful color and light-as-a-feather texture make these rolls our family's favorite for holiday meals. I won the reserve champion award at a 4-H yeast bread competition with this recipe.
—*LeAnne Hofferichter-Tieken, Floresville, TX*

Prep: 55 min. + rising • **Bake:** 20 min.
Makes: 2½ dozen

- 2 medium potatoes, peeled and quartered
- 1½ cups water
- 2 pkg. (¼ oz. each) active dry yeast
- 1 tsp. sugar
- ½ cup butter, melted
- ½ cup honey
- ¼ cup canola oil
- 2 large eggs, room temperature
- 2 tsp. salt
- 6 to 7 cups all-purpose flour

1. In a large saucepan, bring potatoes and water to a boil. Reduce heat; cover and simmer for 15-20 minutes or until tender. Drain, reserving 1 cup cooking liquid; cool liquid to 110° to 115°. Mash potatoes; set aside 1 cup to cool to 110°-115° (save remaining potatoes for another use).
2. In a large bowl, dissolve the yeast and sugar in the reserved potato liquid; let stand for 5 minutes. Add the reserved mashed potatoes, butter, honey, oil, eggs, salt and 1½ cups flour; beat until smooth. Stir in enough of the remaining flour to form a soft dough.
3. Turn onto a floured surface; knead until smooth and elastic, 6-8 minutes. Place in a greased bowl, turning once to grease top. Cover and let rise in a warm place until doubled, about 1 hour.
4. Punch dough down and turn onto a floured surface; divide into 30 pieces. Shape each piece into a ball. Place 10 balls each in 3 greased 9-in. round baking pans. Cover and let rise until doubled, about 30 minutes.
5. Meanwhile, preheat oven to 400°. Bake rolls until golden brown, 20-25 minutes. Remove from pans to wire racks to cool.

1 roll: 165 cal., 5g fat (2g sat. fat), 22mg chol., 193mg sod., 26g carb. (5g sugars, 1g fiber), 3g pro.

BACON-MAPLE COFFEE CAKE

The sleepyheads will roll out of bed when they smell this sweet and savory coffee cake baking. Nuts and bacon in the cake's crumbly topping blend well with the flavors of maple, nutmeg and cinnamon.

—*Angela Spengler, Niceville, FL*

Prep: 25 min. • **Bake:** 35 min. + cooling
Makes: 24 servings

- 2½ cups all-purpose flour
- 1 cup packed brown sugar
- ½ tsp. salt
- ⅓ cup cold butter
- 2 tsp. baking powder
- ½ tsp. baking soda
- ½ tsp. ground cinnamon
- ¼ tsp. ground nutmeg
- 2 large eggs, room temperature
- 1½ cups buttermilk
- ½ cup maple syrup
- ⅓ cup unsweetened applesauce
- 5 bacon strips, cooked and crumbled
- ½ cup chopped walnuts

1. In a large bowl, combine the flour, brown sugar and salt. Cut in the butter until crumbly. Set aside ½ cup for the topping. Combine the baking powder, baking soda, cinnamon and nutmeg; stir into remaining flour mixture.

2. In a bowl, whisk the eggs, buttermilk, syrup and applesauce until well blended. Gradually stir into the flour mixture just until combined.

3. Spread batter into a 13x9-in. baking pan coated with cooking spray. Sprinkle with reserved topping, then bacon and walnuts. Bake at 350° for 35-40 minutes or until a toothpick inserted in the center comes out clean. Cool on a wire rack.

1 piece: 160 cal., 5g fat (2g sat. fat), 27mg chol., 183mg sod., 25g carb. (14g sugars, 1g fiber), 3g pro. **Diabetic exchanges:** 1½ starch, 1 fat.

CINNAMON FRUIT BISCUITS

Because these sweet treats are so easy, I'm almost embarrassed when people ask for the recipe. With refrigerated buttermilk biscuits, sugar, cinnamon and your favorite fruit preserves, they're a snap to make.

—*Ione Burham, Washington, IA*

Prep: 15 min. • **Bake:** 15 min. + cooling
Makes: 10 servings

- ½ cup sugar
- ½ tsp. ground cinnamon
- 1 tube (12 oz.) refrigerated buttermilk biscuits, separated into 10 biscuits
- ¼ cup butter, melted
- 10 tsp. strawberry preserves

1. In a small bowl, combine the sugar and cinnamon. Dip top and sides of biscuits in butter, then in cinnamon-sugar.

2. Place on ungreased baking sheets. With the end of a wooden spoon handle, make a deep indentation in the center of each biscuit; fill with 1 tsp. preserves.

3. Bake at 375° for 15-18 minutes or until golden brown. Cool for 15 minutes before serving (preserves will be hot).

1 biscuit: 178 cal., 5g fat (3g sat. fat), 12mg chol., 323mg sod., 31g carb. (14g sugars, 0 fiber), 3g pro. **Diabetic exchanges:** 2 starch, 1 fat.

CALZONE ROLLS

Big pizza flavor comes through in these rolls. My recipe makes two pans because you'll need 'em! It's so easy to make the dough in my bread machine.

—*Barb Downie, Peterborough, ON*

Prep: 20 min. + rising • **Bake:** 20 min.
Makes: 2 dozen

1⅔ cups water (70° to 80°)
2 Tbsp. nonfat dry milk powder
2 Tbsp. sugar
2 Tbsp. shortening
1¼ tsp. salt
4½ cups all-purpose flour
2¼ tsp. active dry yeast
½ cup chopped onion
½ cup sliced fresh mushrooms
½ cup chopped green pepper
½ cup chopped sweet red pepper
1 Tbsp. olive oil
⅓ cup pizza sauce
½ cup diced pepperoni
1 cup shredded pizza cheese blend
¼ cup chopped ripe olives
2 Tbsp. grated Parmesan cheese

1. In bread machine pan, place the first 7 ingredients in the order suggested by the manufacturer. Select dough setting (check dough after 5 minutes of mixing; add 1-2 Tbsp. of water or flour if needed).
2. In a small skillet, saute chopped onion, mushrooms and peppers in olive oil until tender; cool.
3. When the bread machine cycle is completed, turn the dough onto a lightly floured surface; divide in half. Let rest for 5 minutes. Roll each dough portion into a 16x10-in. rectangle; spread with the pizza sauce. Top dough with the onion mixture, pepperoni, pizza cheese and olives. Roll up each rectangle jelly-roll style, starting with a long side; pinch seam to seal. Cut each into 12 slices (discard end pieces).
4. Place slices cut side down in 2 greased 10-in. cast-iron skillets or 9-in. round baking pans. Sprinkle with the Parmesan cheese. Cover and let rise until doubled, about 30 minutes.
5. Bake rolls at 375° until golden brown, 20-30 minutes. Serve warm.
Note: To make the dough without a bread machine, dissolve the yeast in warm water (110°-115°). Add milk powder, sugar, shortening, salt and 3 cups flour. Beat on medium speed until smooth. Stir in enough remaining flour to form a soft dough. Turn dough onto a floured surface; knead until smooth and elastic, 6-8 minutes. Place in a greased bowl, turning once to grease top. Cover bowl and let rise in a warm place until doubled, about 1 hour. Punch dough down. Proceed with recipe as written.
1 roll: 144 cal., 5g fat (2g sat. fat), 7mg chol., 244mg sod., 21g carb. (2g sugars, 1g fiber), 5g pro.

CELERY-ONION POPOVERS

I found this handwritten recipe in a cookbook I received from my mom. With onion and celery, these pleasing popovers taste a little like stuffing.

—*Barbara Carlucci, Orange Park, FL*

Prep: 15 min. • **Bake:** 40 min.
Makes: 9 servings

2 cups all-purpose flour
1 tsp. onion salt
⅛ tsp. celery salt
4 large eggs, room temperature
2 cups whole milk
¼ cup grated onion
¼ cup grated celery
3 Tbsp. butter, melted

1. In a large bowl, combine flour, onion salt and celery salt. Combine eggs, milk, onion, celery and butter; whisk into dry ingredients just until blended. Grease and flour the bottom and sides of 9 popover cups; fill two-thirds full with batter.
2. Bake at 450° for 15 minutes. Reduce heat to 350° (do not open oven door). Bake 25 minutes longer or until deep golden brown (do not underbake). Immediately cut a slit in the top of each popover to allow steam to escape.
1 popover: 202 cal., 8g fat (4g sat. fat), 98mg chol., 306mg sod., 25g carb. (3g sugars, 1g fiber), 7g pro.

GOLDEN HONEY PAN ROLLS

A cousin in North Carolina gave me the recipe for these delicious honey-glazed rolls. Using my bread machine to make the dough saves me time compared to the traditional method. The rich buttery тaste of these rolls is so popular with family and friends that I usually make two batches so I have enough!

—Sara Wing, Philadelphia, PA

- -

Prep: 35 min. + rising • **Bake:** 20 min.
Makes: 2 dozen

- 1 cup warm 2% milk (70° to 80°)
- 1 large egg, room temperature
- 1 large egg yolk, room temperature
- ½ cup canola oil
- 2 Tbsp. honey
- 1½ tsp. salt
- 3½ cups bread flour
- 2¼ tsp. active dry yeast
- GLAZE
- ⅓ cup sugar
- 2 Tbsp. butter, melted
- 1 Tbsp. honey
- 1 large egg white
  Additional honey, optional

1. In bread machine pan, place the first 8 ingredients in the order suggested by the manufacturer. Select dough setting (check dough after 5 minutes of mixing; add 1-2 Tbsp. of water or flour if needed.)

2. When cycle is completed, turn dough onto a lightly floured surface. Punch down; cover and let rest for 10 minutes. Divide into 24 pieces; shape each into a ball. Place 12 balls each in 2 greased 8-in. square baking pans. Cover and let rise in a warm place until doubled, about 30 minutes.

3. For glaze, combine the sugar, butter, honey and egg white; drizzle over dough. Bake at 350° until golden brown, 20-25 minutes. Brush rolls with additional honey if desired.

Note: To make the dough without a bread machine, dissolve the yeast in warm milk (110°-115°). In another bowl, combine egg, egg yolk, oil, honey, salt, yeast mixture and 2 cups of flour; beat on medium speed until smooth. Stir in enough remaining flour to form a soft dough (dough will be sticky). Turn onto a floured surface; knead until smooth and elastic, 6-8 minutes. Place in a greased bowl, turning once to grease top. Cover and let rise in a warm place until doubled, about 1 hour. Punch down dough; cover and let rest 10 minutes. Turn onto a lightly floured surface. Divide and shape into 24 balls; place 12 each in 2 greased 8x8-in. baking pans. Cover and let rise in a warm place until doubled, about 30 minutes. Preheat oven to 350° glaze and bake as directed.

1 roll: 139 cal., 6g fat (2g sat. fat), 22mg chol., 168mg sod., 18g carb. (5g sugars, 1g fiber), 3g pro.

EVERYTHING BREAD

I love to make bread from scratch. This has become one of our tried-and-true favorites to serve with any meal, casual or formal.
—*Traci Wynne, Denver, PA*

- -

Prep: 45 min. + rising • **Bake:** 25 min.
Makes: 1 loaf (25 slices)

- 1   **pkg. (¼ oz.) active dry yeast**
- ¾   **cup warm water (110° to 115°)**
- 1   **cup warm 2% milk (110° to 115°)**
- ¼   **cup butter, softened**
- 2   **Tbsp. sugar**
- 1   **large egg yolk, room temperature**
- 1½ **tsp. salt**
- 4   **to 4½ cups all-purpose flour**
- 1   **large egg white**
- 2   **tsp. water**
- 1   **tsp. coarse sea salt or kosher salt**
- 1   **tsp. dried minced onion**
- 1   **tsp. each sesame, caraway and poppy seeds**

1. In a large bowl, dissolve yeast in warm water. Add milk, butter, sugar, egg yolk, salt and 2 cups flour. Beat on medium speed for 3 minutes. Stir in enough remaining flour to form a firm dough.
2. Turn onto a floured surface; knead until smooth and elastic, about 6-8 minutes. Place in a greased bowl, turning once to grease the top. Cover and let rise until doubled, about 1 hour.
3. Punch the dough down. Turn onto a lightly floured surface; divide dough into thirds. Shape each into a 20-in. rope. Place ropes on a large greased baking sheet and braid; pinch ends to seal and tuck under. Cover braid and let rise until doubled, about 45 minutes.
4. Preheat oven to 375°. Combine egg white and water; brush over the dough. Combine salt, onion and seeds; sprinkle over bread. Bake 22-28 minutes or until golden brown. Remove from pan to a wire rack to cool.

1 slice: 102 cal., 2g fat (1g sat. fat), 14mg chol., 237mg sod., 17g carb. (2g sugars, 1g fiber), 3g pro. **Diabetic exchanges:** 1 starch, ½ fat.

SWEET POTATO SPICE BREAD

It's a good thing this recipe makes two mini loaves because they'll go fast! For a small household, eat one loaf now and freeze the other for later.

—*Ronnie Littles, VA Beach, VA*

- -

Prep: 15 min. • **Bake:** 25 min. + cooling
Makes: 2 mini loaves (6 slices each)

- 1 cup all-purpose flour
- 1½ tsp. baking powder
- ¼ tsp. each ground cinnamon, nutmeg and allspice
- ⅛ tsp. salt
- 1 large egg, room temperature
- ⅓ cup mashed sweet potato
- ⅓ cup honey
- 3 Tbsp. canola oil
- 2 Tbsp. molasses
- ⅓ cup chopped walnuts

1. In a small bowl, combine the flour, baking powder, spices and salt. In another small bowl, whisk the egg, sweet potato, honey, oil and molasses. Stir into the dry ingredients just until moistened. Fold in chopped walnuts.

2. Transfer to two 5¾x3x2-in. loaf pans coated with cooking spray. Bake at 325° for 25-30 minutes or until a toothpick inserted in the center comes out clean. Cool for 10 minutes before removing from pans to wire racks.

1 slice: 142 cal., 6g fat (1g sat. fat), 18mg chol., 85mg sod., 20g carb. (10g sugars, 1g fiber), 3g pro. **Diabetic exchanges:** 1½ starch, 1 fat.

Contest Winner

MUENSTER BREAD

With cheese peeking out from every slice, this beautiful loaf is worth the effort.

—*Melanie Mero, Ida, MI*

- -

Prep: 20 min. + rising • **Bake:** 40 min. + cooling
Makes: 1 loaf (16 slices)

- 2 pkg. (¼ oz. each) active dry yeast
- 1 cup warm 2% milk (110° to 115°)
- ½ cup butter, softened
- 2 Tbsp. sugar
- 1 tsp. salt
- 3¼ to 3¾ cups all-purpose flour
- 1 large egg plus 1 large egg yolk, room temperature
- 4 cups shredded Muenster cheese
- 1 large egg white, beaten

1. In a large bowl, dissolve yeast in milk. Add the butter, sugar, salt and 2 cups flour; beat until smooth. Stir in enough remaining flour to form a soft dough.

2. Turn onto a floured surface; knead until smooth and elastic, 6-8 minutes. Place in a greased bowl, turning once to grease top. Cover and let rise in a warm place until doubled, about 1 hour.

3. In a large bowl, beat egg and yolk; stir in cheese. Punch down dough; roll into a 16-in. circle.

4. Place in a greased 10-in. cast-iron skillet or 9-in. round baking pan, letting dough drape over the edges. Spoon the cheese mixture into center of the dough. Gather dough up over the filling in 1½-in. pleats. Gently squeeze pleats together at top and twist to make a topknot. Let rise 10-15 minutes.

5. Brush loaf with egg white. Bake at 375° for 40-45 minutes. Cool on a wire rack for 20 minutes. Serve warm.

1 slice: 273 cal., 16g fat (9g sat. fat), 71mg chol., 399mg sod., 22g carb. (3g sugars, 1g fiber), 11g pro.

Playful Bubble Breads

Breads you pick apart with your hands go by many names: bubble bread, pull-aparts, puzzle bread, monkey bread, and even pinch-me cake! No matter the moniker, these showstoppers command the spotlight when they're placed on the table. Dig in!

PULL-APART GARLIC BREAD

People go wild over this golden, garlicky loaf whenever I serve it. There's intense flavor in every bite.
—*Carol Shields, Summerville, PA*

Prep: 10 min. + rising • **Bake:** 30 min.
Makes: 16 servings

- ¼ cup butter, melted
- 1 Tbsp. dried parsley flakes
- 1 tsp. garlic powder
- ¼ tsp. garlic salt
- 1 loaf (1 lb.) frozen white bread dough, thawed

1. In a small bowl, combine the butter, parsley, garlic powder and garlic salt. Cut dough into 1-in. pieces; dip into butter mixture. Layer in a greased 9x5-in. loaf pan. Cover and let rise until doubled, about 1 hour.
2. Bake at 350° for 30 minutes or until golden brown.

1 serving: 104 cal., 4g fat (2g sat. fat), 8mg chol., 215mg sod., 15g carb. (1g sugars, 1g fiber), 3g pro.

CINNAMON APPLE CIDER MONKEY BREAD

I use the cold-weather staple apple cider— plus apples and more cinnamon— to turn plain cinnamon rolls into monkey bread. My boys love the sticky sweetness.
—*Kelly Walsh, Aviston, IL*

Prep: 20 min. • **Bake:** 45 min. + standing
Makes: 16 servings

- 5 envelopes (.74 oz. each) instant spiced cider mix
- 3 tubes (12.4 oz. each) refrigerated cinnamon rolls with icing
- 2 medium Granny Smith apples, peeled and chopped
- 1 cup chopped pecans or walnuts
- 6 Tbsp. butter, melted
- 2 tsp. ground cinnamon

1. Preheat oven to 350°. Combine cider mixes. Separate cinnamon rolls, setting aside icings; cut each roll into quarters. Add to cider mixture; toss to coat.
2. Arrange a third of the dough pieces in a well-greased 10-in. fluted tube pan; top with half of the apples and half of the pecans. Repeat the layers once. Top with remaining dough.
3. Mix melted butter, cinnamon and icing from 1 container until blended. Drizzle over top of rolls. Bake until golden brown, 45-50 minutes. (If needed, cover the top loosely with foil during last 5 minutes to prevent overbrowning.)
4. Immediately invert the monkey bread onto a serving plate; keep pan inverted 10 minutes, allowing the bread to release. Remove the pan. Meanwhile, microwave the remaining icing, uncovered, until it is softened, about 10 seconds. Drizzle over monkey bread. Serve warm.

1 serving: 329 cal., 17g fat (5g sat. fat), 11mg chol., 553mg sod., 41g carb. (5g sugars, 1g fiber), 4g pro.

BUTTERY BUBBLE BREAD

Homemade bread can be time-consuming, difficult and tricky to make. But this fun-to-eat monkey bread, baked in a fluted tube pan, is easy and almost foolproof. If I'm going to serve it for breakfast, I add some cinnamon and drizzle it with icing.

—*Pat Stevens, Granbury, TX*

Prep: 25 min. + rising • **Bake:** 30 min.
Makes: 16 servings

- 1 pkg. (¼ oz.) active dry yeast
- 1 cup warm water (110° to 115°)
- ½ cup sugar
- ½ cup shortening
- 1 large egg, room temperature
- ½ tsp. salt
- 4 to 4½ cups all-purpose flour, divided
- 6 Tbsp. butter, melted

1. In a large bowl, dissolve yeast in warm water. Add the sugar, shortening, egg, salt and 1 cup of flour. Beat until smooth. Stir in enough of the remaining flour to form a soft dough.

2. Turn onto a floured surface; knead dough until smooth and elastic, about 6-8 minutes. Place in a greased bowl, turning once to grease top. Cover and let rise in a warm place until doubled, about 1 hour.

3. Punch dough down. Turn onto a lightly floured surface; shape into 1½-in. balls. Dip the balls in butter and arrange evenly in a greased 9-in. fluted tube pan. Drizzle with remaining butter. Cover and let rise in a warm place until doubled, about 45 minutes.

4. Bake at 350° for 30-35 minutes or until golden brown. Cool for 5 minutes before inverting onto a serving platter. Serve the bread warm.

1 serving: 237 cal., 11g fat (4g sat. fat), 25mg chol., 122mg sod., 30g carb. (7g sugars, 1g fiber), 4g pro.

Contest Winner

BACON PULL-APART BREAD

I made this tender and tasty bread for my husband, and he just loved it! When I'm out of bacon, I substitute bacon bits.

—*Terri Christensen, Montague, MI*

Prep: 15 min. • **Bake:** 25 min.
Makes: 12 servings

- 12 bacon strips, diced
- 2 tubes (12 oz. each) refrigerated buttermilk biscuits
- 2 cups shredded part-skim mozzarella cheese
- 1 Tbsp. Italian salad dressing mix
- 2 tsp. olive oil

1. Preheat oven to 375°. In a large skillet, cook the bacon over medium heat until cooked but not crisp. Using a slotted spoon, remove to paper towels to drain. Separate biscuits; cut each into quarters.

2. In a large bowl, combine the cheese, dressing mix, oil and bacon. Place half of the biscuit pieces in a greased 10-in. fluted tube pan; sprinkle with half of the cheese mixture. Top with remaining biscuit pieces and cheese mixture.

3. Bake 25-30 minutes or until golden brown. Cool 5 minutes before inverting onto a serving plate. Serve immediately.

1 serving: 227 cal., 8g fat (3g sat. fat), 18mg chol., 800mg sod., 28g carb. (1g sugars, 0 fiber), 11g pro.

Main Dishes

When it's time for dinner, wow your family with a hearty and delicious home-cooked entree. From roasts to casseroles, stews to main-dish salads, the 37 recipes in this chapter will become your family's new favorites. Plus, take a new look at an old classic, with four outside-the-box ways to make meat loaf something special!

HORSERADISH-ENCRUSTED BEEF TENDERLOIN

Wow friends and family with this tender beef in a golden horseradish crust. Roasted garlic boosts the robust flavor even more.
—*Laura Bagozzi, Dublin, OH*

- -

Prep: 35 min. + cooling
Bake: 45 min. + standing • **Makes:** 8 servings

1	whole garlic bulb
1	tsp. olive oil
⅓	cup prepared horseradish
¼	tsp. salt
¼	tsp. dried basil
¼	tsp. dried thyme
¼	tsp. pepper
⅓	cup soft bread crumbs
1	beef tenderloin roast (3 lbs.)

1. Preheat oven to 425°. Remove the papery outer skin from garlic (do not peel or separate cloves). Cut the top off the garlic bulb; brush with oil. Wrap in heavy-duty foil. Bake until softened, 30-35 minutes. Cool for 10-15 minutes. Reduce oven temperature to 400°.

2. Squeeze softened garlic into a small bowl; stir in the horseradish, salt, basil, thyme and pepper. Add bread crumbs; toss to coat. Spread over top of the tenderloin. Place on a rack in a large shallow roasting pan.

3. Bake until the meat reaches the desired doneness (for medium-rare, a thermometer should read 135°; medium, 140°; medium-well, 145°), 45-55 minutes. Let stand for 10 minutes before slicing.

5 oz. cooked beef: 268 cal., 11g fat (4g sat. fat), 75mg chol., 119mg sod., 4g carb. (1g sugars, 1g fiber), 37g pro. **Diabetic exchanges:** 5 lean meat.

SLOPPY JOE UNDER A BUN

Our kids just love sloppy joes, so I usually keep a can of the sauce in the pantry. But I don't always have buns on hand. With this fun casserole, we can enjoy the flavor they adore any time.
—*Trish Bloom, Ray, MI*

Prep: 15 min. • **Bake:** 25 min.
Makes: 8 servings

1½ lbs. ground beef
1 can (15½ oz.) sloppy joe sauce
2 cups shredded cheddar cheese
2 cups biscuit/baking mix
2 large eggs, lightly beaten
1 cup 2% milk
1 Tbsp. sesame seeds

1. Preheat oven to 400°. In a large skillet, cook beef over medium heat until no longer pink; drain. Stir in sauce. Transfer to a lightly greased 13x9-in. baking dish; sprinkle with cheese.
2. In a large bowl, combine the biscuit mix, eggs and milk just until blended. Pour over cheese; sprinkle with sesame seeds. Bake, uncovered, for 25 minutes or until golden brown.
1 serving: 423 cal., 23g fat (12g sat. fat), 129mg chol., 961mg sod., 26g carb. (6g sugars, 1g fiber), 27g pro.

Contest Winner

APPLE CIDER CHICKEN & DUMPLINGS

I came up with this recipe one fall when I had an abundance of apple cider. Adding some to a down-home classic was a delectable decision.
—*Margaret Sumner-Wichmann, Questa, NM*

Prep: 10 min. • **Bake:** 65 min.
Makes: 4 servings

8 bone-in chicken thighs (3 lbs.), skin removed
2 Tbsp. butter
1 medium red onion, chopped
1 celery rib, chopped
2 Tbsp. minced fresh parsley
 Salt and pepper to taste
3 Tbsp. all-purpose flour
3 cups chicken broth
1 cup apple cider or juice
DUMPLINGS
2 cups all-purpose flour
1 Tbsp. baking powder
½ tsp. salt
1 Tbsp. cold butter
1 large egg, lightly beaten
⅔ cup 2% milk

1. Preheat oven to 350°. In a Dutch oven, brown chicken in butter; remove and set aside. In the same pan, combine onion, celery, parsley, salt and pepper; cook and stir until vegetables are tender. Sprinkle with flour and mix well. Add broth and cider. Bring to a boil; cook and stir until thickened, 2 minutes. Add chicken. Cover and bake for 45-50 minutes. Increase heat to 425°.
2. For the dumplings, combine flour, baking powder and salt in a bowl; cut in butter until crumbly. Combine egg and milk; stir into the dry ingredients just until moistened. Drop the batter into 12 mounds onto the hot broth.
3. Bake, uncovered, for 10 minutes. Cover and bake until a toothpick inserted into a dumpling comes out clean, 10 minutes longer.
1 serving: 721 cal., 27g fat (11g sat. fat), 220mg chol., 1548mg sod., 65g carb. (12g sugars, 3g fiber), 50g pro.

BACON-WRAPPED PESTO PORK TENDERLOIN

I love to serve this family-favorite tenderloin—maybe because of the compliments that come with it! When the weather warms up, we grill it instead.
—*Megan Riofski, Frankfort, IL*

Prep: 30 min. • **Bake:** 20 min.
Makes: 4 servings

- 10 bacon strips
- 1 pork tenderloin (1 lb.)
- ¼ tsp. pepper
- ⅓ cup prepared pesto
- 1 cup shredded Italian cheese blend
- 1 cup fresh baby spinach

1. Preheat oven to 425°. Arrange the bacon strips lengthwise in a foil-lined 15x10x1-in. pan, overlapping slightly.
2. Cut tenderloin lengthwise through the center to within ½ in. of bottom. Open tenderloin flat; pound with a meat mallet to ½-in. thickness. Place tenderloin on center of bacon, perpendicular to strips.
3. Sprinkle pepper over pork. Spread with pesto; layer with cheese and spinach. Close tenderloin; wrap with bacon so the ends overlap. Tie with kitchen string at 3-in. intervals; secure with toothpicks.
4. In a 12-in. skillet, brown roast on all sides, about 8 minutes. Return to baking pan; roast in oven 17-20 minutes or until a thermometer inserted in pork reads 145°. Remove string and toothpicks; let stand 5 minutes before slicing.

1 serving: 402 cal., 25g fat (9g sat. fat), 104mg chol., 864mg sod., 4g carb. (1g sugars, 1g fiber), 37g pro.

Contest Winner

CHICKEN SWISS BUNDLES

These yummy sandwich buns made with frozen dinner rolls are a favorite at our house. They're great hot from the oven but they also freeze well. I serve them with tomato soup, and just watch as they disappear.
—*Trisha Kruse, Eagle, ID*

Prep: 30 min. • **Bake:** 20 min.
Makes: 6 servings

- 1 small onion, finely chopped
- ½ cup sliced fresh mushrooms
- 1½ tsp. butter
- 1 garlic clove, minced
- 1 cup cubed cooked chicken breast
- ½ cup chopped roasted sweet red peppers
- 1 Tbsp. honey mustard
- ¼ tsp. salt
- ¼ tsp. lemon-pepper seasoning
- ¼ tsp. Italian seasoning
- 2 cups shredded Swiss cheese
- 12 frozen bread dough dinner rolls, thawed
- 2 Tbsp. butter, melted

1. Preheat oven to 350°. In a large skillet, saute onion and mushrooms in butter until tender. Add garlic; cook 1 minute longer. Add chicken, peppers, mustard and seasonings; heat through. Remove from heat; stir in cheese.
2. Flatten each roll into a 5-in. circle. Place ¼ cup of the chicken mixture in the center of 6 of the circles. Brush the edges with water; top with the remaining circles. Press edges with a fork to seal.
3. Place the bundles on greased baking sheets; brush with butter. Bake until golden brown, 18-22 minutes. Cut bundles in half to serve.

Freeze option: Cover and freeze unbaked bundles on a waxed paper-lined baking sheet until firm. Transfer to a resealable freezer container; return to freezer. To use, bake bundles as directed, increasing time as necessary to heat through.

1 bundle: 434 cal., 20g fat (10g sat. fat), 64mg chol., 722mg sod., 40g carb. (5g sugars, 3g fiber), 24g pro.

CURRIED BEEF STEW

My mother, who was Japanese, made an amazing beef curry stew. After much experimenting, I came up with a version close to hers. This recipe is special to me because it brings back memories of her.
—*Gloria J. Gowins, Massillon, OH*

Prep: 15 min. • **Cook:** 2 hours
Makes: 4 servings

- ¾ lb. beef stew meat (1 to 1½-in. pieces)
- ¼ tsp. salt
- ⅛ tsp. pepper
- 2 Tbsp. all-purpose flour
- 1 Tbsp. canola oil
- 1 large onion, cut into ¾-in. pieces
- 2 Tbsp. curry powder
- 2 tsp. reduced-sodium soy sauce
- 2 bay leaves
- 3 cups beef stock
- 1½ lbs. potatoes (about 3 medium), cut into 1-in. cubes
- 2 large carrots, thinly sliced
- 1 Tbsp. white vinegar
- Hot cooked brown rice, optional

1. Sprinkle beef with salt and pepper; toss with flour. In a Dutch oven, heat oil over medium heat; cook beef and onion until lightly browned, stirring occasionally. Stir in curry powder, soy sauce, bay leaves and stock; bring to a boil. Reduce heat; simmer, covered, 45 minutes.

2. Stir in potatoes and carrots; return to a boil. Reduce heat; simmer, covered, until the meat and vegetables are tender, 1-1¼ hours, stirring occasionally. Remove bay leaves; stir in vinegar. If desired, serve with rice.

1½ cups: 362 cal., 10g fat (3g sat. fat), 53mg chol., 691mg sod., 44g carb. (7g sugars, 7g fiber), 24g pro. **Diabetic exchanges:** 3 starch, 3 lean meat, ½ fat.

EASY CHEESY LOADED GRITS

A tasty bowl of grits inspired me to develop my own with sausage, green chiles and cheeses. It just might be better than the original recipe!
—*Joan Hallford, North Richland Hills, TX*

Prep: 35 min. • **Bake:** 50 min. + standing
Makes: 8 servings

- 1 lb. mild or spicy bulk pork sausage
- 1 small onion, chopped
- 4 cups water
- ½ tsp. salt
- 1 cup quick-cooking grits
- 3 cans (4 oz. each) chopped green chiles
- 1½ cups shredded sharp cheddar cheese, divided
- 1½ cups shredded Monterey Jack cheese, divided
- 2 Tbsp. butter
- ¼ tsp. hot pepper sauce
- 2 large eggs, lightly beaten
- ¼ tsp. paprika
- Chopped fresh cilantro

1. Preheat oven to 325°. In a large skillet, cook sausage and onion over medium heat 6-8 minutes or until the sausage is no longer pink, breaking up the sausage into crumbles; drain.

2. In a large saucepan, bring water and salt to a boil. Slowly stir in grits. Reduce heat to medium-low; cook, covered, about 5 minutes or until thickened, stirring occasionally. Remove from heat.

3. Add green chiles, ¾ cup cheddar cheese, ¾ cup Monterey Jack cheese, butter and pepper sauce; stir until the cheese is melted. Stir in eggs, then the sausage mixture.

4. Transfer to a greased 13x9-in. baking dish. Top with the remaining cheeses; sprinkle with paprika. Bake, uncovered, 50-60 minutes or until golden brown and set. Let stand 10 minutes before serving. Sprinkle with cilantro.

1 cup: 399 cal., 28g fat (15g sat. fat), 116mg chol., 839mg sod., 19g carb. (2g sugars, 2g fiber), 18g pro.

FAVORITE DEEP-DISH PIZZA

My kids love to get pizza delivered, but it's expensive and isn't very healthy. I came up with a one-bowl pizza that is healthier than delivery pizza and allows the kids to add the toppings of their choice.
—Sara LaFountain, Rockville, MD

- -

Prep: 20 min. • **Bake:** 20 min.
Makes: 8 servings

1¾ cups whole wheat flour
1¾ cups all-purpose flour
2 pkg. (¼ oz. each) quick-rise yeast
4 tsp. sugar
1 tsp. salt
1½ cups warm water (120° to 130°)
¼ cup olive oil
1 can (8 oz.) pizza sauce
8 oz. fresh mozzarella cheese, sliced

2 cups shredded Italian cheese blend
½ tsp. dried oregano
½ tsp. Italian seasoning
Optional: Fresh oregano leaves and crushed red pepper flakes

1. Preheat oven to 400°. In a large bowl, combine wheat flour, 1 cup all-purpose flour, the yeast, sugar and salt. Add water and oil; beat until smooth. Stir in enough remaining flour to form a soft dough. Press dough onto the bottom and up the sides of a greased 13x9-in. baking dish.
2. Top with pizza sauce. Place mozzarella slices over sauce. Sprinkle with shredded cheese, oregano and Italian seasoning. Bake, uncovered, for 20-25 minutes or until golden brown. If desired, top with fresh oregano leaves and crushed red pepper flakes.

1 slice: 449 cal., 20g fat (9g sat. fat), 42mg chol., 646mg sod., 47g carb. (4g sugars, 5g fiber), 19g pro.

WHY WHOLE WHEAT FLOUR?

Whole wheat flour is an easy way to sneak extra fiber into your diet. An equal amount of all-purpose flour can be used in place of the whole wheat flour and this recipe will still work, but keep in mind that a crust made that way will be less dense, perhaps not what you're looking for in this deep-dish pizza.

SKILLET CHICKEN STEW

It's been 20 years since I first adapted this from a recipe for beef stew. We like it so much that, in all that time, I have never changed any ingredients or amounts—unless it was to double them!
—*Valerie Jordan, Kingmont, WV*

- -

Prep: 15 min. • **Cook:** 25 min.
Makes: 6 servings

- ⅓ cup all-purpose flour
- ½ tsp. salt
  Dash pepper
- 1½ lbs. boneless skinless chicken breasts, cut into 1-in. pieces
- 3 Tbsp. butter
- 1 medium onion, sliced
- 3 celery ribs, sliced
- 2 medium potatoes, peeled and cut into ¾-in. cubes
- 3 medium carrots, cut into ¼-in. slices
- 1 cup chicken broth
- ½ tsp. dried thyme
- 1 Tbsp. ketchup
- 1 Tbsp. cornstarch

1. In a large shallow dish, combine the flour, salt and pepper. Add chicken, a few pieces at a time, and turn to coat.
2. In a large skillet, melt butter; cook the chicken until chicken juices run clear. Add onion and celery; cook for 3 minutes. Stir in potatoes and carrots.
3. In a small bowl, combine the broth, thyme, ketchup and cornstarch; stir into skillet. Bring to a boil. Reduce heat; cover and simmer for 15-20 minutes or until the vegetables are tender.
1½ cups: 275 cal., 9g fat (4g sat. fat), 78mg chol., 524mg sod., 23g carb. (5g sugars, 3g fiber), 26g pro.

FAMOUS BBQ CHICKEN

This chicken is topped with a sticky, lip-smackin' sauce that everyone—including my kids—loves. I make it in big batches now and give jars of it to family and friends.
—*Stacey Nerness, Spencer, IA*

- -

Prep: 45 min. • **Grill:** 40 min.
Makes: 4 servings (plus 3 cups leftover sauce)

- 2½ cups ketchup
- ½ cup packed brown sugar
- ½ cup honey
- ¼ cup liquid smoke
- ¼ cup molasses
- 1 serrano pepper, finely chopped
- 2 Tbsp. prepared mustard
- 1 Tbsp. white wine vinegar
- 1 Tbsp. Worcestershire sauce
- 2 tsp. onion powder
- 2 tsp. garlic powder
- ¼ tsp. cayenne pepper
- 4 chicken leg quarters
- ½ tsp. salt
- ½ tsp. pepper

1. In a large saucepan, combine the first 12 ingredients. Bring to a boil. Reduce heat; simmer, uncovered, for 30 minutes to allow flavors to blend. Set aside ½ cup sauce for basting; cover and refrigerate remaining sauce for later use.
2. Sprinkle chicken with salt and pepper. Place chicken skin side down on a lightly oiled grilled rack over a drip pan; grill over indirect medium heat for 20 minutes. Turn; grill 20-30 minutes longer or until a thermometer reads 170°-175°, basting occasionally with reserved sauce.
Note: Wear disposable gloves when cutting hot peppers; the oils can burn skin. Avoid touching your face.
1 chicken leg quarter: 340 cal., 16g fat (4g sat. fat), 105mg chol., 673mg sod., 17g carb. (16g sugars, 0 fiber), 30g pro.

PORK & GREEN CHILE CASSEROLE

In addition to working at a local hospital, I also work part time for some area doctors, so I'm always on the lookout for good, quick recipes to fix for my family. This zippy casserole is one that a co-worker brought to a picnic at my house. People raved about it!
—*Dianne Esposite, New Middletown, OH*

- -

Prep: 20 min. • **Bake:** 30 min.
Makes: 6 servings

- 1½ lbs. boneless pork, cut into ½-in. cubes
- 1 Tbsp. canola oil
- 1 can (15 oz.) black beans, rinsed and drained
- 1 can (10¾ oz.) condensed cream of chicken soup, undiluted
- 1 can (14½ oz.) diced tomatoes, undrained
- 2 cans (4 oz. each) chopped green chiles
- 1 cup quick-cooking brown rice
- ¼ cup water
- 2 to 3 Tbsp. salsa
- 1 tsp. ground cumin
- ½ cup shredded cheddar cheese
  Sliced jalapeno pepper, optional

1. Preheat oven to 350°. In a large skillet, brown pork in oil; drain. Stir in the beans, soup, tomatoes, chiles, rice, water, salsa and cumin.

2. Pour into an ungreased 2-qt. baking dish. Bake, uncovered, until bubbly, about 30 minutes. Sprinkle with cheese; let stand 5 minutes before serving. If desired, serve with jalapeno slices.

Freeze option: Sprinkle cheese over cooled unbaked casserole. Cover and freeze. To use, partially thaw in refrigerator overnight. Remove from refrigerator 30 minutes before baking. Preheat oven to 350°. Bake casserole as directed, increasing time as necessary to heat through and for a thermometer inserted in center to read 165°. If desired, serve with jalapeno slices.

1 serving: 390 cal., 15g fat (6g sat. fat), 81mg chol., 814mg sod., 29g carb. (3g sugars, 6g fiber), 32g pro.

FIG-GLAZED CHICKEN WITH WHITE BEANS

Sauteed shallots, fig jam, rosemary, lemon and sherry vinegar make a delightful sauce for both the chicken and beans. My husband couldn't believe how well the white beans absorbed the flavor, making this a grand slam. Try adding matchstick carrots to the bean mixture for extra color, flavor and crunch.
—*Arlene Erlbach, Morton Grove, IL*

- -

Prep: 15 min. • **Cook:** 30 min.
Makes: 6 servings

- ¾ cup fig preserves
- ⅓ cup water
- 2 Tbsp. lemon juice
- 2 Tbsp. sherry vinegar
- 4 tsp. minced fresh rosemary or 1 tsp. dried rosemary, crushed
- 1 Tbsp. Worcestershire sauce
- ¼ tsp. salt
- ¼ tsp. pepper
- 6 bone-in chicken thighs (about 2¼ lbs.)
- 4 shallots, coarsely chopped
- 1 can (15 oz.) cannellini beans, rinsed and drained

1. Mix the first 8 ingredients. In a large skillet over medium-high heat, brown the chicken in batches, starting skin side down. Remove chicken from the pan, reserving the drippings.

2. Saute shallots in the drippings until golden brown, 2-3 minutes. Stir in the preserves mixture; bring to a boil, stirring to loosen any browned bits from the pan. Add the chicken. Reduce heat; simmer, covered, for 5 minutes.

3. Add the beans; return to a boil. Cook, uncovered, until a thermometer inserted in chicken reads 170°-175°, 12-15 minutes.

1 serving: 405 cal., 15g fat (4g sat. fat), 81mg chol., 287mg sod., 42g carb. (25g sugars, 3g fiber), 26g pro.

Contest Winner

ARTICHOKE CHICKEN

Rosemary, mushrooms and artichokes combine to give chicken a wonderful savory flavor. I've served this dish for a large group by doubling the recipe. It's always a big hit with everyone—especially my family!
—*Ruth Stenson, Santa Ana, CA*

- -

Prep: 15 min. • **Bake:** 40 min.
Makes: 8 servings

- 8   boneless skinless chicken breast halves (4 oz. each)
- 2   Tbsp. butter
- 2   jars (6 oz. each) marinated quartered artichoke hearts, drained
- 1   jar (4½ oz.) whole mushrooms, drained
- ½   cup chopped onion
- ⅓   cup all-purpose flour
- 1½ tsp. dried rosemary, crushed
- ¾   tsp. salt
- ¼   tsp. pepper
- 2   cups chicken broth or 1 cup broth and 1 cup dry white wine
     Hot cooked noodles
     Minced fresh parsley

1. Preheat oven to 350°. In a large skillet, brown chicken in butter. Remove chicken to an ungreased 13x9-in. baking dish. Arrange artichokes and mushrooms on top of the chicken; set aside.
2. Saute onion in pan juices until crisp-tender. Combine the flour, rosemary, salt and pepper. Stir into pan until blended. Add chicken broth. Bring to a boil; cook and stir until thickened and bubbly, about 2 minutes. Spoon over the chicken.
3. Bake, uncovered, until a thermometer inserted in the chicken reads 165°, about 40 minutes. Serve with cooked noodles and sprinkle with parsley.

Freeze option: Cool unbaked casserole; cover and freeze. To use, partially thaw in refrigerator overnight; remove refrigerator 30 minutes before baking. Bake casserole as directed, increasing time as necessary to heat through and for a thermometer inserted in the chicken to read 165°.

1 serving: 232 cal., 9g fat (3g sat. fat), 81mg chol., 752mg sod., 7g carb. (1g sugars, 1g fiber), 28g pro. **Diabetic exchanges:** 4 lean meat, 1½ fat, ½ starch.

TURKEY SAUSAGE PIZZA

If pizza night is a must in your home, give this distinctly different, lighter pizza a try.
—*Melissa Jelinek, Apple Valley, MN*

Prep: 20 min. • **Bake:** 15 min. • **Makes:** 8 slices

- 1 loaf (1 lb.) frozen bread dough, thawed
- ¾ lb. Italian turkey sausage links, casings removed
- ½ cup sliced onion
- ½ cup sliced fresh mushrooms
- ½ cup chopped green pepper
- ½ cup pizza sauce
- 2 cups shredded part-skim mozzarella cheese

1. Preheat oven to 400°. With greased fingers, press dough onto a 12-in. pizza pan coated with cooking spray. Prick dough thoroughly with a fork. Bake until lightly browned, 10-12 minutes.
2. In a large skillet, cook sausage, onion, mushrooms and green pepper over medium heat until the sausage is no longer pink, 6-8 minutes, breaking up sausage into crumbles; drain.
3. Spread crust with pizza sauce. Top with the sausage mixture; sprinkle with cheese. Bake until crust is golden brown and cheese is melted, 12-15 minutes longer.
Freeze option: Wrap and freeze cooled pizza. To use, thaw overnight in the refrigerator. Unwrap; bake on a pizza pan at 400° until heated through, 18-22 minutes.
1 slice: 283 cal., 9g fat (4g sat. fat), 32mg chol., 668mg sod., 30g carb. (4g sugars, 3g fiber), 18g pro. **Diabetic exchanges:** 2 starch, 2 lean meat, ½ fat.

JAMBALAYA RICE SALAD

My cold rice salad has a little hint of spice for a classic jambalaya-style kick. Shrimp, tomatoes, ham and peppers give it bright colors and a delightful texture.
—*Karen Rahn, Hixon, TN*

Prep: 20 min. • **Cook:** 15 min. + chilling
Makes: 8 servings

- 1⅓ cups uncooked long grain rice
- 2 Tbsp. olive oil
- 2 cups cubed fully cooked ham
- ⅓ cup chopped onion
- 2 garlic cloves, minced
- 1 tsp. dried oregano
- 1 tsp. dried thyme
- ½ to 1 tsp. salt
- ¼ to ½ tsp. cayenne pepper
- ¼ tsp. pepper
- ⅓ cup red wine vinegar
- 1½ lbs. peeled and deveined cooked shrimp (31-40 per lb.)
- 2 celery ribs, thinly sliced
- 1 small green pepper, julienned
- 1 small sweet red pepper, julienned
- 1 pint cherry tomatoes, halved
- 2 green onions, sliced

1. Prepare rice according to the package directions; cool. In a large skillet, heat oil over medium heat. Add ham and onion; cook and stir until the onion is tender, about 5 minutes. Add next 6 ingredients; cook and stir 2 minutes. Remove from heat; stir in vinegar.
2. Combine the rice, ham mixture, shrimp, celery and peppers. Refrigerate, covered, for at least 2 hours. Add tomatoes; toss to combine. Sprinkle with onions.
1¼ cups: 309 cal., 7g fat (1g sat. fat), 150mg chol., 709mg sod., 32g carb. (2g sugars, 2g fiber), 28g pro. **Diabetic exchanges:** 4 lean meat, 2 starch, 1 vegetable, 1 fat.

FONTINA ROLLED CHICKEN

Good food has a way of transporting you to far-off places. Eating this delicious chicken dish is like dining in Italy without ever leaving home—no passport required!
—*Tammy Rex, New Tripoli, PA*

- -

Prep: 30 min. • **Bake:** 30 min.
Makes: 4 servings

- 4   oz. cream cheese, softened
- 1   cup shredded fontina cheese
- 5   bacon strips, cooked and crumbled
- 4   green onions, chopped
- ¼   cup chopped fresh Italian parsley
- ¼   cup julienned oil-packed sun-dried tomatoes, drained, chopped and patted dry
- ½   tsp. salt, divided
- ¾   tsp. pepper, divided
- 1   large egg
- 1½ cups panko bread crumbs
- 1   tsp. paprika
- 4   boneless skinless chicken breast halves (6 oz. each)
- 1   Tbsp. olive oil

1. Preheat oven to 375°. In a bowl, mix the first 6 ingredients; stir in ¼ tsp. each salt and pepper. In a shallow bowl, whisk egg and the remaining salt and pepper. In another shallow bowl, toss bread crumbs with paprika.

2. Carefully pound the chicken breasts with a meat mallet to ¼-in. thickness. Spread cheese mixture over chicken. Roll up each chicken breast from a short side; secure with toothpicks.

3. Dip each chicken breast in egg, then coat with crumbs. Place in a foil-lined 15x10x1-in. baking pan, seam side down. Drizzle tops with oil.

4. Bake, uncovered, for 30-35 minutes or until crust is golden brown and the chicken is no longer pink. Let stand for 5 minutes; discard the toothpicks before serving.

1 serving: 561 cal., 32g fat (14g sat. fat), 213mg chol., 962mg sod., 15g carb. (2g sugars, 2g fiber), 51g pro.

GRILLED APPLE-BRINED TURKEY

The sweet apple juice-based brine helps produce a juicy, amber-colored bird bursting with flavor. You won't regret planning for the long marinating time—this tasty turkey is worth every minute.
—*Trudy Williams, Shannonville, ON*

- -

Prep: 30 min. + marinating
Grill: 3 hours + standing
Makes: 14 servings

- 2   qt. unsweetened apple juice
- 2½   cups packed brown sugar
- 1   cup kosher salt
- 4   oz. fresh gingerroot, peeled and thinly sliced
- 15   whole cloves
- 6   garlic cloves, crushed
- 3   bay leaves
- 3   medium oranges, quartered
- 3   qt. cold water
- 1   turkey (12 to 14 lbs.)
- 2   Tbsp. canola oil

1. To make the brine, in a large kettle, combine the first 7 ingredients. Bring to a boil; cook and stir until the salt and sugar are dissolved. Stir in oranges. Remove from the heat. Add cold water to cool the brine to room temperature.

2. Remove giblets from turkey (discard or save for another use). Place a turkey-sized oven roasting bag inside a second roasting bag; add the turkey. Carefully pour cooled brine into bag. Squeeze out as much air as possible; seal bags and turn to coat. Place in a roasting pan or other large container. Refrigerate 18-24 hours, turning occasionally.

3. Prepare grill for indirect heat. Drain turkey, discarding brine. Rinse turkey under cold water; pat dry. Rub oil over skin. Skewer turkey openings; tie drumsticks together.

4. Place turkey breast side up on a rack in a disposable foil roasting pan. Grill, covered, over indirect medium heat for 30-40 minutes. Tent turkey with foil; grill, covered, until a thermometer reads 165°, 2½-3 hours longer. Cover and let stand for 15 minutes before carving.

8 oz. cooked turkey: 473 cal., 23g fat (6g sat. fat), 210mg chol., 213mg sod., 1g carb. (1g sugars, 0 fiber), 62g pro.

Contest Winner

HOMEMADE MANICOTTI

These tender manicotti are much easier to stuff than the purchased variety. People are always amazed when I say I make my own noodles. My son fixed this recipe for friends, and they were extremely impressed with his cooking skills!

—Richard Bunt, Painted Post, NY

- -

Prep: 70 min. • **Bake:** 40 min
Makes: 6 servings

CREPE NOODLES
1½ cups all-purpose flour
1 cup whole milk
3 large eggs
½ tsp. salt

FILLING
1½ lbs. ricotta cheese
¼ cup grated Romano cheese
1 large egg
1 Tbsp. minced fresh parsley or
1 tsp. dried parsley flakes
1 jar (26 oz.) meatless spaghetti sauce
Grated Romano cheese, optional

1. Preheat oven to 350°. Place flour in a bowl; whisk in milk, eggs and salt until smooth. Heat a lightly greased 8-in. skillet; pour about 2 Tbsp. batter into center of skillet. Spread into a 5-in. circle. Cook over medium heat until set; do not brown or turn. Repeat with remaining batter, making 18 crepes. Stack crepes with waxed paper in between; set aside.
2. For filling, combine the cheeses, egg and parsley. Spoon 3-4 Tbsp. down the center of each crepe; roll up.
3. Pour half of the spaghetti sauce into an ungreased 13x9-in. baking dish. Place crepes, seam side down, over the sauce; pour the remaining sauce over top.
4. Cover and bake for 20 minutes. Uncover and bake 20 minutes longer or until heated through. Sprinkle with Romano cheese if desired.
3 manicotti: 480 cal., 22g fat (11g sat. fat), 201mg chol., 1128mg sod., 44g carb. (17g sugars, 3g fiber), 27g pro.

TACOS DELUXE

I first tried this recipe in my junior high school home economics class some 20 years ago. As an adult, I wrote home for the recipe and have enjoyed it ever since!

—Katie Dreibelbis, Santa Clara, CA

- -

Prep: 25 min. • **Bake:** 10 min.
Makes: 8 servings

1 lb. ground beef
2 Tbsp. chopped onion
1 can (15 oz.) tomato sauce
1 tsp. white vinegar
1 tsp. Worcestershire sauce
2 to 3 drops hot pepper sauce
1 tsp. sugar
1 tsp. chili powder
½ tsp. garlic salt
¼ tsp. celery salt
¼ tsp. onion salt
⅛ tsp. ground allspice
⅛ tsp. ground cinnamon
Dash pepper
½ cup shredded cheddar cheese
8 taco shells
Shredded lettuce
Chopped tomatoes

SWEET-AND-SOUR DRESSING
1 cup Miracle Whip
⅓ cup sugar
2 Tbsp. white vinegar
¼ tsp. salt
½ tsp. hot pepper sauce

1. Preheat oven to 400°. In a large skillet, cook beef and onion over medium heat until no longer pink; drain. Add the next 12 ingredients to meat mixture. Simmer, uncovered, 10-15 minutes or until liquid is almost completely reduced, stirring occasionally. Cool slightly; stir in cheese.
2. Place taco shells open end up in a baking pan; place a scoop of meat mixture into each shell. Bake 10-15 minutes until the meat is hot and the cheese is melted.
3. Sprinkle lettuce and tomatoes over tacos. In a small bowl, combine dressing ingredients; drizzle over tacos.
1 taco: 312 cal., 19g fat (6g sat. fat), 44mg chol., 874mg sod., 21g carb. (12g sugars, 1g fiber), 13g pro.

THE BEST BEEF STEW

Our recipe for the best beef stew has tons of flavor, thanks to its blend of herbs and the addition of red wine and balsamic vinegar. It's a comfort classic stepped up a notch.
—*James Schend, Pleasant Prairie, WI*

Prep: 30 min. • **Cook:** 2 hours
Makes: 6 servings (2¼ qt.)

- 1½ **lbs. beef stew meat, cut into 1-in. cubes**
- ½ **tsp. salt, divided**
- 6 **Tbsp. all-purpose flour, divided**
- ½ **tsp. smoked paprika**
- 1 **Tbsp. canola oil**
- 3 **Tbsp. tomato paste**
- 2 **tsp. herbes de Provence**
- 2 **garlic cloves, minced**
- 2 **cups dry red wine**
- 2 **cups beef broth**
- 1½ **tsp. minced fresh rosemary, divided**
- 2 **bay leaves**
- 3 **cups cubed peeled potatoes**
- 3 **cups coarsely chopped onions (about 2 large)**
- 2 **cups sliced carrots**
- 2 **Tbsp. cold water**
- 2 **Tbsp. balsamic or red wine vinegar**
- 1 **cup fresh or frozen peas**

1. In a small bowl, toss beef and ¼ tsp. salt. In a large bowl, combine 4 Tbsp. flour and paprika. Add beef, a few pieces at a time, and toss to coat.

2. In a Dutch oven, brown beef in oil over medium heat. Stir in tomato paste, herbes de Provence and garlic; cook until fragrant and the color starts to darken slightly. Add wine; cook until mixture just comes to a boil. Simmer until reduced by half, about 5 minutes. Stir in broth, 1 tsp. rosemary and bay leaves. Bring to a boil. Reduce heat; cover and simmer until the meat is almost tender, about 1½ hours.

3. Add potatoes, onions and carrots. Cover; simmer until meat and vegetables are tender, about 30 minutes longer.

4. Discard bay leaves. In a small bowl, combine the remaining ½ tsp. rosemary, remaining ¼ tsp. salt and remaining 2 Tbsp. flour. Add cold water and vinegar; stir until smooth. Stir into stew. Bring to a boil; add frozen peas. Cook, stirring, until thickened, about 2 minutes. If desired, top with additional fresh rosemary.

1½ cups: 366 cal., 11g fat (3g sat. fat), 71mg chol., 605mg sod., 40g carb. (9g sugars, 6g fiber), 28g pro. **Diabetic exchanges:** 3 lean meat, 2½ starch, ½ fat.

PLAN AHEAD FOR POTPIE

When I fix beef stew, I usually make extra and reheat it another night with a pastry crust on top. My family looks forward to the beef potpie almost as much as the original stew.
—**Amelia Law** Ardmore, PA

TWO-FOR-ONE CHICKEN TETRAZZINI

A good friend shared a version of this recipe with me 35 years ago. I pay it forward by making this casserole for friends when they are unable to cook.

—Helen McPhee, Savoy, IL

- -

Prep: 30 min. • **Bake:** 20 min.
Makes: 2 casseroles (4 servings each)

- 1 pkg. (12 oz.) spaghetti
- ⅓ cup butter, cubed
- ⅓ cup all-purpose flour
- ¾ tsp. salt
- ¼ tsp. white pepper
- 1 can (14½ oz.) chicken broth
- 1½ cups half-and-half cream
- 1 cup heavy whipping cream
- 4 cups cubed cooked chicken
- 3 cans (4 oz. each) mushroom stems and pieces, drained
- 1 jar (4 oz.) sliced pimientos, drained
- ½ cup grated Parmesan cheese

1. Preheat oven to 350°. Cook spaghetti according to the package directions. Meanwhile, in a Dutch oven, melt butter. Stir in the flour, salt and pepper until smooth. Gradually add the broth, half-and-half and whipping cream. Bring to a boil; cook and stir until thickened, about 2 minutes.

2. Remove from the heat. Stir in the chicken, mushrooms and pimientos. Drain spaghetti; add to the chicken mixture and toss to coat.

3. Transfer to 2 greased 11x7-in. baking dishes. Sprinkle with cheese. Cover and freeze 1 casserole for up to 2 months. Bake the second casserole, uncovered, until heated through, 20-25 minutes.

To use frozen casserole: Thaw in the refrigerator overnight. Cover and bake at 350° for 30 minutes. Uncover; bake until heated through, 15-20 minutes more. Stir before serving.

1 cup: 572 cal., 31g fat (17g sat. fat), 150mg chol., 746mg sod., 40g carb. (4g sugars, 2g fiber), 31g pro.

SAUSAGE & KALE LENTIL STEW

I made a pot of this soup when visiting my sister and her family. Now I bring it along when I stop by, or I pack up a few containers for my nephew, who appreciates a home-cooked meal while he's away at college.
—*Tiffany Ihle, Bronx, NY*

Prep: 20 min. • **Cook:** 45 min.
Makes: 6 servings (2 qt.)

- 1 lb. bulk pork sausage
- 10 baby carrots, chopped (about ¾ cup)
- 1 small onion, finely chopped
- 4 garlic cloves, minced
- 4 plum tomatoes, halved
- ¾ cup roasted sweet red peppers
- 1 cup dried lentils, rinsed
- 2 cans (14½ oz. each) vegetable broth
- 1 bay leaf
- ½ tsp. ground cumin
- ¼ tsp. pepper
- 2 cups coarsely chopped fresh kale

1. In a Dutch oven, cook sausage, carrots and onion over medium-high heat until the sausage is no longer pink, breaking up sausage into crumbles, 8-10 minutes. Stir in garlic; cook 2 minutes longer. Drain.
2. Place tomatoes and red peppers in a food processor; process until finely chopped. Add to the sausage mixture; stir in lentils, broth and seasonings. Bring to a boil. Reduce heat; simmer, covered, 20 minutes, stirring occasionally.
3. Stir in kale; cook until the lentils and kale are tender, 10-15 minutes. Remove bay leaf.
Freeze option: Freeze cooled stew in freezer containers. To use, partially thaw in refrigerator overnight. Heat through in a saucepan, stirring occasionally.
1⅓ cups: 339 cal., 17g fat (5g sat. fat), 41mg chol., 1007mg sod., 29g carb. (5g sugars, 5g fiber), 17g pro.

RASPBERRY-WALNUT PORK SALAD

Raspberry, rosemary, Gorgonzola and walnuts combine to make a pork dish that's simply bursting with flavor.
—*Virginia C. Anthony, Jacksonville, FL*

Prep: 30 min. • **Cook:** 20 min.
Makes: 6 servings

- 1½ lbs. pork tenderloins, cut into 1-in. slices
- ⅓ cup ground walnuts
- 2 Tbsp. all-purpose flour
- ½ tsp. salt, divided
- ½ tsp. coarsely ground pepper, divided
- 4½ tsp. walnut oil
- ⅓ cup chopped shallot
- 1 medium pear, chopped
- ¾ cup reduced-sodium chicken broth
- ¾ cup seedless raspberry preserves
- ½ cup raspberry vinegar
- 2 tsp. minced fresh rosemary or ½ tsp. dried rosemary, crushed
- 2 tsp. minced fresh sage
- 2 pkg. (6 oz. each) fresh baby spinach
- ½ cup crumbled Gorgonzola cheese
- ½ cup chopped walnuts, toasted

1. Flatten pork slices to ½-in. thickness. In a shallow dish, combine the ground walnuts, flour, ¼ tsp. salt and ¼ tsp. pepper. Add pork, a few pieces at a time, and turn to coat.
2. In a large skillet over medium heat, cook the pork in oil in batches until the meat is no longer pink, 2-3 minutes on each side. Remove and keep warm.
3. In the same skillet, saute shallot until tender. Add pear; cook 1 minute longer. Add the broth, preserves and vinegar. Bring to a boil; cook for 6-8 minutes or until slightly thickened. Stir in the rosemary, sage and remaining salt and pepper. Remove from the heat.
4. Place spinach in a large bowl. Add the pear mixture; toss to coat. Divide among 6 plates; top each with pork. Sprinkle with cheese and chopped walnuts.
1 serving: 398 cal., 17g fat (4g sat. fat), 71mg chol., 415mg sod., 34g carb. (25g sugars, 2g fiber), 30g pro.

INDIVIDUAL SHEPHERD'S PIES

These comforting little pies make a fun St. Patrick's Day surprise for the family. Extras are easy to freeze and eat later on busy weeknights.
—*Ellen Osborne, Clarksville, TN*

Prep: 30 min. • **Bake:** 20 min.
Makes: 10 mini pies

- 1 lb. ground beef
- 3 Tbsp. chopped onion
- ½ tsp. minced garlic
- ⅓ cup chili sauce or ketchup
- 1 Tbsp. cider vinegar
- 2 cups hot mashed potatoes (with added milk and butter)
- 3 oz. cream cheese, softened
- 1 tube (12 oz.) refrigerated buttermilk biscuits
- ½ cup crushed potato chips
  Paprika, optional

1. Preheat oven to 375°. In a large skillet, cook beef and onion over medium heat until beef is no longer pink, 5-7 minutes, breaking up the beef into crumbles. Add the garlic; cook 1 minute or until tender. Drain. Stir in chili sauce and vinegar.
2. In a small bowl, mix mashed potatoes and cream cheese until blended. Press 1 biscuit onto bottom and up sides of each of 10 greased muffin cups. Fill with beef mixture. Spread the potato mixture over tops. Sprinkle with potato chips, pressing down lightly.
3. Bake 20-25 minutes or until golden brown. If desired, sprinkle with paprika.
Freeze option: Freeze cooled shepherd's pies in a single layer in freezer containers. To use, partially thaw in refrigerator overnight. Bake on a baking sheet in a preheated 375° oven until heated through, 15-18 minutes.
2 mini pies: 567 cal., 30g fat (12g sat. fat), 84mg chol., 1378mg sod., 51g carb. (9g sugars, 2g fiber), 23g pro.

SHEPHERD'S STROGANOFF

My family's favorite version of shepherd's pie is when I stir sour cream and paprika into the beef mixture before baking. It gives the traditional recipe a beef stroganoff spin!
—**Tanya S.** Stoney Creek, ON

Contest Winner

ROASTED CHICKEN WITH ROSEMARY

Herbs, garlic and butter give this hearty meal-in-one a classic flavor. It's a lot like pot roast, only it uses chicken instead of beef.
—*Isabel Zienkosky, Salt Lake City, UT*

Prep: 20 min. • **Bake:** 2 hours + standing
Makes: 9 servings

- ½ cup butter, cubed
- 4 Tbsp. minced fresh rosemary or 2 Tbsp. dried rosemary, crushed
- 2 Tbsp. minced fresh parsley
- 1 tsp. salt
- ½ tsp. pepper
- 3 garlic cloves, minced
- 1 whole roasting chicken (5 to 6 lbs.)
- 6 small red potatoes, halved
- 6 medium carrots, halved lengthwise and cut into 2-in. pieces
- 2 medium onions, quartered

1. Preheat the oven to 350°. In a small saucepan, melt butter; stir in seasonings and garlic. Place the chicken breast side up on a rack in a shallow roasting pan; tie drumsticks together with kitchen string. Spoon half of the butter mixture over chicken. Place the potatoes, carrots and onions around chicken. Drizzle the remaining butter mixture over vegetables.
2. Bake for 1½ hours. Baste with the cooking juices; bake 30-60 minutes longer, basting occasionally, until a thermometer inserted in thickest part of thigh reads 170°-175°. (Cover loosely with foil if chicken browns too quickly.)
3. Let stand 10-15 minutes, tented with foil if necessary, before carving. Serve with vegetables.
1 serving: 449 cal., 28g fat (11g sat. fat), 126mg chol., 479mg sod., 16g carb. (5g sugars, 3g fiber), 33g pro.

BLEND OF THE BAYOU

My sister-in-law shared this recipe when I first moved to Louisiana. It's been handed down in my husband's family for generations, and I've passed it on to my children, too.
—*Ruby Williams, Bogalusa, LA*

Prep: 20 min. • **Bake:** 25 min.
Makes: 8 servings

- 1 pkg. (8 oz.) cream cheese, cubed
- 4 Tbsp. butter, divided
- 1 large onion, chopped
- 2 celery ribs, chopped
- 1 large green pepper, chopped
- 1 lb. cooked medium shrimp, peeled and deveined
- 2 cans (6 oz. each) crabmeat, drained, flaked and cartilage removed
- 1 can (10¾ oz.) condensed cream of mushroom soup, undiluted
- ¾ cup cooked rice
- 1 jar (4½ oz.) sliced mushrooms, drained
- 1 tsp. garlic salt
- ¾ tsp. hot pepper sauce
- ½ tsp. cayenne pepper
- ¾ cup shredded cheddar cheese
- ½ cup crushed butter-flavored crackers (about 12 crackers)

1. Preheat the oven to 350°. In a small saucepan, cook and stir cream cheese and 2 Tbsp. butter over low heat until melted and smooth.
2. In a large cast-iron or other ovenproof skillet, saute onion, celery and green pepper in the remaining butter until tender. Stir in shrimp, crab, soup, rice, mushrooms, garlic salt, pepper sauce, cayenne and the cream cheese mixture.
3. Combine the cheddar cheese and cracker crumbs; sprinkle over top. Bake, uncovered, until bubbly, 25-30 minutes.
1 cup: 366 cal., 23g fat (13g sat. fat), 164mg chol., 981mg sod., 17g carb. (3g sugars, 2g fiber), 23g pro.

MAPLE-PEACH GLAZED HAM

This is one of my husband's favorite recipes. He makes it regularly on the weekends for his group of friends because it's so good and so easy.
—*Bonnie Hawkins, Elkhorn, WI*

Prep: 5 min. • **Bake:** 2 hours
Makes: 16 servings (about 2 cups sauce)

- 1 fully cooked bone-in ham (7 to 9 lbs.)
- 2 cups peach preserves or orange marmalade
- ½ cup maple syrup
- ⅓ cup orange juice
- 2 Tbsp. ground ancho chili pepper, optional

1. Preheat oven to 325°. Place ham on a rack in a shallow roasting pan. Cover and bake for 1¾-2¼ hours or until a thermometer reads 130°.
2. Meanwhile, in a small saucepan, mix the preserves, syrup, orange juice and, if desired, chili pepper until blended. Remove ¾ cup mixture for glaze.
3. Remove the ham from oven; brush with some of the glaze. Bake, uncovered, for 15-20 minutes longer or until a thermometer reads 140°, brushing occasionally with the remaining glaze.
4. In a saucepan over medium heat, bring the preserves mixture to a boil, stirring occasionally. Cook and stir until mixture is slightly thickened, 1-2 minutes. Serve as a sauce with ham.
4 oz. cooked ham with 2 Tbsp. sauce: 294 cal., 5g fat (2g sat. fat), 87mg chol., 1040mg sod., 34g carb. (31g sugars, 0 fiber), 29g pro.

Contest Winner

STUFFED WHOLE CABBAGE

My husband's great about trying new recipes—like this one. He gave me feedback on all my experiments until I got it just right!
—*Wyn Jespersen, Suffield, CT*

- -

Prep: 30 min. • **Cook:** 1¾ hours
Makes: 8 servings

SAUCE
- 1 **can (28 oz.) diced tomatoes, undrained**
- 1 **can (6 oz.) tomato paste**
- 1 **garlic clove, minced**
- 1½ **tsp. dried oregano**
- 1 **tsp. dried thyme**
- 1 **tsp. brown sugar**
- ½ **tsp. salt**

FILLING
- 1 **large head cabbage (4 lbs.), such as savoy**
- 1 **medium onion, chopped**
- 2 **tsp. vegetable oil**
- 1 **lb. ground beef**
- ¾ **cup cooked rice**
- 1 **large egg, beaten**

- 1 **tsp. salt**
- ½ **tsp. pepper**
- 1¼ **cups water, divided**
- 3 **Tbsp. cornstarch**
- 2 **Tbsp. shredded Parmesan cheese**

1. Combine sauce ingredients; set aside. Line a medium bowl with cheesecloth, allowing 6 in. to overhang edges of bowl. Place cabbage in bowl with core facing upward; leaving a 1-in. shell, remove core and center of cabbage. Discard core; chop the center cabbage leaves. In a skillet, cook onion and 1 cup chopped cabbage in oil until tender, 4-5 minutes; remove from the heat and cool slightly. In a small bowl, mix together beef, onion mixture, 1 cup sauce, rice, egg, salt and pepper; mix well. Spoon beef mixture into cabbage shell. Gather cheesecloth around cabbage and twist tightly to securely enclose cabbage leaves and filling.
2. Place 1 cup water, the remaining chopped cabbage and the remaining sauce in a Dutch oven; mix well. Carefully add stuffed cabbage, with twisted

cheesecloth facing down. Cover and bring to a boil. Reduce heat; and simmer, covered until the whole cabbage is tender and thermometer inserted in the middle of the cabbage reads 160°, 1-1¼ hours. Remove the cabbage and discard the cheesecloth. Place cabbage on a serving platter; keep warm.
3. To thicken the sauce, combine the cornstarch and the remaining ¼ cup water; add to the Dutch oven. Bring to a boil, stirring constantly; boil for 2 minutes. Cut cabbage into wedges and if desired, top with fresh thyme and oregano leaves. Serve with sauce and Parmesan cheese.
1 serving: 306 cal., 14g fat (5g sat. fat), 64mg chol., 724mg sod., 31g carb. (14g sugars, 8g fiber), 17g pro.

═══════════════════════

TWINE IF NEEDED
If needed, secure cheesecloth around the cabbage with kitchen twine. Discard cheesecloth and twine prior to serving.

CHICKEN POTPIE CASSEROLE

I always have leftover chicken broth on hand and use it for many things, including this comforting family favorite. You can buy biscuits at the store, or make your own, like I do—I always like to bake extra to eat with butter and jam.

—Liliane Jahnke, Cypress, TX

Prep: 40 min. • **Bake:** 15 min.
Makes: 8 servings

- ⅓ cup butter, cubed
- 1½ cups sliced fresh mushrooms
- 2 medium carrots, sliced
- ½ medium onion, chopped
- ¼ cup all-purpose flour
- 1 cup chicken broth
- 1 cup 2% milk
- 4 cups cubed cooked chicken
- 1 cup frozen peas
- 1 jar (2 oz.) diced pimientos, drained
- ½ tsp. salt

BISCUIT TOPPING

- 2 cups all-purpose flour
- 4 tsp. baking powder
- 2 tsp. sugar
- ½ tsp. salt
- ½ tsp. cream of tartar
- ½ cup cold butter, cubed
- ⅔ cup 2% milk

1. Preheat the oven to 400°. In a large saucepan, heat butter over medium heat. Add mushrooms, carrots and onion; cook and stir until tender.

2. Stir in flour until blended; gradually stir in broth and milk. Bring to a boil, stirring constantly; cook and stir for 2 minutes or until thickened. Stir in chicken, peas, pimientos and salt; heat through. Transfer to a greased 11x7-in. baking dish.

3. For the topping, in a large bowl, whisk flour, baking powder, sugar, salt and cream of tartar. Cut in butter until the mixture resembles coarse crumbs. Add milk; stir just until moistened.

4. Turn onto a lightly floured surface; knead gently 8-10 times. Pat or roll dough to ½-in. thickness; cut with a floured 2½-in. biscuit cutter. Place over chicken mixture. Bake, uncovered, 15-20 minutes or until the biscuits are golden brown.

1 serving: 489 cal., 26g fat (14g sat. fat), 118mg chol., 885mg sod., 36g carb. (6g sugars, 3g fiber), 27g pro.

SANTA MARIA ROAST BEEF

A simple dry rub makes this roast beef a real crowd-pleaser. The slightly spicy meat is irresistible—if there are any leftovers, pile them on top of fresh, crusty bread for a delicious second-day treat.

—Allison Ector, Ardmore, PA

Prep: 20 min. + marinating
Grill: 1 hour + standing • **Makes:** 6 servings

- 4 Tbsp. paprika
- 3 Tbsp. brown sugar
- 2 Tbsp. chili powder
- 1 Tbsp. garlic powder
- 1 Tbsp. white pepper
- 1 Tbsp. celery salt
- 1 Tbsp. ground cumin
- 1 Tbsp. dried oregano
- 1 Tbsp. pepper
- 2 tsp. cayenne pepper
- 1 tsp. ground mustard
- 1 beef tri-tip roast or beef sirloin tip roast (2 to 3 lbs.)
- 2 cups soaked hickory wood chips or chunks
- 2 Tbsp. canola oil

1. Combine the first 11 ingredients; rub desired amount over roast. Wrap and refrigerate overnight. Store leftover dry rub in an airtight container for up to 6 months.

2. Remove roast from the refrigerator 1 hour before grilling. Prepare grill for indirect heat, using a drip pan. Add wood chips according to the manufacturer's directions.

3. Unwrap roast and brush with oil; place over drip pan. Grill, covered, over medium-low indirect heat until the meat reaches the desired doneness (for medium-rare, a thermometer should read 135°; medium, 140°; medium-well, 145°), 1-1½ hours or. Let stand for 10-15 minutes before slicing.

4 oz. cooked beef: 294 cal., 16g fat (4g sat. fat), 91mg chol., 324mg sod., 5g carb. (3g sugars, 1g fiber), 32g pro. **Diabetic exchanges:** 4 lean meat, 1 fat.

ORANGE-GLAZED PORK LOIN

This is one of the best pork recipes I've ever tried. My family looks forward to this roast for dinner, and guests always want the recipe. You don't have to save it for a roast night; the flavorful rub and a glaze sparked with orange juice are also outstanding on pork chops.

—Lynnette Miete, Alna, ME

- -

Prep: 10 min. • **Bake:** 1 hour 20 min. + standing
Makes: 16 servings

- 1 tsp. salt
- 1 garlic clove, minced
- 2 to 3 fresh thyme sprigs or
  ¼ tsp. dried thyme
- ¼ tsp. ground ginger
- ¼ tsp. pepper
- 1 boneless pork loin roast (5 lbs.)

GLAZE

- 1 cup orange juice
- ¼ cup packed brown sugar
- 1 Tbsp. Dijon mustard
- ⅓ cup cold water
- 1 Tbsp. cornstarch

1. Preheat oven to 350°. Combine the first 5 ingredients; rub over the roast. Place roast fat side up on a rack in a shallow roasting pan. Bake, uncovered, for 1 hour.

2. Meanwhile, in a saucepan over medium heat, combine the orange juice, brown sugar and mustard. In a small bowl, mix water and cornstarch until smooth. Add to the orange juice mixture. Bring to a boil; cook and stir for 2 minutes. Reserve 1 cup of glaze for serving; brush half of the remaining glaze over roast.

3. Bake until a thermometer reads 145°, 20-40 minutes longer, brushing occasionally with the remaining glaze. Let stand 10 minutes before slicing. Reheat reserved glaze; serve with roast.

4 oz. cooked pork with 1 Tbsp. glaze: 199 cal., 7g fat (2g sat. fat), 71mg chol., 212mg sod., 6g carb. (5g sugars, 0 fiber), 28g pro.
Diabetic exchanges: 4 lean meat, ½ starch.

❄ HAM & COLLARDS QUICHE

I love quiche and wanted to make something that celebrates my southern roots, so I came up with this recipe. With eggs, cheese, ham and collard greens in a flaky crust, it's a complete meal.

—Billie Williams-Henderso, Bowie, MD

- -

Prep: 20 min. • **Bake:** 35 min. + standing
Makes: 6 servings

- 1 sheet refrigerated pie crust
- 2 Tbsp. olive oil
- 1 cup frozen chopped collard greens, thawed and drained
- 1 small onion, chopped
- 1 garlic clove, minced
- ¼ tsp. salt
- ¼ tsp. pepper
- 2 cups shredded Colby-Monterey Jack cheese
- ¾ cup cubed fully cooked ham
- 6 large eggs
- 1 cup 2% milk

1. Preheat oven to 375°. Unroll crust into a 9-in. pie plate; flute edge. Chill crust while preparing filling.

2. In a large skillet, heat oil over medium-high heat. Add collard greens and onion; cook and stir until the onion is tender, 5-7 minutes. Add garlic; cook 1 minute longer. Stir in salt and pepper. Cool slightly; stir in the cheese and ham. Spoon into the crust.

3. In a large bowl, whisk eggs and milk until blended. Pour over top.

4. Bake on lower oven rack until a knife inserted in the center comes out clean, 35-40 minutes. Cover edge loosely with foil during the last 15 minutes if needed to prevent overbrowning. Remove foil. Let stand 10 minutes before cutting.

Freeze option: Cover and freeze unbaked quiche. To use, remove from freezer 30 minutes before baking (do not thaw). Preheat oven to 375°. Place quiche on a baking sheet. Bake as directed, increasing time to 50-60 minutes.

1 piece: 457 cal., 31g fat (15g sat. fat), 240mg chol., 766mg sod., 23g carb. (4g sugars, 1g fiber), 21g pro.

TUNA MUSHROOM CASSEROLE

The first time I made this dish, my uncle asked for seconds even though tuna casseroles are not usually his favorite. The green beans add nice texture, color and flavor.
—*Jone Furlong, Santa Rosa, CA*

Prep: 30 min. • **Bake:** 25 min.
Makes: 6 servings

- ½ cup water
- 1 tsp. chicken bouillon granules
- 1 pkg. (9 oz.) frozen cut green beans
- 1 cup chopped onion
- 1 cup sliced fresh mushrooms
- ¼ cup chopped celery
- 1 garlic clove, minced
- ½ tsp. dill weed
- ½ tsp. salt
- ⅛ tsp. pepper
- 4 tsp. cornstarch
- 1½ cups cold whole milk
- ½ cup shredded Swiss cheese
- ¼ cup mayonnaise
- 2½ cups egg noodles, cooked and drained
- 1 can (12 oz.) light tuna in water, drained and flaked
- ⅓ cup dry bread crumbs
- 1 Tbsp. butter

1. Preheat the oven to 350°. In a large saucepan, bring water and bouillon to a boil; stir until the bouillon is dissolved. Add the next 8 ingredients; bring to a boil. Reduce heat; cover and simmer until the vegetables are tender, about 5 minutes.
2. In a small bowl, combine cornstarch and milk until smooth; gradually add to vegetable mixture. Bring to a boil; cook and stir until thickened, about 2 minutes. Remove from heat; stir in cheese and mayonnaise until the cheese is melted. Fold in noodles and tuna.
3. Pour into a greased 2½-qt. baking dish. In a small skillet, brown bread crumbs in butter; sprinkle over the casserole. Bake, uncovered, until heated through, 25-30 minutes.

1 serving: 343 cal., 15g fat (5g sat. fat), 57mg chol., 770mg sod., 27g carb. (7g sugars, 2g fiber), 24g pro.

Reimagining Meat Loaf

Take the all-time family favorite in a new direction with these homey, delicious spins on the classic meat loaf recipe. From new flavors to new forms, meat loaf is new again!

PIZZA MEAT LOAF CUPS

These moist little meat loaves are packed with pizza flavor. Try reheating one or two for an after-school snack. My family likes to drizzle extra pizza sauce on top.
—*Susan Wollin, Marshall, WI*

Takes: 30 min. • **Makes:** 1 dozen

- 1 large egg, lightly beaten
- ½ cup pizza sauce
- ¼ cup seasoned bread crumbs
- ½ tsp. Italian seasoning
- 1½ lbs. ground beef
- 1½ cups shredded part-skim mozzarella cheese
- Optional: Additional pizza sauce and basil leaves

1. Preheat oven to 375°. In a large bowl, mix the first 4 ingredients. Add beef; mix lightly but thoroughly. Divide into 12 portions; press each onto the bottom and up sides of a greased muffin cup. Add cheese to centers.
2. Bake until the meat is cooked through, 15-18 minutes. If desired, top with additional sauce and basil before serving.
2 meat loaf cups: 327 cal., 20g fat (8g sat. fat), 119mg chol., 416mg sod., 6g carb. (2g sugars, 1g fiber), 29g pro.

MINI BARBECUE MEAT LOAVES

I gave meat loaf a tasty twist by adding barbecue sauce. My kids usually get bored with beef entrees, but they keep asking for this dish. It's become a staple at my house.
—*Vicki Smith, Okeechobee, FL*

Prep: 15 min. • **Bake:** 20 min. • **Makes:** 1 dozen

- ⅔ cup barbecue sauce
- ⅓ cup salsa
- 2 tsp. Worcestershire sauce
- 1 cup dry bread crumbs
- 1 small onion, finely chopped
- 1 small green pepper, finely chopped
- 1 large egg, lightly beaten
- 2 Tbsp. Montreal steak seasoning
- 1½ lbs. lean ground beef (90% lean)

1. Preheat oven to 400°. In a large bowl, mix barbecue sauce, salsa and Worcestershire sauce; reserve ½ cup mixture for topping. Add bread crumbs, onion, pepper, egg and steak seasoning to the remaining sauce mixture. Add beef; mix lightly but thoroughly.
2. Place ⅓ cup of the beef mixture in each of 12 greased muffin cups. Spoon the reserved sauce mixture over tops.
3. Bake for 20-25 minutes or until a thermometer reads 160°. Let stand for 5 minutes before removing from pan.
1 mini meat loaf: 163 cal., 6g fat (2g sat. fat), 51mg chol., 633mg sod., 14g carb. (6g sugars, 1g fiber), 13g pro. **Diabetic exchanges:** 2 lean meat, 1 starch.

FESTIVE SWIRLED MEAT LOAF

This crowd-sized pinwheel features ham, Swiss cheese and a homemade tomato sauce. I like to serve this during the holidays.
—*Vera Sullivan, Amity, OR*

Prep: 20 min. • **Bake:** 1¼ hours
Makes: 20 servings

- 3 large eggs
- 1 cup dry bread crumbs
- ½ cup finely chopped onion
- ½ cup finely chopped green pepper
- ¼ cup ketchup
- 2 tsp. minced fresh parsley
- 1 tsp. dried basil
- 1 tsp. dried oregano
- 1 garlic clove, minced
- 2 tsp. salt
- ½ tsp. pepper
- 5 lbs. lean ground beef (90% lean)
- ¾ lb. thinly sliced deli ham
- ¾ lb. thinly sliced Swiss cheese

TOMATO PEPPER SAUCE

- ½ cup finely chopped onion
- 2 celery ribs, chopped
- ½ cup chopped green pepper
- 1 garlic clove, minced
- 1 to 2 tsp. olive oil
- 2 cups chopped fresh tomatoes
- 1 cup beef broth
- 1 bay leaf
- 1 tsp. sugar
- ¼ tsp. salt
- ¼ tsp. dried thyme
- 1 Tbsp. cornstarch
- 2 Tbsp. cold water

1. Preheat oven to 350°. In a large bowl, combine the first 11 ingredients. Crumble beef over mixture and mix lightly but thoroughly. On a piece of heavy-duty foil, pat the beef mixture into a 17x15-in. rectangle. Cover with ham and Swiss cheese slices to within ½ in. of edges.
2. Roll up tightly jelly-roll style, starting with a short side. Place seam side down in a roasting pan. Bake, uncovered, until a thermometer reads 160°, 1¼-1½ hours.
3. In a large saucepan, saute onion, celery, green pepper and garlic in oil until tender, 3-5 minutes. Add tomatoes, broth, bay leaf, sugar, salt and thyme. Simmer, uncovered, for 30 minutes. Discard the bay leaf.
4. Combine cornstarch and water until smooth; stir into the sauce. Bring to a boil; cook and stir until thickened, about 2 minutes. Drain the meat loaf before serving; serve with sauce.
1 slice: 319 cal., 17g fat (7g sat. fat), 124mg chol., 732mg sod., 8g carb. (2g sugars, 1g fiber), 32g pro.

ITALIAN MUSHROOM MEAT LOAF

Healthful oats and flaxseed amp up the nutrition in this tasty Italian meat loaf.
—*Kylie Werning, Candler, NC*

Prep: 30 min. • **Bake:** 1 hour
Makes: 8 servings

- 1 large egg, lightly beaten
- ¼ lb. fresh mushrooms, chopped
- ½ cup old-fashioned oats
- ½ cup chopped red onion
- ¼ cup ground flaxseed
- ½ tsp. pepper
- 1 pkg. (19½ oz.) Italian turkey sausage links, casings removed, crumbled
- 1 lb. lean ground beef (90% lean)
- 1 cup marinara or spaghetti sauce
  Shredded Parmesan cheese, optional

1. Preheat oven to 350°. In a large bowl, combine the egg, mushrooms, oats, onion, flax and pepper. Crumble turkey and beef over the mixture and mix lightly but thoroughly.
2. Shape into a 10x4-in. loaf. Place in a 13x9-in. baking dish coated with cooking spray. Bake, uncovered, for 50 minutes; drain. Top with marinara sauce. Bake 10-15 minutes longer or until no pink remains and a thermometer reads 165°. If desired, top with Parmesan cheese.
1 slice: 261 cal., 14g fat (3g sat. fat), 103mg chol., 509mg sod., 10g carb. (3g sugars, 2g fiber), 25g pro. **Diabetic exchanges:** 3 lean meat, ½ starch.

Meals in Minutes

On the busiest nights, when dinner needs to be on the table fast, here are the dishes you can turn to. Start to finish, each of these 28 delicious recipes takes just a half-hour— or less!—and the results are downright scrumptious. Your family will think you're a magic worker!

LEMONY SHRIMP & SNOW PEA PASTA

This pretty pasta is a family favorite—the kids love the light lemony flavor and I love that they devour the fresh veggies. You can use other types of pasta noodles for variety, like bow ties or corkscrews.
—*Jennifer Fisher, Austin, TX*

Takes: 30 min. • **Makes:** 6 servings

- 1¾ cups uncooked gemelli or spiral pasta
- 2 Tbsp. olive oil, divided
- 2 cups fresh snow peas
- 1 lb. uncooked shrimp (26-30 per lb.), peeled and deveined
- 3 garlic cloves, minced
- ¾ tsp. salt, divided
- ¼ tsp. plus ⅛ tsp. pepper, divided
- 1 cup grape tomatoes, halved

DRESSING
- ¼ cup lemon juice
- 2 Tbsp. chopped fresh parsley
- 2 Tbsp. olive oil
- 2 garlic cloves, minced
- 2 tsp. grated lemon zest
  Additional grated lemon zest and chopped fresh parsley, optional

1. Cook pasta according to the package directions. Meanwhile, in a large cast-iron or other heavy skillet, heat 1 Tbsp. oil over medium heat. Add peas; cook and stir until crisp-tender, 2-3 minutes. Remove and keep warm.
2. In the same pan, heat the remaining oil over medium-high heat. Add shrimp; cook and stir until the shrimp turn pink, 2-3 minutes. Add the garlic, ½ tsp. salt and ¼ tsp. pepper; cook and stir for 1 minute longer.
3. Drain pasta, reserving ½ cup pasta water. Add pasta to the shrimp mixture; stir in peas and tomatoes. In a small bowl, whisk the lemon juice, parsley, oil, garlic, lemon zest and the remaining salt and pepper until blended. Pour over the shrimp mixture; toss to coat, adding enough of the reserved pasta water to moisten pasta. If desired, sprinkle with additional lemon zest and parsley.
1⅓ cups: 279 cal., 11g fat (2g sat. fat), 92mg chol., 390mg sod., 28g carb. (3g sugars, 2g fiber), 18g pro. **Diabetic exchanges:** 3 lean meat, 2 starch, 1 fat.

SALMON & SPUD SALAD

I headed straight for the kitchen when I decided to pick up a healthier lifestyle. This salmon with veggies proves that smart choices can be simple and satisfying.
—*Matthew Teixeira, Milton, ON*

Takes: 30 min. • **Makes:** 4 servings

- 1 lb. fingerling potatoes
- ½ lb. fresh green beans
- ½ lb. fresh asparagus
- 4 salmon fillets (6 oz. each)
- 1 Tbsp. plus ⅓ cup red wine vinaigrette, divided
- ¼ tsp. salt
- ¼ tsp. pepper
- 4 cups fresh arugula or baby spinach
- 2 cups cherry tomatoes, halved
- 1 Tbsp. minced fresh chives

1. Cut potatoes lengthwise in half. Trim and cut green beans and asparagus into 2-in. pieces. Place the potatoes in a 6-qt. stockpot; add water to cover. Bring to a boil. Reduce heat; cook, uncovered, until tender, 10-15 minutes, adding green beans and asparagus during the last 4 minutes of cooking. Drain.
2. Meanwhile, brush salmon with 1 Tbsp. vinaigrette; sprinkle with salt and pepper. Place fish on oiled grill rack, skin side down. Grill, covered, over medium-high heat or broil 4 in. from heat until the fish just begins to flake easily with a fork, 6-8 minutes.
3. In a large bowl, combine the potato mixture, arugula, tomatoes and chives. Drizzle with the remaining vinaigrette; toss to coat. Serve with salmon.
1 salmon fillet with 2 cups salad: 480 cal., 23g fat (4g sat. fat), 85mg chol., 642mg sod., 33g carb. (8g sugars, 6g fiber), 34g pro.
Diabetic exchanges: 5 lean meat, 2 vegetable, 1½ starch, 1½ fat.

PIEROGI CHICKEN SUPPER

This change-of-pace dish combines chicken, cheese and onion with frozen pierogies for a complete meal in just 30 minutes.
—*Barbara Scott, Walkersville, MD*

Takes: 30 min. • **Makes:** 4 servings

- 1 pkg. (16 oz.) frozen pierogi
- 1 lb. boneless skinless chicken breasts, cut into 2x½-in. strips
- ¼ tsp. salt
- ⅛ tsp. pepper
- 2 Tbsp. butter, divided
- ½ large sweet onion, thinly sliced
- ½ cup shredded cheddar cheese

1. Cook pierogi according to the package directions; drain. Meanwhile, toss the chicken strips with salt and pepper. In a large nonstick skillet, heat 1 Tbsp. butter over medium-high heat; saute chicken and onion until the chicken is no longer pink. Remove from pan.
2. In the same pan, heat the remaining butter over medium heat; saute pierogi until lightly browned. Stir in the chicken mixture; sprinkle with cheese. Cover; remove from heat and let stand until the cheese is melted.
1 cup: 444 cal., 16g fat (8g sat. fat), 101mg chol., 762mg sod., 40g carb. (10g sugars, 3g fiber), 33g pro.

WEEKDAY BEEF STEW

Beef stew capped with flaky puff pastry adds hearty comfort to your weeknight menu. Make a salad and call your crowd to the table.
—*Daniel Anderson, Kenosha, WI*

Takes: 30 min. • **Makes:** 4 servings

- 1 sheet frozen puff pastry, thawed
- 1 pkg. (15 oz.) refrigerated beef roast au jus
- 2 cans (14½ oz. each) diced tomatoes, undrained
- 1 pkg. (16 oz.) frozen vegetables for stew
- ¾ tsp. pepper
- 2 Tbsp. cornstarch
- 1¼ cups water

1. Preheat oven to 400°. Unfold puff pastry. Using a 4-in. round cookie cutter, cut out 4 circles. Place circles 2 in. apart on a greased baking sheet. Bake until pastry is golden brown, 14-16 minutes.
2. Meanwhile, shred beef with 2 forks and transfer to a large saucepan. Add tomatoes, vegetables and pepper; bring to a boil. In a small bowl, mix cornstarch and water until smooth; stir into the beef mixture. Return to a boil, stirring constantly; cook and stir until thickened, 1-2 minutes. Ladle stew into 4 bowls; top each with a pastry round.
1½ cups with 1 pastry round: 604 cal., 25g fat (8g sat. fat), 73mg chol., 960mg sod., 65g carb. (10g sugars, 9g fiber), 32g pro.

TURKEY & APPLE ARUGULA SALAD

Try turkey anytime and not just at the holidays. Enjoy its flavor year-round in this refreshing salad with fresh fruit and salad greens.
—*Nancy Heishman, Las Vegas, NV*

Takes: 20 min. • **Makes:** 6 servings

- ½ cup orange juice
- 3 Tbsp. red wine vinegar
- 3 Tbsp. sesame oil
- 2 Tbsp. minced fresh chives
- ¼ tsp. salt
- ¼ tsp. coarsely ground pepper

SALAD
- 4 cups cubed cooked turkey
- 4 tsp. curry powder
- ½ tsp. freshly ground pepper
- ¼ tsp. salt
- 1 large apple, chopped
- 1 cup green grapes, halved
- 3 cups fresh arugula or baby spinach
- 1 can (11 oz.) mandarin oranges, drained
- ½ cup chopped walnuts
- ½ cup pomegranate seeds

1. For dressing, whisk together the first 6 ingredients.
2. Place turkey in a large bowl; sprinkle with seasonings and toss to combine. Stir in apple and grapes. Add arugula and mandarin oranges. Drizzle with the dressing; toss lightly to combine.
3. Sprinkle salad with walnuts and pomegranate seeds. Serve immediately.
1½ cups: 354 cal., 17g fat (3g sat. fat), 94mg chol., 301mg sod., 22g carb. (17g sugars, 3g fiber), 30g pro.

PORK CHOPS WITH TOMATO-BACON TOPPING

My husband and I collaborated on these chops with sun-dried tomatoes, bacon and rosemary. They're easy enough for any day and fancy enough for special events.
—*Trisha Klempel, Sidney, MT*

Takes: 30 min. • **Makes:** 4 servings

- 4 thick-sliced bacon strips, chopped
- 4 boneless pork loin chops (6 oz. each)
- ½ tsp. salt
- ¼ tsp. pepper
- ¼ cup julienned oil-packed sun-dried tomatoes
- 2 Tbsp. brown sugar
- 2 tsp. minced fresh rosemary or ½ tsp. dried rosemary, crushed

1. Preheat broiler. In a large cast-iron or other ovenproof skillet, cook bacon over medium heat until crisp, stirring occasionally. Remove with a slotted spoon; drain on paper towels.
2. Sprinkle pork chops with salt and pepper. Add the chops to the drippings; cook until a thermometer reads 145°, 3-4 minutes on each side. Meanwhile, in a small bowl, mix bacon, tomatoes, brown sugar and rosemary.
3. Spoon the tomato mixture over chops. Broil 3-4 in. from heat until the brown sugar is melted, 1-2 minutes.
1 pork chop: 457 cal., 33g fat (12g sat. fat), 108mg chol., 636mg sod., 2g carb. (0 sugars, 0 fiber), 37g pro.

TILAPIA WITH CORN SALSA

My family loves fish, and this super fast and delicious dish is popular at my house. Though it tastes like it takes a long time, it cooks in minutes under the broiler. We like it garnished with lemon wedges and with couscous on the side.
—*Brenda Coffey, Singer Island, FL*

Takes: 10 min. • **Makes:** 4 servings

- 4 tilapia fillets (6 oz. each)
- 1 Tbsp. olive oil
- ¼ tsp. salt
- ¼ tsp. pepper
- 1 can (15 oz.) black beans, rinsed and drained
- 1 can (11 oz.) whole kernel corn, drained
- ½ cup Italian salad dressing
- 2 Tbsp. chopped green onion
- 2 Tbsp. chopped sweet red pepper

1. Drizzle both sides of fillets with oil; sprinkle with salt and pepper. Broil 4-6 in. from the heat until the fish flakes easily with a fork, 5-7 minutes.
2. Meanwhile, in a small bowl, combine the remaining ingredients. Serve with the fish.
1 fillet with ¾ cup salsa: 354 cal., 10g fat (2g sat. fat), 83mg chol., 934mg sod., 25g carb. (7g sugars, 6g fiber), 38g pro.

SPICY CAJUN SAUSAGE & RICE SKILLET

I created this easy skillet dish to use up the boil-in-a-bag rice in my cabinet. The result packs a lot of flavor. If you're watching your salt intake, replace half the sausage with lean ground turkey and use unsalted chicken broth—you'll save almost 700 milligrams sodium per serving.
—*Sonali Ruder, New York, NY*

Takes: 30 min. • **Makes:** 4 servings

- 1 pkg. (16 oz.) hot lean turkey breakfast sausage
- 1 large onion, chopped
- 1 medium green pepper, chopped
- 1 can (14½ oz.) diced tomatoes with garlic and onion, undrained
- 1 can (14½ oz.) reduced-sodium chicken broth
- 3 tsp. Cajun seasoning
- ¼ tsp. pepper
- 2 bags boil-in-bag white rice Louisiana-style hot sauce, optional

1. In a large nonstick skillet, cook and crumble sausage with onion and pepper over medium-high heat until sausage is no longer pink, 5-7 minutes.

2. Stir in the tomatoes, broth, Cajun seasoning, pepper and the contents of the rice bags; bring to a boil. Reduce heat; simmer, covered, until liquid is absorbed and the rice is tender, 8-10 minutes. If desired, serve with hot sauce.

1½ cups: 461 cal., 12g fat (3g sat. fat), 122mg chol., 1816mg sod., 52g carb. (6g sugars, 4g fiber), 35g pro.

TURKEY BUNDLES

This recipe is a must-try—creamy turkey filling in crescent dough. Make double, if you want enough leftovers for lunch the next day!
—*Lydia Garrod, Tacoma, WA*

Takes: 30 min. • **Makes:** 6 servings

- 4 oz. cream cheese, softened
- 2 Tbsp. 2% milk
- ½ tsp. dill weed
- ¼ tsp. celery salt
- ¼ tsp. pepper
- 2 cups cubed cooked turkey
- ¼ cup chopped water chestnuts
- 1 green onion, chopped
- 2 tubes (one 8 oz., one 4 oz.) refrigerated crescent rolls
- 2 Tbsp. butter, melted
- 2 Tbsp. seasoned bread crumbs

1. Preheat oven to 375°. In a large bowl, beat the first 5 ingredients until smooth. Stir in the turkey, water chestnuts and green onion.

2. Unroll both tubes of crescent dough and separate dough into 6 rectangles; press perforations to seal. Place ⅓ cup turkey mixture in the center of each rectangle. Bring the 4 corners of dough together above the filling; twist and pinch seams to seal.

3. Place the bundles on an ungreased baking sheet. Brush tops with butter; sprinkle with bread crumbs. Bake for 15-20 minutes or until golden brown.

1 bundle: 418 cal., 25g fat (10g sat. fat), 67mg chol., 674mg sod., 26g carb. (5g sugars, 0 fiber), 20g pro.

CHICKEN, NECTARINE & AVOCADO SALAD

This summery salad comes together very, very quickly. The crunch of the granola sets it apart from the expected chicken salad. I've tried different types of granola—our favorites are ones that have a lot of nuts and aren't very sweet. This is not the time for chocolate granola!
—*Elisabeth Larsen, Pleasant Grove, UT*

Takes: 15 min. • **Makes:** 4 servings

- 6 oz. fresh baby spinach (about 8 cups)
- 2 medium nectarines, thinly sliced
- 2 cups cubed cooked chicken
- 1 cup crumbled feta cheese
- ½ cup poppy seed salad dressing
- 1 medium ripe avocado, peeled and sliced
- 1 cup granola with fruit and nuts

In a large bowl, combine the spinach, nectarines, chicken and feta. Drizzle with dressing; toss to coat. Top with avocado and granola. Serve immediately.

1½ cups: 561 cal., 32g fat (7g sat. fat), 87mg chol., 539mg sod., 38g carb. (18g sugars, 7g fiber), 30g pro.

PEPPERONI PIZZA BAKED POTATOES

These tasty taters are a true mash-up dish that combines two dinnertime favorites into one super fun meal.
—*Dawn E. Lowenstein, Huntingdon Valley, PA*

Takes: 30 min. • **Makes:** 4 servings

- 4 medium russet potatoes (about 8 oz. each)
- 1 Tbsp. olive oil
- 1 cup sliced fresh mushrooms
- 1 small green pepper, chopped
- 1 small onion, chopped
- 1 garlic clove, minced
- 1 can (8 oz.) pizza sauce
- ⅓ cup mini sliced turkey pepperoni
- ½ cup shredded Italian cheese blend
  Fresh oregano leaves or dried oregano

1. Preheat oven to 400°. Scrub potatoes; place on a microwave-safe plate. Pierce several times with a fork. Microwave, uncovered, on high until tender, 12-15 minutes.

2. In a large skillet, heat oil over medium-high heat; saute mushrooms, pepper and onion until tender, 6-8 minutes. Add garlic; cook and stir 1 minute. Stir in pizza sauce and pepperoni; heat through.

3. Place potatoes on a baking sheet; cut an X in the top of each. Fluff pulp with a fork. Top with vegetable mixture; sprinkle with cheese. Bake until cheese is melted, 5-7 minutes. Sprinkle with oregano.

1 baked potato with toppings: 311 cal., 9g fat (3g sat. fat), 23mg chol., 515mg sod., 46g carb. (5g sugars, 6g fiber), 13g pro. **Diabetic exchanges:** 3 starch, 1 medium-fat meat, ½ fat.

CHICKEN ARTICHOKE SKILLET

This stovetop chicken entree featuring artichokes and olives has a real Greek flair. Seasoned with lemon juice and oregano, the chicken turns out moist and tender.
—Carol Latimore, Arvada, CO

- -

Takes: 25 min. • **Makes:** 4 servings

4	boneless skinless chicken breast halves (4 oz. each)
¼	tsp. salt
¼	tsp. pepper
2	tsp. olive oil
1	can (14 oz.) water-packed quartered artichoke hearts, rinsed and drained
⅔	cup reduced-sodium chicken broth
¼	cup halved pimiento-stuffed olives
¼	cup halved pitted Greek olives
2	Tbsp. minced fresh oregano or 2 tsp. dried oregano
1	Tbsp. lemon juice

Sprinkle chicken with salt and pepper. In a large skillet, heat oil over medium-high heat; brown chicken on both sides. Add the remaining ingredients; bring to a boil. Reduce heat; simmer, covered, until a thermometer inserted in chicken reads 165°, 4-5 minutes.

1 serving: 225 cal., 9g fat (1g sat. fat), 63mg chol., 864mg sod., 9g carb. (0 sugars, 0 fiber), 26g pro. **Diabetic exchanges:** 3 lean meat, 1 vegetable.

BEEF & BACON GNOCCHI SKILLET

This gnocchi dish tastes like a bacon cheeseburger in a bowl! My kids like to top it just like a burger—with ketchup, mustard and pickles.
—Ashley Lecker, Green Bay, WI

- -

Takes: 30 min. • **Makes:** 6 servings

1	pkg. (16 oz.) potato gnocchi
1¼	lbs. lean ground beef (90% lean)
1	medium onion, chopped
8	cooked bacon strips, crumbled and divided
1	cup water
½	cup heavy whipping cream
1	Tbsp. ketchup
¼	tsp. salt
¼	tsp. pepper
1½	cups shredded cheddar cheese
½	cup chopped tomatoes
2	green onions, sliced

1. Preheat broiler. Cook potato gnocchi according to package directions; drain.
2. Meanwhile, in a large cast-iron or other ovenproof skillet, cook ground beef and chopped onion, crumbling beef, over medium heat until meat is no longer pink, 4-6 minutes. Drain.
3. Stir in half the bacon; add gnocchi, water, cream and ketchup. Bring to a boil. Cook, stirring, over medium heat until sauce has thickened, 3-4 minutes. Add salt and pepper. Sprinkle with cheese.
4. Broil 3-4 in. from heat until the cheese has melted, 1-2 minutes. Top with tomatoes, green onions and the remaining bacon.
Note: Look for potato gnocchi in the pasta or frozen foods section.

1 cup: 573 cal., 31g fat (16g sat. fat), 136mg chol., 961mg sod., 35g carb. (7g sugars, 2g fiber), 36g pro.

FAJITA-STYLE SHRIMP & GRITS

I combined two of my favorite dishes—fajitas and shrimp with cheesy grits—into this spicy one-dish meal. For more heat, use pepper jack cheese instead of the mild Mexican cheese blend.

—*Arlene Erlbach, Morton Grove, IL*

- -

Takes: 30 min. • **Makes:** 4 servings

- 1 lb. uncooked shrimp (16-20 per lb.), peeled and deveined
- 2 Tbsp. fajita seasoning mix
- 1 cup quick-cooking grits
- 4 cups boiling water
- 1½ cups shredded Mexican cheese blend
- 3 Tbsp. 2% milk
- 2 Tbsp. canola oil
- 3 medium sweet peppers, seeded and cut into 1-in. strips
- 1 medium sweet onion, cut into 1-in. strips
- 1 jar (15½ to 16 oz.) medium chunky salsa
- ¼ cup orange juice
- ¼ cup plus 1 Tbsp. fresh cilantro leaves, divided

1. Sprinkle shrimp with fajita seasoning; toss to coat. Set aside.

2. Slowly stir the grits into boiling water. Reduce heat to medium; cook, covered, stirring occasionally, until thickened, 5-7 minutes. Remove from heat. Stir in cheese until melted; stir in milk. Keep warm.

3. In a large skillet, heat canola oil over medium-high heat. Add peppers and onion; cook and stir until vegetables are tender and the pepper edges are slightly charred. Add the salsa, orange juice and shrimp. Cook, stirring constantly, until the shrimp turn pink, 4-6 minutes. Stir in ¼ cup cilantro. Remove from heat.

4. Spoon the grits into serving bowls; top with the shrimp mixture. Sprinkle with the remaining cilantro.

1 serving: 561 cal., 23g fat (8g sat. fat), 176mg chol., 1324mg sod., 55g carb. (12g sugars, 4g fiber), 33g pro.

FIVE-SPICE GLAZED SMOKED CHOPS

I started out fixing another recipe but didn't have all the ingredients, so I came up with this one! The spice gives it a flavorful kick. If you don't have five-spice powder, you can make a tasty imitation by combining cloves, cinnamon, anise and nutmeg. I love that I can make this on the stovetop or the grill.

—*Jill Thomas, Washington, IN*

Takes: 25 min. • **Makes:** 4 servings

- ¼ cup unsweetened apple juice
- ¼ cup grape jelly
- 2 Tbsp. cider vinegar
- ½ tsp. Chinese five-spice powder
- ½ tsp. minced fresh gingerroot
- ¼ tsp. crushed red pepper flakes
- 1 Tbsp. butter
- 4 smoked bone-in pork chops (7½ oz. each)

1. Place the first 6 ingredients in a small saucepan; bring just to a boil. Reduce heat; simmer, uncovered, 10 minutes.
2. In a 12-in. skillet, heat butter over medium-high heat. Add pork chops; cook until bottoms are browned, 4-5 minutes. Turn chops; spoon glaze over top. Cook, uncovered, until the chops are glazed and heated through, 3-4 minutes.
1 pork chop: 363 cal., 22g fat (10g sat. fat), 77mg chol., 1345mg sod., 16g carb. (15g sugars, 0 fiber), 27g pro.

JEZEBEL CHICKEN THIGHS

This easy-to-prepare, sweet and spicy baked chicken dish is a quick favorite that we make throughout the year. Tender and moist, it's a filling dish for busy weeknights.

—*Judy Armstrong, Prairieville, LA*

Takes: 25 min. • **Makes:** 4 servings

- 4 bone-in chicken thighs
- ½ tsp. salt
- ½ tsp. paprika
- ¼ tsp. pepper
- 1 Tbsp. olive oil
- 1 shallot, finely chopped
- 2 garlic cloves, minced
- ½ cup apricot preserves
- ¼ cup chicken broth
- 1 to 2 Tbsp. horseradish sauce
- 4 green onions, sliced, divided

1. Sprinkle chicken with seasonings. In a large nonstick skillet, heat oil over medium-high heat; brown chicken on both sides, beginning skin side down. Remove from pan, reserving drippings.
2. In the same pan, saute shallot and garlic in the drippings over medium-high heat until tender, 1-2 minutes. Stir in the apricot preserves, broth, horseradish sauce and half the green onions. Add the chicken; cook, covered, over medium heat until a thermometer reads 170°-175°, 10-12 minutes.
3. To serve, spoon sauce over chicken; sprinkle with remaining green onions.
1 chicken thigh with 2 Tbsp. sauce: 380 cal., 19g fat (5g sat. fat), 82mg chol., 474mg sod., 30g carb. (19g sugars, 1g fiber), 23g pro.

SAVORY STEAK SALAD

Caramelized onion and sirloin steak seasoned with a cinnamon rub make this main-dish salad different from typical versions. It's easy to toss together with packaged greens, blue cheese, dried cranberries and store-bought vinaigrette.

—Taste of Home *Test Kitchen*

Takes: 30 min. • **Makes:** 4 servings

- 2 **Tbsp. brown sugar, divided**
- 1 **tsp. salt**
- ¾ **tsp. ground cinnamon**
- ¼ **tsp. cayenne pepper**
- ¼ **tsp. pepper**
- 1 **beef top sirloin steak (1 in. thick and 1 lb.)**
- ¾ **cup balsamic vinaigrette, divided**
- 1 **medium onion, sliced**
- 2 **Tbsp. butter**
- 1 **pkg. (5 oz.) spring mix salad greens**
- ½ **cup dried cranberries**
- ¼ **cup crumbled blue cheese**

1. In a small bowl, combine 1 Tbsp. brown sugar with the salt, cinnamon, cayenne and pepper. Rub over both sides of the steak. Brush with ¼ cup vinaigrette.

2. Place steak on a broiler pan. Broil 4 in. from heat 5-6 minutes on each side or until meat reaches desired doneness (for medium-rare, a thermometer should read 135°; medium, 140°; medium-well, 145°).

3. Meanwhile, in a large skillet, saute the onion in butter until tender, about 10 minutes. Add remaining brown sugar; cook and stir over medium heat until the onion is browned, 5-10 minutes.

4. Cut steak across the grain into thin slices. In a large bowl, combine greens, cranberries, blue cheese, onion and beef. Drizzle with the remaining vinaigrette; toss to coat.

1½ cups: 407 cal., 21g fat (8g sat. fat), 85mg chol., 1200mg sod., 30g carb. (24g sugars, 3g fiber), 24g pro.

BACON & SPINACH PIZZA

Our go-to pizza is a snap to make using packaged pizza crust and ready-to-serve bacon. The kids don't even mind the spinach on top!

—Annette Riva, Naperville, IL

Takes: 20 min. • **Makes:** 6 servings

- 1 **prebaked 12-in. pizza crust**
- ⅓ **cup pizza sauce**
- 1 **cup shaved Parmesan cheese**
- 2 **cups fresh baby spinach, thinly sliced**
- 8 **ready-to-serve fully cooked bacon strips, cut into 1-in. pieces**

Preheat oven to 450°. Place crust on an ungreased baking sheet. Spread with sauce; top with ½ cup cheese, spinach and bacon. Sprinkle with remaining cheese. Bake until cheese is melted, 8-10 minutes.

1 slice: 269 cal., 10g fat (4g sat. fat), 10mg chol., 726mg sod., 31g carb. (2g sugars, 2g fiber), 15g pro. **Diabetic exchanges:** 2 starch, 2 medium-fat meat.

══

TO SHAVE OR BUY?

You can buy shaved Parmesan cheese in bags, but it's easy to shave your own from a block. Use a vegetable peeler, a cheese slicer or a mandoline on a fine setting. While prepackaged is more convenient, shaving your own gives you flexibility—shave, grate or shred the rest as needed. Another bonus: Unused cheese stays fresher in block form.

SPICY CHICKEN & BACON MAC

I've been working to perfect a creamy, spicy mac and cheese for years. After adding smoky bacon, chicken, jalapenos and spicy cheese, this is the ultimate! I use rotisserie chicken and precooked bacon when I'm pressed for time.

—*Sarah Gilbert, Beaverton, OR*

- -

Takes: 30 min. • **Makes:** 6 servings

- 1½ **cups uncooked cavatappi pasta or elbow macaroni**
- 3 **Tbsp. butter**
- 3 **Tbsp. all-purpose flour**
- 1½ **cups heavy whipping cream**
- ½ **cup 2% milk**
- 1 **tsp. Cajun seasoning**
- ¼ **tsp. salt**
- ¼ **tsp. pepper**
- 2 **cups shredded pepper jack cheese**
- 2 **cups shredded cooked chicken**
- 6 **bacon strips, cooked and crumbled**
- 1 **jalapeno pepper, seeded and chopped**
- 1 **cup crushed kettle-cooked potato chips or panko bread crumbs**

1. Cook pasta according to the package directions for al dente; drain. Preheat the broiler.
2. In a 10-in. cast-iron or other ovenproof skillet, heat butter over medium heat. Stir in flour until blended; cook and stir until lightly browned, 1-2 minutes (do not burn). Gradually whisk in cream, milk, Cajun seasoning, salt and pepper. Bring to a boil, stirring constantly. Reduce the heat; cook and stir until thickened, about 5 minutes. Stir in cheese until melted. Add pasta, chicken, bacon and jalapeno; cook and stir until heated through. Sprinkle chips over top.
3. Broil 3-4 in. from heat until chips are browned, about 30 seconds.
1 cup: 673 cal., 50g fat (28g sat. fat), 175mg chol., 705mg sod., 26g carb. (3g sugars, 1g fiber), 32g pro.

SPICE IT UP!
If your family likes food on the spicy side, add more Cajun seasoning or jalapeno. You can also use a spicier pepper, like a serrano or habanero.

SAGE-RUBBED SALMON

If you've always thought of sage with turkey, try it with salmon for a little taste of heaven. We serve this with rice, salad and sauteed green beans.

—*Nicole Raskopf, Beacon, NY*

- -

Takes: 20 min. • **Makes:** 6 servings

- 2 **Tbsp. minced fresh sage**
- 1 **tsp. garlic powder**
- 1 **tsp. kosher salt**
- 1 **tsp. freshly ground pepper**
- 1 **skin-on salmon fillet (1½ lbs.)**
- 2 **Tbsp. olive oil**

1. Preheat oven to 375°. Mix the first 4 ingredients; rub onto the flesh side of the salmon. Cut into 6 portions.
2. In a large cast-iron skillet, heat oil over medium heat. Add salmon, skin side down; cook 5 minutes. Transfer skillet to oven; bake just until fish flakes easily with a fork, about 10 minutes.
3 oz. cooked fish: 220 cal., 15g fat (3g sat. fat), 57mg chol., 377mg sod., 1g carb. (0 sugars, 0 fiber), 19g pro.
Diabetic exchanges: 3 lean meat.

TENDER SWEET & SOUR PORK CHOPS

My best friend gave me the recipe for these delightful pork chops years ago. It's become one of my family's favorites, and I prepare them often.
—Gina Young, Lamar, CO

- -

Takes: 25 min. • **Makes:** 6 servings

6	boneless pork loin chops (4 oz. each)
¾	tsp. pepper
½	cup water
⅓	cup cider vinegar
¼	cup packed brown sugar
2	Tbsp. reduced-sodium soy sauce
1	Tbsp. Worcestershire sauce
1	Tbsp. cornstarch
2	Tbsp. cold water

1. Sprinkle pork chops with pepper. In a large skillet coated with cooking spray, cook the pork over medium heat for 4-6 minutes on each side or until lightly browned. Remove and keep warm.

2. Add the water, vinegar, brown sugar, soy sauce and Worcestershire sauce to skillet; stir to loosen browned bits. Bring to a boil. Combine cornstarch and cold water until smooth; stir into skillet. Bring to a boil; cook and stir for 2 minutes or until thickened.

3. Return chops to the pan. Reduce heat; cover and simmer for 4-5 minutes or until meat is tender.

1 pork chop with 3 Tbsp. sauce: 198 cal., 6g fat (2g sat. fat), 55mg chol., 265mg sod., 12g carb. (10g sugars, 0 fiber), 22g pro.
Diabetic exchanges: 3 lean meat, 1 starch.

DUMP THE LUMPS

To prevent lumps in a sauce thickened with flour or cornstarch, be sure to stir the mixture constantly while boiling. If lumps do form, break them up by beating briskly with a wire whisk.

STRAWBERRY-BLUE CHEESE STEAK SALAD

At lunch one day, a friend told me about a steak salad she'd had at a party. It sounded so fantastic, I had to try it for myself. My family would eat it nonstop if we could. We can't get enough of that tangy dressing!

—*Alma Winberry, Great Falls, MT*

- -

Takes: 30 min. • **Makes:** 4 servings

1	beef top sirloin steak (¾ in. thick and 1 lb.)
½	tsp. salt
¼	tsp. pepper
2	tsp. olive oil
2	Tbsp. lime juice

SALAD

1	bunch romaine, torn (about 10 cups)
2	cups fresh strawberries, halved
¼	cup thinly sliced red onion
¼	cup crumbled blue cheese
¼	cup chopped walnuts, toasted Reduced-fat balsamic vinaigrette

1. Season steak with salt and pepper. In a large skillet, heat oil over medium heat. Add steak; cook 5-7 minutes on each side until meat reaches desired doneness (for medium-rare, a thermometer should read 135°; medium, 140°; medium-well, 145°). Remove from pan; let stand 5 minutes. Cut steak into bite-sized strips; toss with lime juice.

2. On a serving platter, combine romaine, strawberries and onion; top with steak. Sprinkle with cheese and walnuts. Serve with vinaigrette.

Note: To toast nuts, cook in a skillet over low heat until lightly browned, stirring occasionally.

1 serving: 289 cal., 15g fat (4g sat. fat), 52mg chol., 452mg sod., 12g carb. (5g sugars, 4g fiber), 29g pro. **Diabetic exchanges:** 4 lean meat, 2 vegetable, 2 fat, ½ fruit.

MAKE IT LIGHTER

An easy way to trim calories from this dish is simply to leave off the walnuts and blue cheese; they add almost 40 calories per serving.

PRETZEL-CRUSTED CATFISH

I'm not a big fish lover, so any concoction that has me enjoying fish is a keeper in my book. This combination of flavors works for me. It's awesome served with corn muffins, butter and honey! Spicy brown or honey mustard also work well in place of Dijon.

—*Kelly Williams, Forked River, NJ*

- -

Takes: 30 min. • **Makes:** 4 servings

- 4 **catfish fillets (6 oz. each)**
- ½ **tsp. salt**
- ½ **tsp. pepper**
- 2 **large eggs**
- ⅓ **cup Dijon mustard**
- 2 **Tbsp. 2% milk**
- ½ **cup all-purpose flour**
- 4 **cups honey mustard miniature pretzels, coarsely crushed**
  Oil for frying
  Lemon slices, optional

1. Sprinkle catfish with salt and pepper. Whisk the eggs, mustard and milk in a shallow bowl. Place flour and pretzels in separate shallow bowls. Coat fillets with flour, then dip in the egg mixture and coat with pretzels.
2. Heat ¼ in. oil to 375° in an electric skillet. Fry fillets, a few at a time, until fish flakes easily with a fork, 3-4 minutes on each side. Drain on paper towels. Serve with lemon slices if desired.
1 fillet: 610 cal., 31g fat (4g sat. fat), 164mg chol., 1579mg sod., 44g carb. (2g sugars, 2g fiber), 33g pro.

BAVARIAN APPLE-SAUSAGE HASH

This awesome recipe reflects my German roots. In the cooler months, nothing is as comforting as a hearty hash. Serve this versatile recipe as a side dish at a holiday meal or as a brunch entree over cheddar grits or topped with a fried egg.

—*Crystal Schlueter, Northglenn, CO*

- -

Takes: 30 min. • **Makes:** 4 servings

- 2 **Tbsp. canola oil**
- ½ **cup chopped onion**
- 4 **fully cooked apple chicken sausages or flavor of your choice, sliced**
- 1½ **cups thinly sliced Brussels sprouts**
- 1 **large tart apple, peeled and chopped**
- 1 **tsp. caraway seeds**
- ¼ **tsp. salt**
- ⅛ **tsp. pepper**
- 2 **Tbsp. finely chopped walnuts**
- 1 **Tbsp. brown sugar**
- 1 **Tbsp. whole grain mustard**
- 1 **Tbsp. cider vinegar**

In a large skillet, heat oil over medium-high heat; saute the onion until tender, 1-2 minutes. Add the sausage, Brussels sprouts, apple and seasonings; saute until lightly browned, 6-8 minutes. Stir in walnuts, brown sugar, mustard and vinegar; cook and stir 2 minutes.
1 cup: 310 cal., 17g fat (3g sat. fat), 60mg chol., 715mg sod., 25g carb. (19g sugars, 3g fiber), 16g pro.

Sensational Stir-Fry

When it comes to quick, easy and delicious, a great stir-fry is the gold standard. Fresh and fast, these dishes come together in a single skillet almost effortlessly!

GINGER PORK STIR-FRY

An easy homemade stir-fry sauce is the perfect base for this weeknight dish. It comes together quickly, but tastes impressive.
—*Adeline Russell, Hartford, WI*

Takes: 20 min. • **Makes:** 4 servings

- 2 Tbsp. cornstarch
- 1 cup beef broth
- 3 Tbsp. soy sauce
- 1 Tbsp. sugar
- 1½ tsp. ground ginger
- ½ tsp. garlic powder
- ½ tsp. crushed red pepper flakes
- 1 pork tenderloin (1 lb.), cut into 2-in. strips
- 2 Tbsp. canola oil, divided
- 1 pkg. (16 oz.) frozen sugar snap stir-fry vegetable blend, thawed
  Hot cooked rice
  Minced fresh cilantro, optional

1. In a small bowl, combine cornstarch and broth until smooth. Stir in soy sauce, sugar, ginger, garlic powder and pepper flakes; set aside.
2. In a wok or large skillet, stir-fry pork in 1 Tbsp. oil until juices run clear. Remove and keep warm. In the same pan, stir-fry vegetables in the remaining oil until crisp-tender.
3. Stir the broth mixture and add to the vegetables. Bring to a boil; cook and stir for 1 minute or until thickened. Return pork to the pan; heat through. Serve with rice and, if desired, sprinkle with cilantro.
1 cup: 278 cal., 11g fat (2g sat. fat), 63mg chol., 958mg sod., 16g carb. (7g sugars, 4g fiber), 27g pro.
Ginger-Orange Pork Stir-Fry: Omit first 7 ingredients. Combine 1 Tbsp. cornstarch with 1 cup orange juice and 2 Tbsp. soy sauce until smooth. Stir in 2 minced garlic cloves and ¾ tsp. ground ginger. Proceed as directed.

ASPARAGUS TURKEY STIR-FRY

When people try this dish, they ask for the recipe, just as I did when I first tasted it at a friend's home. Tossed in a delicious lemon sauce, this simple skillet dish is sure to satisfy on the busiest of nights. What a way to use leftover turkey!
—*May Evans, Corinth, KY*

Takes: 20 min. • **Makes:** 4 servings

- 2 tsp. cornstarch
- ¼ cup chicken broth
- 1 Tbsp. lemon juice
- 1 tsp. soy sauce
- 1 lb. turkey breast tenderloins, cut into ½-in. strips
- 1 garlic clove, minced
- 2 Tbsp. canola oil, divided
- 1 lb. fresh asparagus, trimmed and cut into 1½-in. pieces
- 1 jar (2 oz.) sliced pimientos, drained

1. In a small bowl, combine cornstarch, broth, lemon juice and soy sauce until smooth; set aside. In a large skillet or wok, stir-fry turkey and garlic in 1 Tbsp. oil until the turkey is no longer pink; remove and keep warm.
2. Stir-fry asparagus in the remaining oil until crisp-tender. Add pimientos. Stir broth mixture and add to the pan; cook and stir for 1 minute or until thickened. Return turkey to the pan; heat through.
1¼ cups: 205 cal., 9g fat (1g sat. fat), 56mg chol., 204mg sod., 5g carb. (1g sugars, 1g fiber), 28g pro. **Diabetic exchanges:** 3 lean meat, 1½ fat, 1 vegetable.

SHRIMP & CORN STIR-FRY

I make this seafood stir-fry at summer's end when my garden has plenty of tomatoes, squash, garlic and corn. For a quick supper, my family loves it over rice.
—Lindsay Honn, Huntingdon, PA

Takes: 20 min. • **Makes:** 4 servings

- 2 Tbsp. olive oil
- 2 small yellow summer squash, sliced
- 1 small onion, chopped
- 1 lb. uncooked shrimp (26-30 per lb.), peeled and deveined
- 1½ cups fresh or frozen corn, thawed
- 1 cup chopped tomatoes
- 4 garlic cloves, minced
- ½ tsp. salt
- ¼ tsp. pepper
- ¼ tsp. crushed red pepper flakes, optional
- ¼ cup chopped fresh basil
  Hot cooked brown rice, optional

1. In a large skillet, heat oil over medium-high heat. Add squash and onion; stir-fry until squash is crisp-tender, 2-3 minutes.
2. Add the next 6 ingredients and, if desired, pepper flakes; stir-fry until the shrimp turn pink, 3-4 minutes longer. Top with basil. Serve with rice if desired.
1 serving: 239 cal., 9g fat (1g sat. fat), 138mg chol., 443mg sod., 19g carb. (8g sugars, 3g fiber), 22g pro. **Diabetic exchanges:** 3 lean meat, 1½ fat, 1 starch, 1 vegetable.

CARIBBEAN CHICKEN STIR-FRY

Fruit cocktail in stir-fry? You might be surprised by how good this dish is! It's a promising go-to option when time's tight.
—Jeanne Holt, Mendota Heights, MN

Takes: 25 min. • **Makes:** 4 servings

- 2 tsp. cornstarch
- ¼ cup water
- 1 lb. boneless skinless chicken breasts, cut into ½-in. strips
- 2 tsp. Caribbean jerk seasoning
- 1 can (15 oz.) mixed tropical fruit, drained and coarsely chopped
- 2 pkg. (8.8 oz. each) ready-to-serve brown rice

1. In a small bowl, mix cornstarch and water until smooth.
2. Coat a large skillet with cooking spray; heat over medium-high heat. Add chicken strips; sprinkle with jerk seasoning. Stir-fry for 3-5 minutes or until no longer pink. Stir cornstarch mixture and add to pan with fruit. Bring to a boil; cook and stir for 1-2 minutes or until sauce is thickened.
3. Meanwhile, heat rice according to package directions. Serve with chicken.
½ cup stir-fry with ½ cup rice: 432 cal., 5g fat (1g sat. fat), 63mg chol., 210mg sod., 60g carb. (0 sugars, 3g fiber), 28g pro.

Cooking for Two

Empty nesters, newlyweds, or any two-person household— it can be tough to find great recipes that suit you. But these 24 scrumptious recipes are sized just right to work for you, without doing math or stuffing your fridge with leftovers that get boring by Day 3!

Contest Winner

MEATLESS TACO SALAD

This colorful salad blends together all your favorite taco ingredients—minus the ground beef. And you won't miss the meat at all! The guacamole dressing is thick and creamy.
—*Kimberly Dray, Pflugerville, TX*

- -

Takes: 20 min. • **Makes:** 2 servings

⅓ cup guacamole
¼ cup sour cream
2 Tbsp. chopped green pepper
1 Tbsp. chopped green onions
1 Tbsp. prepared Italian salad dressing
¼ tsp. chili powder
¼ tsp. pepper
3 cups shredded lettuce
8 cherry tomatoes, halved
½ cup canned kidney beans, rinsed and drained
¼ cup sliced ripe olives
½ cup crushed corn chips
½ cup shredded cheddar cheese

In a small bowl, combine the first 7 ingredients; set aside. In a large bowl, combine the lettuce, tomatoes, beans and olives. Arrange lettuce mixture on a serving plate; top with guacamole mixture. Sprinkle with corn chips and shredded cheese.

1 serving: 486 cal., 33g fat (12g sat. fat), 35mg chol., 849mg sod., 34g carb. (7g sugars, 9g fiber), 16g pro.,

═══════════════════════════════

FREEZE YOUR PEPPERS

Diced peppers can be frozen for easy use—simply wash and dry the peppers, remove the stems and seeds, and chop as desired. Pack into freezer bags, containers or canning jars. Peppers will keep in your freezer for up to 6 months. When a dish calls for diced peppers, you can use them directly from the freezer.

STOVETOP MEAT LOAVES

Who says meat loaf has to bake in the oven for hours? For this convenient recipe, all you need is your stovetop and 30 minutes. I appreciate that it's a quick, simple dish to make for one or two people that tastes as if you were in the kitchen all day.

—*Emily Sund, Geneseo, IL*

Takes: 30 min. • **Makes:** 2 servings

- 3 Tbsp. 2% milk
- 2 Tbsp. quick-cooking oats
- 1 Tbsp. chopped onion
- ⅛ tsp. salt
- ½ lb. lean ground beef
- ½ tsp. cornstarch
- ½ cup Italian tomato sauce
- ¼ cup cold water

1. In a small bowl, combine the milk, oats, onion and salt. Crumble beef over mixture and mix well. Shape into 2 loaves.

2. In a small nonstick skillet, brown loaves on all sides; drain. Combine cornstarch, tomato sauce and water until smooth. Pour over the meat loaves. Bring to a boil. Reduce heat to medium-low; cover and cook until the meat is no longer pink, for 15-20 minutes.

1 meat loaf: 292 cal., 13g fat (5g sat. fat), 99mg chol., 548mg sod., 10g carb. (2g sugars, 2g fiber), 33g pro. **Diabetic exchanges:** 3 lean meat, ½ starch.

SOUTHERN SUNSHINE EGGS

This breakfast dish is a fresh take on the classic bacon-and-eggs combo. Make sure your bowls are ovenproof for baking!

—*Carol Forcum, Marion, IL*

Prep: 20 min. • **Bake:** 20 min.
Makes: 2 servings

- 4 bacon strips
- 4 large eggs
- ⅓ cup half-and-half cream
- ⅛ tsp. pepper
- ½ cup shredded cheddar cheese
- 2 green onions, chopped

1. Preheat oven to 350°. In a small skillet, cook the bacon over medium heat until cooked but not crisp. Remove to paper towels to drain; keep warm. Coat the inside of two 8-oz. ramekins or custard cups with cooking spray; set aside.

2. In a small bowl, whisk 2 eggs, the cream and pepper. Wrap 2 bacon strips around the inside edges of each of the prepared ramekins.

3. Sprinkle each with half of the cheese and onions. Divide egg mixture between ramekins. Break 1 of the remaining eggs into each ramekin. Sprinkle with the remaining cheese and onion. Bake until eggs are completely set, 18-22 minutes.

1 serving: 380 cal., 28g fat (14g sat. fat), 486mg chol., 521mg sod., 5g carb. (3g sugars, 0 fiber), 24g pro.

MEXICAN-STYLE CHICKEN MANICOTTI

Combining an Italian pasta and Mexican ingredients created an exceptional dish. Folks like this recipe a lot, even here in Cajun country, Louisiana!

—*Larry Phillips, Shreveport, LA*

- -

Prep: 25 min. • **Bake:** 25 min
Makes: 2 servings

- 4 uncooked manicotti shells
- 1 cup cubed cooked chicken breast
- 1 cup salsa, divided
- ½ cup reduced-fat ricotta cheese
- 2 Tbsp. sliced ripe olives
- 4 tsp. minced fresh parsley
- 1 Tbsp. diced pimientos
- 1 green onion, thinly sliced
- 1 small garlic clove, minced
- ¼ to ½ tsp. hot pepper sauce
- ⅓ cup shredded Monterey Jack cheese

1. Preheat oven to 400°. Cook manicotti according to package directions. In a small bowl, combine chicken, ¼ cup salsa, the ricotta cheese, olives, parsley, pimientos, green onion, garlic and pepper sauce. Drain manicotti; fill with chicken mixture.
2. Spread ¼ cup salsa in an 8-in. square baking dish coated with cooking spray. Top with the manicotti shells and the remaining ½ cup salsa.
3. Cover dish and bake for 20 minutes. Uncover; sprinkle with Monterey Jack cheese and bake until the cheese is melted and the filling is heated through, 5-10 minutes longer.
2 shells: 352 cal., 10g fat (4g sat. fat), 71mg chol., 708mg sod., 34g carb. (6g sugars, 2g fiber), 30g pro. **Diabetic exchanges:** 4 lean meat, 2 starch.

HEARTY MULTIGRAIN PANCAKES

Oats and whole wheat flour make these tasty pancakes extra hearty. Try them with applesauce spooned on top.

—*Jeri Tirmenstein, Apache Junction, AZ*

- -

Takes: 20 min. • **Makes:** 4 pancakes

- ¼ cup all-purpose flour
- ¼ cup whole wheat flour
- ¼ cup quick-cooking oats
- 1 Tbsp. brown sugar
- 1 tsp. baking powder
- ¼ tsp. salt
- ½ cup plus 1 Tbsp. fat-free milk
- 2 Tbsp. egg substitute
- 2 tsp. canola oil
  Fresh berries, maple syrup and butter, optional

1. In a large bowl, combine the first 6 ingredients. Combine the milk, egg substitute and oil; add to the dry ingredients just until moistened.
2. Pour batter by ¼ cupfuls onto a greased hot griddle. Turn when bubbles form on top; cook until the second side is golden brown. If desired, serve pancakes with optional toppings.
2 pancakes: 243 cal., 6g fat (1g sat. fat), 1mg chol., 559mg sod., 40g carb. (11g sugars, 3g fiber), 9g pro.
Vanilla Pancakes: Omit whole wheat flour and oats. Use ¾ cup all-purpose flour. Add ¾ tsp. vanilla extract to milk mixture. Proceed as the recipe directs.

HOMEMADE FISH STICKS

As a nutritionist, I needed a healthy fish fix. Moist inside and crunchy outside, these are outstanding with oven fries or roasted veggies and low-fat homemade tartar sauce.
—*Jennifer Rowland, Elizabethtown, KY*

- -

Takes: 25 min. • **Makes:** 2 servings

- ½ cup dry bread crumbs
- ½ tsp. salt
- ½ tsp. paprika
- ½ tsp. lemon-pepper seasoning
- ½ cup all-purpose flour
- 1 large egg, beaten
- ¾ lb. cod fillets, cut into 1-in. strips
  Butter-flavored cooking spray

1. Preheat oven to 400°. In a shallow bowl, mix bread crumbs and seasonings. Place flour and egg in separate shallow bowls. Dip fish strips in flour to coat both sides; shake off excess. Dip in egg, then in crumb mixture, patting to help the coating adhere.

2. Place fish on a baking sheet coated with cooking spray; spritz with butter-flavored cooking spray. Bake for 10-12 minutes or until the fish just begins to flake easily with a fork, turning once.

1 serving: 278 cal., 4g fat (1g sat. fat), 129mg chol., 718mg sod., 25g carb. (2g sugars, 1g fiber), 33g pro. **Diabetic exchanges:** 4 lean meat, 1½ starch.

MAPLE SAUSAGE SKILLET

Maple syrup adds a welcome bit of sweetness to this stovetop supper. If I'm looking for even more green, I stir in some broccoli, too.
—*Dottie Tarlton, Malvern, AR*

- -

Takes: 25 min. • **Makes:** 2 servings

- 1 tsp. canola oil
- ½ lb. fully cooked kielbasa or Polish sausage, sliced
- 1½ cups sliced fresh mushrooms
- 1 medium green pepper, thinly sliced
- 1 small onion, halved and sliced
- 1 celery rib, sliced
- 2 Tbsp. maple syrup
- ¼ tsp. pepper
  Hot cooked rice

In a large skillet, heat oil over medium-high heat. Add sausage; cook and stir for 3-4 minutes or until lightly browned. Add the vegetables; cook and stir for 3-4 minutes longer or until vegetables are crisp-tender. Stir in syrup and pepper; heat through. Serve with rice.

1½ cups: 472 cal., 34g fat (11g sat. fat), 76mg chol., 1244mg sod., 26g carb. (0 sugars, 3g fiber), 17g pro.

ROSEMARY POT ROAST

Come home to a comforting, ready-to-eat entree with this slow-cooker favorite sized just right for two. It's so easy, and it fills the house with a wonderful aroma.

—Marcia Schroeder, River Edge, NJ

- -

Prep: 15 min. • **Cook:** 8 hours
Makes: 2 servings

- 1   boneless beef chuck steak
      (¾ in. thick and ¾ lb.)
- 1   to 2 tsp. canola oil
- ¼   cup beef broth
- ¼   cup tomato sauce
- ¼   cup dry red wine or
      additional beef broth
- 2   Tbsp. chopped onion
- 1   garlic clove, minced
- 1½ tsp. dried parsley flakes
- ¼   tsp. minced fresh rosemary
- ⅛   tsp. salt
- ⅛   tsp. pepper
- 1½ tsp. cornstarch
- 1   Tbsp. water

1. In a large skillet, brown beef in oil on both sides. Transfer to a 1½-qt. slow cooker. In a small bowl, combine the broth, tomato sauce, wine, onion, garlic, parsley, rosemary, salt and pepper; pour over beef. Cover and cook on low until meat is tender, about 8 hours.

2. Remove beef and keep warm. In a small saucepan, combine cornstarch and water until smooth; stir in cooking juices. Bring to a boil; cook and stir until thickened, about 2 minutes. Serve with beef.

5 oz. cooked beef: 358 cal., 19g fat (6g sat. fat), 111mg chol., 472mg sod., 6g carb. (1g sugars, 1g fiber), 34g pro.

═══════════════

MAKE IT A FULL MEAL

Mashed potatoes and a green veggie, like peas or steamed broccoli with lemon butter, make this a hearty meal for two. Since the leftovers are so tender and tasty, you might just want to double this recipe to serve over noodles or in sandwiches the next day.

PUFFY APPLE OMELET

With all the eggs our chickens produce, I could make this omelet every day! It's a pretty festive-looking dish, but you could fix it anytime...including for a light supper.
—*Melissa Davenport, Campbell, MN*

Takes: 30 min. • **Makes:** 2 servings

- 3 Tbsp. all-purpose flour
- ¼ tsp. baking powder
- ⅛ tsp. salt, optional
- 2 large eggs, separated, room temperature
- 3 Tbsp. 2% milk
- 1 Tbsp. lemon juice
- 3 Tbsp. sugar

TOPPING

- 1 large apple, peeled if desired and thinly sliced
- 1 tsp. sugar
- ¼ tsp. ground cinnamon

1. Preheat oven to 375°. Mix flour, baking powder and, if desired, salt. In a small bowl, whisk together egg yolks, milk and lemon juice; stir into flour mixture.

2. In another bowl, beat egg whites on medium speed until foamy. Gradually add sugar, 1 Tbsp. at a time, beating on high after each addition until stiff peaks form. Fold into the flour mixture.

3. Pour into a 9-in. deep-dish pie plate coated with cooking spray. Arrange apple slices over top. Mix sugar and cinnamon; sprinkle over apple.

4. Bake, uncovered, until a knife inserted in the center comes out clean, about 18-20 minutes. Serve immediately.

1 piece: 253 cal., 5g fat (2g sat. fat), 188mg chol., 142mg sod., 44g carb. (32g sugars, 2g fiber), 9g pro.

MUSHROOM & SPINACH SAUTE

Mushrooms and spinach make a super fast combination that's a perfectly elegant side dish for two. It's also easy to double or triple when you're serving guests.
—*Pauline Howard, Lago Vista, TX*

Takes: 10 min. • **Makes:** 2 servings

- 2 tsp. olive oil
- 2 cups sliced fresh mushrooms
- 2 garlic cloves, minced
- 1 pkg. (5 to 6 oz.) fresh baby spinach
- ⅛ tsp. salt
- ⅛ tsp. pepper

In a large skillet, heat the oil over medium-high heat. Add mushrooms; saute until tender, about 2 minutes. Add garlic; cook 1 minute longer. Add spinach in batches; cook and stir until wilted, about 1 minute. Season with salt and pepper. Serve the saute immediately.

¾ cup: 76 cal., 5g fat (1g sat. fat), 0 chol., 208mg sod., 6g carb. (2g sugars, 2g fiber), 4g pro. **Diabetic exchanges:** 1 vegetable, 1 fat.

CHEESY SUMMER SQUASH CASSEROLE

Onion and cheddar cheese perk up the rich flavor of summer squash in this comforting casserole. A crispy cornflake-crumb topping adds crunch.

—Katherine Metz, Jacksonville, FL

- -

Prep: 10 min. • **Bake:** 25 min.
Makes: 2 servings

2   **small yellow summer squash, sliced**
¼   **cup chopped onion**
½   **tsp. salt, divided**
1   **large egg**
¼   **cup mayonnaise**
2   **tsp. sugar**
   Pepper to taste
¼   **cup shredded cheddar cheese**
2   **Tbsp. crushed cornflakes**
1½   **tsp. butter, melted**

1. Preheat the oven to 350°. In a small saucepan, combine squash, onion and ¼ tsp. salt. Cover with water. Bring to a boil. Reduce heat; simmer, uncovered, until the squash is crisp-tender, about 2 minutes. Drain.

2. Whisk egg, mayonnaise, sugar, pepper and the remaining salt until blended. Stir in cheese and squash mixture. Transfer to a greased 2-cup baking dish. Toss the cornflakes and butter; sprinkle over top.

3. Bake, uncovered, until golden brown and bubbly, 25-30 minutes.

¾ cup: 376 cal., 31g fat (8g sat. fat), 117mg chol., 937mg sod., 18g carb. (10g sugars, 2g fiber), 9g pro.

SESAME ALMOND SLAW

Crunchy veggies and noodles are coated in a tangy dressing in this delightful slaw.
—Taste of Home Test Kitchen

- -

Takes: 20 min. • **Makes:** 2 servings

1   **pkg. (3 oz.) ramen noodles**
¾   **cup shredded cabbage**
¾   **cup shredded romaine**
2   **Tbsp. sliced green onion**
2   **tsp. slivered almonds, toasted**
2   **tsp. sesame seeds, toasted**
1   **Tbsp. rice vinegar**
1½   **tsp. sugar**
1½   **tsp. canola oil**
1   **tsp. water**
½   **tsp. sesame oil**
¼   **tsp. reduced-sodium soy sauce**
   Dash salt
   Dash pepper

1. Split ramen noodles in half (save the seasoning and half of the noodles for another use). Break apart the remaining ramen noodles; place in a bowl. Add the cabbage, romaine, onion, almonds and sesame seeds.

2. For dressing, in a jar with a tight-fitting lid, combine the vinegar, sugar, canola oil, water, sesame oil, soy sauce, salt and pepper; shake well. Add dressing to the salad and toss to coat. Serve immediately.

1 cup: 187 cal., 10g fat (3g sat. fat), 0 chol., 193mg sod., 20g carb. (4g sugars, 2g fiber), 4g pro. **Diabetic exchanges:** 1½ fat, 1 starch, 1 vegetable.

PORK CHOPS & PIEROGI

This meal-in-one is a different way to use pierogi—they're traditionally served with applesauce or sour cream.
—Greta Igl, Menomonee Falls, WI

Takes: 25 min. • **Makes:** 2 servings

- 8 frozen potato and onion pierogi
- 2 bone-in pork loin chops (¾ in. thick)
- ½ tsp. salt, divided
- ½ tsp. pepper, divided
- 4 Tbsp. butter, divided
- 1 medium sweet onion, sliced and separated into rings
- 1 medium Golden Delicious apple, cut into ¼-in. slices
- ¼ cup sugar
- ¼ cup cider vinegar

1. Cook pierogi according to the package directions. Sprinkle the pork chops with ¼ tsp. salt and ¼ tsp. pepper. In a large skillet, cook chops in 2 Tbsp. butter over medium heat until meat juices run clear; remove and keep warm.

2. Saute onion in remaining butter for 3 minutes. Add apple; saute until almost tender. Stir in the sugar, vinegar, and remaining salt and pepper. Bring to a boil. Reduce the heat; simmer, uncovered, for 5 minutes. Drain pierogi. Add chops and pierogi to skillet; stir to coat.

1 serving: 730 cal., 33g fat (18g sat. fat), 154mg chol., 1207mg sod., 72g carb. (45g sugars, 5g fiber), 36g pro.

SWEET CARROTS

Here's a flavorful way to dress up carrots without a lot of bother. Simply steam the good-for-you veggies, then season with butter, brown sugar, vinegar and a sprinkling of chives. The carrots not only are colorful, but they taste good, too.
—Taste of Home *Test Kitchen*

Takes: 15 min. • **Makes:** 2 servings

- 1½ cups baby carrots
- 2 tsp. brown sugar
- 1 tsp. butter
- 1 tsp. white wine vinegar
- ⅛ tsp. salt
- 2 tsp. minced chives

Place carrots in a steamer basket. Place in a saucepan over 1 in. of water; bring to a boil. Cover and steam 5-8 minutes, until tender. Transfer carrots to a large bowl. Add the brown sugar, butter, vinegar and salt; toss until the butter is melted and the carrots are coated. Sprinkle with chives.

¾ cup: 72 cal., 2g fat (1g sat. fat), 5mg chol., 247mg sod., 13g carb. (10g sugars, 2g fiber), 1g pro. **Diabetic exchanges:** 1 vegetable, ½ starch, ½ fat.

SPICY CHICKEN ENCHILADAS

Cooked chicken strips and canned enchilada sauce hurry along this zesty entree. I came up with the spicy recipe shortly after getting married. It's a delicious dinner for two that's easy to double for company.
—Amy Dando, Apalachin, NY

- -

Takes: 30 min. • **Makes:** 2 servings

- 1 pkg. (6 oz.) ready-to-use southwestern chicken strips
- 1½ cups shredded cheddar cheese, divided
- 1 can (10 oz.) enchilada sauce, divided
- 1 cup refried beans
- 4 flour tortillas (7 in.), warmed
- 1 can (2½ oz.) sliced ripe olives, drained

Optional toppings: chopped tomato and shredded lettuce

1. Preheat oven to 400°. In a large bowl, combine chicken, 1 cup cheese and ½ cup enchilada sauce. Spread ¼ cup refried beans down the center of each tortilla. Top with chicken mixture; roll up.
2. Place in 2 ungreased small baking dishes. Top with the remaining enchilada sauce and cheese; sprinkle with olives.
3. Cover and bake for 15-20 minutes or until heated through. If desired, top with tomato and lettuce.

2 enchiladas: 868 cal., 46g fat (21g sat. fat), 140mg chol., 2849mg sod., 62g carb. (4g sugars, 9g fiber), 52g pro.

SWEET & SPICY PEANUT BUTTER-BACON SANDWICHES

When I was pregnant, I craved peanut butter and bacon toast. Then I sampled a friend's peanut butter with chile pepper and loved it. The little zip made the sandwich better.
—Carolyn Eskew, Dayton, OH

- -

Takes: 10 min. • **Makes:** 2 servings

- ¼ cup peanut butter
- 4 slices cinnamon-raisin bread
- ⅛ tsp. cayenne pepper
- 4 crisp cooked bacon strips
- 2 tsp. honey

Spread peanut butter on 2 bread slices; sprinkle with cayenne. Top with bacon and drizzle with the honey. Top with the remaining bread.
1 sandwich: 461 cal., 26g fat (6g sat. fat), 23mg chol., 664mg sod., 43g carb. (15g sugars, 6g fiber), 21g pro.

BACON IN BULK

To make sure you always have bacon on hand (and who doesn't want to always have bacon on hand?), fry 2 lbs. or more of bacon at a time, drain the slices well, then freeze them. The slices don't stick together, so it's easy to remove a few from the bag for a sandwich or to crumble for a recipe.

BEEF FILETS WITH PORTOBELLO SAUCE

These tasty steaks seem special but are fast enough for everyday dinners. We enjoy the mushroom-topped filets served with marble rye bread or rolls, mixed salad, and a light but tangy lemon dessert.
—*Christel Stein, Tampa, FL*

Takes: 20 min. • **Makes:** 2 servings

- 2 beef tenderloin steaks (4 oz. each)
- 1¾ cups sliced baby portobello mushrooms (about 4 oz.)
- ½ cup dry red wine or reduced-sodium beef broth
- 1 tsp. all-purpose flour
- ½ cup reduced-sodium beef broth
- 1 tsp. ketchup
- 1 tsp. steak sauce
- 1 tsp. Worcestershire sauce
- ½ tsp. ground mustard
- ¼ tsp. pepper
- ⅛ tsp. salt
- 1 Tbsp. minced fresh chives, optional

1. Place a large skillet coated with cooking spray over medium-high heat; brown steaks on both sides. Remove from pan.
2. Add mushrooms and wine to pan; bring to a boil over medium heat, stirring to loosen browned bits from pan. Cook until liquid is reduced by half, 2-3 minutes. Mix flour and broth until smooth; stir into pan. Stir in all the remaining ingredients except chives; bring to a boil.
3. Return steaks to pan; cook, uncovered, until the meat reaches desired doneness (for medium-rare, a thermometer should read 135°; medium, 140°), 1-2 minutes per side. If desired, sprinkle with chives.

1 steak with ⅓ cup sauce: 247 cal., 7g fat (3g sat. fat), 51mg chol., 369mg sod., 7g carb. (3g sugars, 1g fiber), 27g pro. **Diabetic exchanges:** 3 lean meat, 1 vegetable.

Contest Winner

EASY LAZY LASAGNA

Lasagna may seem as if it's a lot of work for a busy evening, but one day when I had a craving for it, I devised this simple recipe— and it worked out beautifully.
—Carol Mead, Los Alamos, NM

- -

Takes: 30 min. • **Makes:** 2 servings

- 1 **cup spaghetti sauce**
- ¾ **cup shredded part-skim mozzarella cheese**
- ½ **cup 4% cottage cheese**
- 1½ **cups cooked wide egg noodles**
- 2 **Tbsp. grated Parmesan cheese**
   Chopped fresh parsley, optional

1. Preheat oven to 375°. Warm the spaghetti sauce; stir in mozzarella and cottage cheeses. Fold in noodles. Pour mixture into 2 greased 2-cup baking dishes. Sprinkle with Parmesan cheese.
2. Bake, uncovered, until bubbly, about 20 minutes. If desired, top with parsley.
1 lasagna: 399 cal., 16g fat (8g sat. fat), 68mg chol., 1120mg sod., 37g carb. (12g sugars,

PASTA POINTERS

When cooking pasta, many people add oil to the water to prevent the pasta from sticking while cooking. However, oil can also prevent the sauce from sticking to the pasta, making it difficult to eat. It's best to time the pasta so that you add it to the sauce as soon as it's done draining, and let the sauce do the job of separating the noodles.

When using pasta in a baked dish, like this one, drain the pasta thoroughly in a colander without rinsing it. Rinsing can wash away starch that may help to slightly thicken the pasta sauce. On the other hand, pasta can be rinsed in a colander when it is to be served cold, such as in a salad.

PENNE WITH VEGGIES & BLACK BEANS

This pasta dish puts your harvest of zucchini, tomato, peppers and carrots to good use.
—*Vickie Spoerle, Carmel, IN*

Takes: 25 min. • **Makes:** 2 servings

- ¾ cup uncooked penne pasta
- ⅓ cup sliced zucchini
- ⅓ cup sliced fresh carrot
- 4 medium fresh mushrooms, sliced
- ½ small green pepper, thinly sliced
- ½ small onion, thinly sliced
- 1 small garlic clove, minced
- ¼ tsp. each dried basil, oregano and thyme
- ¼ tsp. salt
- ⅛ tsp. pepper
- 2 tsp. olive oil, divided
- 1 cup canned black beans, rinsed and drained
- ¼ cup chopped seeded tomato
- 2 Tbsp. shredded Parmesan cheese
- 2 tsp. minced fresh parsley

1. Cook pasta according to the package directions. In a large nonstick skillet, saute zucchini, carrot, mushrooms, green pepper, onion, garlic and seasonings in 1 tsp. oil until crisp-tender. Stir in beans.

2. Drain pasta; add to the vegetable mixture. Add tomato and the remaining olive oil; toss gently. Sprinkle the top with Parmesan cheese and parsley.

1⅓ cups: 300 cal., 7g fat (2g sat. fat), 4mg chol., 643mg sod., 47g carb. (6g sugars, 8g fiber), 14g pro.

TURKEY SALTIMBOCCA

I kept the traditional prosciutto and sage in this Italian classic, but instead of veal I used turkey breast. This saltimbocca is so divine it really "jumps in your mouth," and you won't believe how quick and easy it is.
—*Deirdre Cox, Kansas City, MO*

Takes: 30 min. • **Makes:** 2 servings

- ¼ cup all-purpose flour
- 1 turkey breast tenderloin (8 oz.)
- ⅛ tsp. pepper
- 1½ tsp. olive oil
- 2 Tbsp. butter, divided
- 1 thin slice prosciutto or deli ham, cut into thin strips
- 2 Tbsp. minced fresh sage
- ¼ cup white wine or chicken broth

1. Place flour in a large shallow bowl. Cut turkey tenderloin horizontally in half; flatten each half with a meat mallet to ½-in. thickness. Sprinkle with pepper. Dip in flour to coat both sides; shake off excess.

2. In a large skillet, heat oil and 1 Tbsp. butter over medium heat. Add turkey; cook 3-4 minutes on each side or until no longer pink. Remove turkey from pan; keep warm.

3. In the same pan, heat 1½ tsp. butter over medium-high heat. Add prosciutto and sage; cook and stir until slightly crisp. Add wine to the pan; increase the heat to medium-high. Cook until liquid is slightly reduced, stirring to loosen any browned bits from the pan. Remove from heat; stir in the remaining 1½ tsp. butter. Serve with turkey.

1 serving: 300 cal., 17g fat (8g sat. fat), 92mg chol., 279mg sod., 4g carb. (0 sugars, 0 fiber), 29g pro.

Date Night Desserts

Make any night a date night by serving up a sweet treat just for two. These delicious desserts are just what you need to finish off your meal in style.

EASY BERRY CHEESECAKE PARFAITS

These sweet little parfaits take everything that's good about cheesecake and make it way easier. You get the rich creaminess, graham cracker crust and bright berry flavor all in a fun individual portion.
—Taste of Home *Test Kitchen*

- -

Takes: 15 min. • **Makes:** 2 servings

- 2 oz. cream cheese, softened
- ⅔ cup marshmallow creme
- ½ cup frozen whipped topping
- 4 Tbsp. graham cracker crumbs
- 1 cup fresh raspberries
- 1 cup fresh blueberries

1. Beat cream cheese and marshmallow creme until blended; fold in the frozen whipped topping.
2. Sprinkle 2 Tbsp. cracker crumbs into each of 2 glasses or dessert dishes. Layer each with ½ cup cream cheese mixture, ¼ cup raspberries and ¼ cup blueberries; repeat layers. Refrigerate the parfaits, covered, until serving.
1 parfait: 396 cal., 15g fat (9g sat. fat), 29mg chol., 174mg sod., 54g carb. (39g sugars, 6g fiber), 4g pro.

MOCHA PUDDING CAKES

Mini chocolate cakes are the perfect treat for two. My mom used to make these for us when I was a little girl. Now I like to whip them up for me and my husband. It's nice that the recipe uses basic pantry ingredients, too!
—*Debora Simmons, Eglon, WV*

- -

Takes: 30 min. • **Makes:** 2 servings

- ¼ cup all-purpose flour
- 3 Tbsp. sugar
- 1½ tsp. baking cocoa
- ½ tsp. baking powder
- ⅛ tsp. salt
- 3 Tbsp. 2% milk
- 1½ tsp. butter, melted
- ¼ tsp. vanilla extract

TOPPING

- 2 Tbsp. brown sugar
- 1½ tsp. baking cocoa
- 3 Tbsp. hot brewed coffee
- 1 Tbsp. hot water
  Whipped topping, optional

1. Preheat oven to 350°. In a small bowl, combine the flour, sugar, cocoa, baking powder and salt. Stir in milk, butter and vanilla until smooth. Spoon into two 4-oz. ramekins coated with cooking spray.
2. Combine brown sugar and cocoa; sprinkle over the batter. Combine coffee and water; pour over the topping. Bake for 15-20 minutes or until a knife inserted in the center comes out clean. Serve the cakes warm or at room temperature, with whipped topping if desired.
1 pudding cake: 227 cal., 4g fat (2g sat. fat), 9mg chol., 294mg sod., 47g carb. (33g sugars, 1g fiber), 3g pro.

BLACKBERRY CRISP

I adapted this sweet, comforting dessert from a recipe my mother-in-law gave to me. Hers fed a family with nine growing kids who were never full, so there was never any left. When I make my downsized version, there are never any leftovers either!
—*Marliss Lee, Independence, MO*

Prep: 15 min. • **Bake:** 20 min.
Makes: 2 servings

- 2 **cups fresh or frozen blackberries**
- 2 **Tbsp. sugar**
- 1 **tsp. cornstarch**
- 1½ **tsp. water**
- ½ **tsp. lemon juice**
- ½ **cup quick-cooking oats**
- ¼ **cup all-purpose flour**
- ¼ **cup packed brown sugar**
- ½ **tsp. ground cinnamon**
- ¼ **cup cold butter**
  Vanilla ice cream

1. Preheat the oven to 375°. Place the blackberries in a greased 1-qt. baking dish. In a small bowl, combine the sugar, cornstarch, water and lemon juice until smooth. Pour over berries. Combine the oats, flour, brown sugar and cinnamon; cut in butter until crumbly. Sprinkle over the berries.

2. Bake, uncovered, until the filling is bubbly, for 20-25 minutes. Serve warm with ice cream.

1¼ cups: 576 cal., 25g fat (14g sat. fat), 61mg chol., 245mg sod., 87g carb. (54g sugars, 6g fiber), 6g pro.

CRUNCHY PEANUT BUTTER TARTS

For a fun, fuss-free dessert, try these darling tarts. They're a satisfying, rich family favorite.
—*Mary Kelley, Wilmington, NC*

Takes: 10 min. + chilling • **Makes:** 2 servings

- 2 **oz. cream cheese, softened**
- ¼ **cup chunky peanut butter**
- 2 **Tbsp. sugar**
- 2 **Tbsp. sour cream**
- ¼ **tsp. vanilla extract**
- 2 **individual graham cracker tart shells**
- 2 **Tbsp. whipped topping**
  Chopped peanuts, optional

In a small bowl, beat the cream cheese, peanut butter and sugar until blended. Stir in the sour cream and vanilla. Spoon into tart shells. Refrigerate for at least 1 hour. Top with whipped topping. Sprinkle with peanuts if desired.

1 tart: 500 cal., 34g fat (12g sat. fat), 32mg chol., 375mg sod., 39g carb. (24g sugars, 3g fiber), 11g pro.

Slow Cooker

For making dips to desserts and everything in between, the slow cooker is the ultimate in kitchen convenience. These 23 recipes deliver slow-cooked appetizers, main courses, sides and sweets that let you step away from the kitchen. Plus, a special selection of Instant Pot recipes is perfect for when you want to cook it fast!

COUNTRY FRENCH PORK WITH DRIED PLUMS & APPLES

The classic flavors of herbes de Provence, apples and dried plums make this easy slow-cooked pork taste like a hearty meal at a French country cafe. For a traditional pairing, serve the pork with braised lentils.
—*Suzanne Banfield, Basking Ridge, NJ*

- -

Prep: 20 min. • **Cook:** 4 hours + standing
Makes: 10 servings

  2 **Tbsp. all-purpose flour**
  1 **Tbsp. herbes de Provence**
1½ **tsp. salt**
 ¾ **tsp. pepper**
  1 **boneless pork loin roast (3 to 4 lbs.)**
  2 **Tbsp. olive oil**
  2 **medium onions, halved and thinly sliced**
  1 **cup apple cider or unsweetened apple juice**
  1 **cup beef stock**
  2 **bay leaves**
  2 **large tart apples, peeled, cored and chopped**
  1 **cup pitted dried plums**

1. Mix flour, herbes de Provence, salt and pepper; rub over pork. In a large skillet, heat oil over medium-high heat. Brown roast on all sides. Place roast in a 5- or 6-qt. slow cooker. Add onions, apple cider, beef stock and bay leaves.
2. Cook, covered, on low 3 hours. Add apples and dried plums. Cook, covered, on low 1-1½ hours longer or until apples and pork are tender. Remove roast, onions, apples and plums to a serving platter, discarding bay leaves; tent with foil. Let stand 15 minutes before slicing.

4 oz. cooked pork with ¾ cup fruit mixture: 286 cal., 9g fat (3g sat. fat), 68mg chol., 449mg sod., 22g carb. (13g sugars, 2g fiber), 28g pro.

NOM DE PLUM

Don't be confused by the term "dried plum"—it's just the new name for the prune. Prunes had come to be seen as unfashionable; calling them "dried plums" is simply a marketing change.

CREAMY RANCHIFIED POTATOES

My daughter-in-law gave me this recipe; over the years, I've adjusted it to our tastes. It's so nice to come home from work to a hot, tasty dish that's ready to serve! You can use any cheese you'd like and also use leftover chicken or another meat in addition to, or in place of, the ham.
—*Jane Whittaker, Pensacola, FL*

Prep: 15 min. • **Cook:** 6 hours
Makes: 8 servings

- 2 lbs. small red potatoes, quartered
- 1 cup cubed fully cooked ham
- 1 can (10¾ oz.) condensed cream of potato soup, undiluted
- 1 carton (8 oz.) spreadable chive and onion cream cheese
- 3 Tbsp. minced chives
- 1 envelope ranch salad dressing mix
- 1 tsp. pepper
- 6 oz. pepper jack cheese, grated

In a 4-qt. slow cooker, combine the first 7 ingredients. Cook, covered, on low until the potatoes are tender, 6-8 hours. Top with cheese; stir to combine.
¾ cup: 297 cal., 15g fat (8g sat. fat), 53mg chol., 933mg sod., 28g carb. (2g sugars, 3g fiber), 14g pro.

SUNDAY CHICKEN SUPPER

Here's a hearty, homespun dinner that will satisfy even the biggest appetites. You're sure to love the convenience of cooking your chicken, veggies and starch all in the same wonderful dish.
—*Ruthann Martin, Louisville, OH*

Prep: 20 min. • **Cook:** 6 hours
Makes: 6 servings

- 4 medium carrots, cut into 2-in. pieces
- 1 medium onion, chopped
- 1 celery rib, cut into 2-in. pieces
- 2 cups cut fresh green beans (2 in.)
- ½ lb. small red potatoes (about 5), quartered
- 4 bacon strips, cooked and crumbled
- 1 broiler/fryer chicken (3 to 3½ lbs.), cut up
- 2 tsp. chicken bouillon granules
- 1 tsp. salt
- ½ tsp. dried thyme
- ½ tsp. dried basil
  Pinch pepper
- 1½ cups water

1. In the order listed, layer the first 7 ingredients in a 5-qt. slow cooker. Sprinkle with bouillon and seasonings. Pour water over top. Do not stir.
2. Cook, covered, until the chicken and vegetables are tender, 6-8 hours. Remove the chicken and vegetables to a platter. If desired, skim fat from cooking juices and thicken for gravy.
1 serving: 385 cal., 19g fat (5g sat. fat), 110mg chol., 898mg sod., 15g carb. (4g sugars, 3g fiber), 37g pro.

Contest Winner

MUSHROOM POT ROAST

Packed with wholesome veggies and tender beef, this is a company-special entree that all ages will enjoy. Serve mashed potatoes alongside to soak up every last drop of the beefy gravy.

—Angie Stewart, Topeka, KS

- -

Prep: 25 min. • **Cook:** 6 hours
Makes: 10 servings

- 1   boneless beef chuck roast (3 to 4 lbs.)
- ½   tsp. salt
- ¼   tsp. pepper
- 1   Tbsp. canola oil
- 1½   lbs. sliced fresh shiitake mushrooms
- 2½   cups thinly sliced onions
- 1½   cups reduced-sodium beef broth
- 1½   cups dry red wine or additional
      reduced-sodium beef broth

- 1   can (8 oz.) tomato sauce
- ¾   cup chopped peeled parsnips
- ¾   cup chopped celery
- ¾   cup chopped carrots
- 8   garlic cloves, minced
- 2   bay leaves
- 1½   tsp. dried thyme
- 1   tsp. chili powder
- ¼   cup cornstarch
- ¼   cup water
      Mashed potatoes

1. Sprinkle roast with salt and pepper. In a Dutch oven, brown roast in oil on all sides. Transfer to a 6-qt. slow cooker. Add the mushrooms, onions, broth, wine, tomato sauce, parsnips, celery, carrots, garlic, bay leaves, thyme and chili powder. Cover and cook on low for 6-8 hours or until the meat is tender.

2. Remove the meat and vegetables to a serving platter; keep warm. Discard bay leaves. Skim fat from the cooking juices; transfer juices to a small saucepan. Bring to a boil. Combine cornstarch and water until smooth; gradually stir into the pan. Return to a boil; then cook and stir for 2 minutes or until thickened. Serve with mashed potatoes, meat and vegetables.
4 oz. cooked beef with ⅔ cup vegetables and ½ cup gravy: 310 cal., 14g fat (5g sat. fat), 89mg chol., 363mg sod., 14g carb. (4g sugars, 3g fiber), 30g pro. **Diabetic exchanges:** 4 lean meat, 2 vegetable, 1½ fat.

BREAD PUDDING WITH BOURBON SAUCE

There's nothing better than this comforting bread pudding on a cold, wintry day. The bourbon sauce tastes extravagant, but it's really simple to prepare. The slow cooker does the most of the work for you!
—*Hope Johnson, Youngwood, PA*

Prep: 15 min. • **Cook:** 3 hours.
Makes: 6 servings

- 3 large eggs
- 1¼ cups 2% milk
- ½ cup sugar
- 3 tsp. vanilla extract
- ½ tsp. ground cinnamon
- ¼ tsp. ground nutmeg
- ⅛ tsp. salt
- 4½ cups day-old cubed brioche or egg bread
- 1¼ cups raisins

BOURBON SAUCE
- ¼ cup butter, cubed
- ½ cup sugar
- ¼ cup light corn syrup
- 3 Tbsp. bourbon

1. In a large bowl, whisk together the first 7 ingredients; stir in bread and raisins. Transfer to a greased 4-qt. slow cooker. Cook, covered, on low 3 hours. (To avoid scorching, rotate the slow cooker insert one-half turn midway through cooking, lifting carefully with oven mitts.)
2. For sauce, place butter, sugar and corn syrup in a small saucepan; bring to a boil, stirring occasionally. Cook and stir until the sugar is dissolved. Remove from heat; stir in bourbon. Serve warm sauce over warm bread pudding.
1 cup with 2 Tbsp. sauce: 477 cal., 12g fat (6g sat. fat), 130mg chol., 354mg sod., 84g carb. (59g sugars, 2g fiber), 8g pro.

HAM & BEAN STEW

You need only five ingredients to fix this thick and flavorful stew. It is so easy to make and is always a favorite with my family. I top bowls of it with a sprinkling of shredded cheese.
—*Teresa D'Amato, East Granby, CT*

Prep: 5 min. • **Cook:** 7 hours
Makes: 6 servings (1½ qt.)

- 2 cans (16 oz. each) baked beans
- 2 medium potatoes, peeled and cubed
- 2 cups cubed fully cooked ham
- 1 celery rib, chopped
- ½ cup water

In a 3-qt. slow cooker, combine all the ingredients; mix well. Cover and cook on low for 7 hours or until the potatoes are tender.
1 cup: 213 cal., 5g fat (2g sat. fat), 30mg chol., 919mg sod., 29g carb. (6g sugars, 5g fiber), 14g pro.

SWEET & TANGY BEETS

Fresh beets are delicious when combined with aromatic cloves and a hint of orange. These have the perfect balance of sweet and sour flavors.
—Taste of Home *Test Kitchen*

- -

Prep: 15 min. • **Cook:** 7 hours
Makes: 6 servings

- 2 lbs. small fresh beets, peeled and halved
- ½ cup sugar
- ¼ cup packed brown sugar
- 2 Tbsp. cornstarch
- ½ tsp. salt
- ¼ cup orange juice
- ¼ cup cider vinegar
- 2 Tbsp. butter
- 1½ tsp. whole cloves

1. Place beets in a 3-qt. slow cooker. Mix sugar, brown sugar, cornstarch and salt. Stir in orange juice and vinegar. Pour over beets; dot with butter.
2. Place cloves on a double thickness of cheesecloth. Gather corners of cloth to enclose seasonings; tie securely with string. Place bag in slow cooker. Cook, covered, on low until the beets are tender, 7-8 hours. Discard spice bag.
¾ cup: 214 cal., 4g fat (2g sat. fat), 10mg chol., 344mg sod., 44g carb. (38g sugars, 3g fiber), 3g pro.

SLOW-COOKER JAMBALAYA RISOTTO

I love risotto, but I don't always love the time and stirring it takes to achieve the creamy goodness. I found a slow-cooker risotto recipe and thought it was too good to be true. I decided to adapt a jambalaya recipe for this dish.
—*Angela Westra, Cambridge, MA*

- -

Prep: 20 min. • **Cook:** 2 hours
Makes: 6 servings

- 2½ cups chicken broth
- 1 can (14½ oz.) diced tomatoes, undrained
- 1½ cups tomato sauce
- 1¼ cups uncooked arborio rice
- 3 Tbsp. finely chopped onion
- 1 Tbsp. dried parsley flakes
- 1 Tbsp. olive oil
- ½ tsp. garlic powder
- ½ tsp. dried thyme
- ½ tsp. pepper
- ¼ tsp. salt
- ¼ tsp. cayenne pepper
- 1 bay leaf
- ½ lb. uncooked shrimp (31-40 per lb.), peeled and deveined and tails removed
- ½ lb. fully cooked andouille sausage links, sliced
- ⅔ cup shredded Parmesan cheese, optional

In a 4- or 5-qt. slow cooker, combine the first 13 ingredients. Cook, covered, on high for 1¾ hours. Stir in shrimp, sausage and, if desired, cheese. Cook until shrimp turn pink and rice is tender, 10-15 minutes longer. Remove bay leaf.
1½ cups: 335 cal., 11g fat (3g sat. fat), 97mg chol., 1276mg sod., 42g carb. (4g sugars, 3g fiber), 19g pro.

FIVE-CHEESE SPINACH & ARTICHOKE DIP

This is the dish I am always asked to bring to events. I have made it for weddings, Christmas parties and more. You also can bake this in the oven—just cook it at about 400° for 30 minutes or until hot and bubbly.

—Noelle Myers, Grand Forks, ND

Prep: 20 min. • **Cook:** 2½ hours
Makes: 16 servings

- 1 jar (12 oz.) roasted sweet red peppers
- 1 jar (6½ oz.) marinated quartered artichoke hearts
- 1 pkg. (10 oz.) frozen chopped spinach, thawed and squeezed dry
- 8 oz. fresh mozzarella cheese, cubed
- 1½ cups shredded Asiago cheese
- 6 oz. cream cheese, softened and cubed
- 1 cup crumbled feta cheese
- ⅓ cup shredded provolone cheese
- ⅓ cup minced fresh basil
- ¼ cup finely chopped red onion
- 2 Tbsp. mayonnaise
- 2 garlic cloves, minced
  Assorted crackers

1. Drain peppers, reserving 1 Tbsp. of the liquid; chop the peppers. Drain artichokes, reserving 2 Tbsp. of the liquid; coarsely chop the artichokes.
2. In a 3-qt. slow cooker coated with cooking spray, combine the spinach, cheeses, basil, onion, mayonnaise, garlic, artichoke hearts and peppers. Stir in reserved pepper and artichoke liquids. Cook, covered, on high for 2 hours. Stir dip, then continue to cook, covered, until cheese is melted, 30-60 minutes longer. Stir before serving; serve with crackers.
¼ cup: 197 cal., 16g fat (8g sat. fat), 38mg chol., 357mg sod., 4g carb. (2g sugars, 1g fiber), 9g pro.

MOIST CORN SPOON BREAD

Enjoy this easy take on a Southern specialty by using the convenience of a slow cooker. Here's an excellent side dish for Thanksgiving, Easter or any special feast.

—Taste of Home Test Kitchen

Prep: 20 min. • **Cook:** 4 hours
Makes: 8 servings

- 1 pkg. (8 oz.) cream cheese, softened
- 2 Tbsp. sugar
- 2 large eggs, beaten
- 1 cup 2% milk
- 2 Tbsp. butter, melted
- ½ tsp. salt
- ¼ tsp. cayenne pepper
- ⅛ tsp. pepper
- 2 cups frozen corn
- 1 can (14¾ oz.) cream-style corn
- 1 cup yellow cornmeal
- 1 cup shredded Monterey Jack cheese
- 3 green onions, thinly sliced
  Optional: Coarsely ground pepper and thinly sliced green onions

1. In a large bowl, beat cream cheese and sugar until smooth. Gradually beat in eggs. Beat in milk, butter, salt, cayenne and pepper until blended. Stir in the remaining ingredients.
2. Pour into a greased 3-qt. slow cooker. Cover and cook on low for 4-5 hours or until a toothpick inserted in the center comes out clean. If desired, top with additional pepper and green onions.
1 serving: 350 cal., 18g fat (11g sat. fat), 54mg chol., 525mg sod., 38g carb. (8g sugars, 3g fiber), 12g pro.

APPLE COMFORT

Years ago, we were without electricity for nine days during an ice storm, but I was able run the slow cooker from our generator. The situation called for dessert, and I pulled it off with this recipe. It's been a favorite ever since!
—*Awynne Thurstenson, Siloam Springs, AR*

Prep: 30 min. • **Cook:** 4 hours
Makes: 8 servings

- 8 medium tart apples, peeled and sliced
- 1 cup sugar
- ¼ cup all-purpose flour
- 2 tsp. ground cinnamon
- 2 large eggs
- 1 cup heavy whipping cream
- 1 tsp. vanilla extract
- 1 cup graham cracker crumbs
- ½ cup chopped pecans
- ¼ cup butter, melted
  Vanilla or cinnamon ice cream, optional

1. In a large bowl, combine the apples, sugar, flour and cinnamon. Spoon into a greased 3-qt. slow cooker. Whisk the eggs, cream and vanilla; pour over apple mixture. Combine the cracker crumbs, pecans and butter; sprinkle over top.
2. Cover and cook on low for 4-5 hours or until the apples are tender. Serve warm, with ice cream if desired.
¾ cup: 443 cal., 25g fat (12g sat. fat), 109mg chol., 133mg sod., 55g carb. (42g sugars, 4g fiber), 4g pro.

Contest Winner

CRAZY DELICIOUS BABY BACK RIBS

My husband often craves baby back ribs, and we cook them multiple ways to keep things interesting. This low and slow method with a tangy sauce is the best we've found.
—*Jan Whitworth, Roebuck, SC*

Prep: 15 min. • **Cook:** 5¼ hours
Makes: 8 servings

- 2 Tbsp. smoked paprika
- 2 tsp. chili powder
- 2 tsp. garlic salt
- 1 tsp. onion powder
- 1 tsp. pepper
- ½ tsp. cayenne pepper
- 4 lbs. pork baby back ribs

SAUCE
- ½ cup Worcestershire sauce
- ½ cup mayonnaise
- ½ cup yellow mustard
- ¼ cup reduced-sodium soy sauce
- 3 Tbsp. hot pepper sauce

1. In a small bowl, combine the first 6 ingredients. Cut ribs into serving-size pieces; rub with seasoning mixture. Place ribs in a 6-qt. slow cooker. Cook, covered, on low until meat is tender, 5-6 hours.
2. Preheat oven to 375°. In a small bowl, whisk the sauce ingredients. Transfer ribs to a foil-lined 15x10x1-in. baking pan; brush with some of the sauce. Bake until browned, 15-20 minutes, turning once and brushing occasionally with sauce. Serve with remaining sauce.
1 serving: 420 cal., 33g fat (9g sat. fat), 86mg chol., 1082mg sod., 6g carb. (2g sugars, 2g fiber), 24g pro.

NEW ZEALAND ROSEMARY LAMB SHANKS

When I was young my family lived in New Zealand for two years. One item that was always available was lamb shanks. Mother cooked them all the time with root vegetables, and to this day I love lamb!
—*Nancy Heishman, Las Vegas, NV*

- -

Prep: 25 min. • **Cook:** 6 hours
Makes: 8 servings

- 1 tsp. salt
- ¾ tsp. pepper
- 4 lamb shanks (about 20 oz. each)
- 1 Tbsp. butter
- ½ cup white wine
- 3 medium parsnips, peeled and cut into 1-in. chunks
- 2 large carrots, peeled and cut into 1-in. chunks
- 2 medium turnips, peeled and cut into 1-in. chunks
- 2 large tomatoes, chopped
- 1 large onion, chopped
- 4 garlic cloves, minced
- 2 cups beef broth
- 1 pkg. (10 oz.) frozen peas, thawed
- ⅓ cup chopped fresh parsley
- 2 Tbsp. minced fresh rosemary

1. Rub salt and pepper over the lamb. In a large skillet, heat butter over medium-high heat; brown meat. Transfer meat to a 6- or 7-qt. slow cooker. Add wine to skillet; cook and stir 1 minute to loosen brown bits. Pour over the lamb. Add parsnips, carrots, turnips, tomatoes, onion, garlic and broth. Cook, covered, on low until the meat is tender, 6-8 hours.

2. Remove lamb; keep warm. Stir in peas, parsley and rosemary; heat through. Serve lamb with vegetables.

½ lamb shank with 1 cup vegetables: 350 cal., 15g fat (6g sat. fat), 103mg chol., 668mg sod., 22g carb. (8g sugars, 6g fiber), 31g pro.
Diabetic exchanges: 4 lean meat, 1 starch, 1 vegetable, ½ fat.

════════════════════════════

SHANKS FOR SLOW COOKING

The shank is the lower leg of the lamb. It is very flavorful but is tough and full of connective tissue—perfectly suited to long, slow cooking times.

SLOW-COOKED TURKEY BREASTS WITH CRANBERRY SAUCE

This is a tasty and easy way to cook a turkey breast in the slow cooker. The sweet cranberry sauce complements the turkey nicely, making it ideal for holiday potlucks.
—*Marie Ramsden, Fairgrove, MI*

Prep: 15 min. • **Cook:** 4 hours
Makes: 10 servings

- 2 boneless skinless turkey breast halves (2 lbs. each)
- 1 can (14 oz.) jellied cranberry sauce
- ½ cup plus 2 Tbsp. water, divided
- 1 envelope onion soup mix
- 3 Tbsp. cornstarch

1. Place turkey breasts in a 5-qt. slow cooker. In a bowl, mix cranberry sauce, ½ cup water and soup mix. Pour half over turkey. Cook, covered, on low until a thermometer reads 165°, 4-6 hours. Remove turkey. Transfer cooking juices and remaining cranberry mixture to a large saucepan.

2. When meat is cool enough to handle, shred with 2 forks. Return to slow cooker; keep warm. Meanwhile, bring cooking juices and cranberry mixture to a boil. Mix cornstarch and remaining water until smooth; gradually stir into cranberry mixture. Cook and stir until thickened, about 2 minutes. Serve with turkey.

6 oz. cooked turkey: 189 cal., 1g fat (trace sat. fat), 90mg chol., 173mg sod., 7g carb. (4g sugars, trace fiber), 36g pro.

CARAMEL PECAN PUMPKIN CAKE

Use your slow cooker as a cake-maker for a seriously yummy dessert that is easy enough for any weekday and tasty enough for a holiday meal—and frees up oven space, too.
—*Julie Peterson, Crofton, MD*

Prep: 15 min. • **Cook:** 2 hours
Makes: 10 servings

- 1 cup butter, softened
- 1¼ cups sugar
- 4 large eggs, room temperature
- 2 cups all-purpose flour
- 2 tsp. baking powder
- 1 tsp. baking soda
- 1 tsp. pumpkin pie spice or ground cinnamon
- ½ tsp. salt
- 1 can (15 oz.) pumpkin
- ½ cup caramel sundae syrup
- ½ cup chopped pecans

1. In large bowl, cream butter and sugar until light and fluffy. Add eggs, 1 at a time, beating well after each addition. In another bowl, whisk together the next 5 ingredients; add to the creamed mixture alternately with pumpkin, beating well after each addition.

2. Line a 5-qt. round slow cooker with heavy duty foil extending over sides; spray with cooking spray. Spread batter evenly into slow cooker. Cook, covered, on high, until a toothpick inserted in the center comes out clean, about 2 hours. To avoid scorching, rotate the slow-cooker insert one-half turn midway through cooking, lifting carefully with oven mitts. Turn off slow cooker; let stand, uncovered, for 10 minutes. Using foil, carefully lift the cake out of slow cooker and invert onto a serving plate.

3. Drizzle caramel syrup over cake; top with pecans. Serve warm.

1 slice: 473 cal., 25g fat (13g sat. fat), 123mg chol., 561mg sod., 59g carb. (35g sugars, 2g fiber), 7g pro.

STUFFED SWEET ONIONS WITH BACON

This distinctive side dish is perfect to serve alongside grilled steak or pork chops. Even if you're not an onion fan, the low heat and long cooking time mellows and sweetens the naturally sharp onion flavors.

—*Erin Chilcoat, Central Islip, NY*

- -

Prep: 45 min. • **Cook:** 4 hours
Makes: 4 servings

- 4 **medium sweet onions**
- 2 **small zucchini, shredded**
- 1 **large garlic clove, minced**
- 1 **Tbsp. olive oil**
- 1 **tsp. dried basil**
- 1 **tsp. dried thyme**
- ¼ **tsp. salt**
- ¼ **tsp. pepper**
- ½ **cup dry bread crumbs**
- 4 **thick-sliced bacon strips, cooked and crumbled**
- ¼ **cup grated Parmesan cheese**
- ¼ **cup reduced-sodium chicken broth**

1. Peel onions and cut a ¼-in. slice from the top and bottom. Carefully cut and remove the center of each onion, leaving a ½-in. shell; chop the removed onion.
2. In a large skillet, saute the zucchini, garlic and chopped onions in oil until tender and the juices are reduced. Stir in the basil, thyme, salt and pepper. Remove from heat. Stir in bread crumbs, bacon and Parmesan cheese. Fill onion shells with the zucchini mixture.
3. Place in a greased 3- or 4-qt. slow cooker. Add broth to the slow cooker. Cover and cook on low for 4-5 hours or until the onions are tender.
1 stuffed onion: 284 cal., 11g fat (3g sat. fat), 14mg chol., 641mg sod., 38g carb. (19g sugars, 5g fiber), 11g pro.

SPICY HONEY SRIRACHA GAME DAY DIP

It's easy to whip up this creamy, spicy and salty dip. I love to make dips for parties—just turn the slow cooker to low once the dip is ready and let guests help themselves. No need to worry about the dip getting cold and having to reheat it.

—*Julie Peterson, Crofton, MD*

- -

Prep: 20 min. • **Cook:** 3 hours
Makes: 3 cups

- 1 **lb. ground chicken**
- 1 **pkg. (8 oz.) cream cheese, cubed**
- 1 **cup shredded white cheddar cheese**
- ¼ **cup chicken broth**
- 2 **to 4 Tbsp. Sriracha chili sauce**
- 2 **Tbsp. honey**
  Tortilla chips
  Chopped green onions, optional

1. In a large skillet, cook chicken over medium heat until no longer pink, 6-8 minutes, breaking into crumbles; drain. Transfer to a greased 3-qt. slow cooker. Stir in cream cheese, cheddar cheese, broth, chili sauce and honey.
2. Cook, covered, on low until cheese is melted, 3-4 hours, stirring every 30 minutes. Serve with tortilla chips. If desired, sprinkle with green onions.
¼ cup: 168 cal., 13g fat (6g sat. fat), 54mg chol., 243mg sod., 5g carb. (4g sugars, 0 fiber), 9g pro.

BUTTERSCOTCH PEARS

This grand finale simmers during dinner and impresses as soon as you bring it to the table. Serve as is, or with vanilla ice cream and a slice of pound cake. The leftover pear nectar is heavenly when added to sparkling wine or simply poured over ice.

—Theresa Kreyche, Tustin, CA

- -

Prep: 20 min. • **Cook:** 2 hours
Makes: 8 servings

4	large firm pears
1	Tbsp. lemon juice
¼	cup packed brown sugar
3	Tbsp. butter, softened
2	Tbsp. all-purpose flour
½	tsp. ground cinnamon
¼	tsp. salt
½	cup chopped pecans
½	cup pear nectar
2	Tbsp. honey

1. Cut pears in half lengthwise; remove cores. Brush pears with lemon juice. In a small bowl, combine the brown sugar, butter, flour, cinnamon and salt; stir in pecans. Spoon brown sugar mixture into the pears; place in a 4-qt. slow cooker.
2. Combine pear nectar and honey; drizzle over pears. Cover and cook on low for 2-3 hours or until the pears are tender. Serve warm.
1 stuffed pear half: 209 cal., 10g fat (3g sat. fat), 11mg chol., 109mg sod., 33g carb. (24g sugars, 4g fiber), 1g pro.

HOW TO CORE A PEAR

To core a fresh pear that's been cut into halves, as in this recipe, you can use a melon baller, a grapefruit spoon, or a sharp knife. To core a whole fresh pear, use an apple corer, a sharp knife or a vegetable peeler to cut the core from the bottom of the pear.

COMFORTING CHEESY POTATOES

As a four-generation Idaho family, we love our potatoes and cook them in every way possible. I have served this dish for weddings, family dinners and more. It has become a favorite of many in our family.

—*Karla Kimball, Emmett, ID*

Prep: 10 min. • **Cook:** 4 hours
Makes: 8 servings

- 1 can (10¾ oz.) condensed cream of chicken soup, undiluted
- 1 cup sour cream
- 1 small onion, finely chopped
- ¼ cup butter, melted
- ¾ tsp. salt
- ¼ tsp. pepper
- 1 pkg. (32 oz.) frozen cubed hash brown potatoes, thawed
- 2 cups shredded cheddar cheese, divided

In a 4-qt. slow cooker, combine the first 6 ingredients. Stir in hash browns and 1½ cups cheese. Cook, covered, on low until the potatoes are tender, 4-5 hours, sprinkling with the remaining cheese during the last 5 minutes.

¾ cup: 358 cal., 24g fat (13g sat. fat), 53mg chol., 764mg sod., 27g carb. (3g sugars, 2g fiber), 11g pro.

Contest Winner

❄ STUFFED CHICKEN ROLLS

Just thinking about this dish sparks my appetite! The ham and cheese rolled inside are a tasty surprise. Leftovers reheat well and make a perfect lunch with green salad.

—*Jean Sherwood, Kenneth City, FL*

Prep: 25 min. + chilling • **Cook:** 4 hours
Makes: 6 servings

- 6 boneless skinless chicken breast halves (8 oz. each)
- 6 slices fully cooked ham
- 6 slices Swiss cheese
- ¼ cup all-purpose flour
- ¼ cup grated Parmesan cheese
- ½ tsp. rubbed sage
- ¼ tsp. paprika
- ¼ tsp. pepper
- ¼ cup canola oil
- 1 can (10¾ oz.) condensed cream of chicken soup, undiluted
- ½ cup chicken broth
  Chopped fresh parsley, optional

1. Flatten chicken to ¼-in. thickness; top with ham and cheese. Roll up and tuck in ends; secure with toothpicks.

2. In a shallow bowl, combine flour, cheese, sage, paprika and pepper; coat chicken on all sides. In a large skillet, brown the chicken in oil over medium-high heat.

3. Transfer to a 5-qt. slow cooker. Combine the soup and broth; pour over the chicken. Cover and cook on low for 4-5 hours or until the chicken is tender. Remove toothpicks. Garnish with parsley if desired.

Freeze option: Cool chicken mixture. Freeze in freezer containers. To use, partially thaw in refrigerator overnight. Heat through slowly in a covered skillet, stirring occasionally, until a thermometer inserted in chicken reads 165°.

1 stuffed chicken breast half: 525 cal., 26g fat (10g sat. fat), 167mg chol., 914mg sod., 9g carb. (1g sugars, 1g fiber), 60g pro.

TOMATO APPLE CHUTNEY

I love to make different kinds of chutney during the holidays and give jars to family and friends for gifts. Cook the chutney in a slow cooker, and you don't have to fuss with it until you are ready to serve.

—*Nancy Heishman, Las Vegas, NV*

Prep: 15 min. • **Cook:** 5 hours
Makes: 30 servings

- 3 cans (14½ oz. each) fire-roasted diced tomatoes with garlic, undrained
- 2 medium red onions, chopped
- 1 large apple, peeled and chopped
- 1 cup golden raisins
- ¾ cup cider vinegar
- ½ cup packed brown sugar
- 1 Tbsp. chopped seeded jalapeno pepper
- 1 Tbsp. minced fresh cilantro
- 2 tsp. curry powder
- ½ tsp. salt
- ¼ tsp. ground allspice
  Baked pita chips

Combine the first 11 ingredients in a greased 3-qt. slow cooker. Cook, uncovered, on high, until thickened, 5-6 hours. Serve warm with pita chips.
¼ cup: 48 cal., 0 fat (0 sat. fat), 0 chol., 152mg sod., 11g carb. (8g sugars, 1g fiber), 1g pro.

CREAMY BRATWURST STEW

I adapted a baked stew recipe from the newspaper to create a simple slow-cooked version. Rich, hearty and creamy, it is the best comfort food for cold winter nights.

—*Susan Holmes, Germantown, WI*

Prep: 20 min. • **Cook:** 6½ hours
Makes: 8 servings (2 qt.)

- 1¾ lbs. potatoes (about 4 medium), peeled and cubed
- 2 medium carrots, chopped
- 2 celery ribs, chopped
- 1 medium onion, chopped
- 1 medium green pepper, chopped
- 2 lbs. uncooked bratwurst links
- ½ cup chicken broth
- 1 tsp. salt
- 1 tsp. dried basil
- ½ tsp. pepper
- 2 cups half-and-half cream
- 1 Tbsp. cornstarch
- 3 Tbsp. cold water

1. Place the first 5 ingredients in a 5-qt. slow cooker; toss to combine. Top with bratwurst. Mix broth and seasonings; pour over top.
2. Cook, covered, on low until sausage is cooked through and the vegetables are tender, 6-7 hours. Remove sausages from slow cooker; cut into 1-in. slices. Return sausages to potato mixture; stir in cream.
3. Mix cornstarch and water until smooth; stir into the stew. Cook, covered, on high until thickened, about 30 minutes.
1 cup: 544 cal., 39g fat (15g sat. fat), 114mg chol., 1367mg sod., 25g carb. (5g sugars, 2g fiber), 19g pro.

SHREDDED LAMB & MINT-BASIL PESTO SLIDERS

Lamb, a wonderful special-occasion meat, is a big crowd-pleaser in these delicious sliders. I served up about 1,500 in two days when I made them for the Great American Beer Fest, using every little bit to satisfy the very last customer.
—*Craig Kuczek, Aurora, CO*

- -

Prep: 45 min. • **Cook:** 6 hours
Makes: 2 dozen

- 1 **boneless lamb shoulder roast (3½ to 4¼ lbs.)**
- 1½ **tsp. salt**
- ½ **tsp. pepper**
- 1 **Tbsp. olive oil**
- 2 **medium carrots, chopped**
- 4 **shallots, chopped**
- 6 **garlic cloves**
- 2 **cups beef stock**

PESTO
- ¾ **cup fresh mint leaves**
- ¾ **cup loosely packed basil leaves**
- ⅓ **cup pine nuts**
- ¼ **tsp. salt**
- ¾ **cup olive oil**
- ¾ **cup shredded Parmesan cheese**
- ⅓ **cup shredded Asiago cheese**
- 24 **slider buns**
- 1 **pkg. (4 oz.) crumbled feta cheese**

1. Sprinkle the roast with salt and pepper. In a large skillet, heat oil over medium-high heat; brown meat. Transfer meat to a 6- or 7-qt. slow cooker. In the same skillet, cook and stir carrots, shallots and garlic until the vegetables are crisp-tender, about 4 minutes. Add stock, stirring to loosen any browned bits from the pan. Pour over the lamb. Cook, covered, on low until the lamb is tender, 6-8 hours.

2. Meanwhile for the pesto, place mint, basil, pine nuts and salt in a food processor; pulse until chopped. Continue processing while gradually adding oil in a steady stream. Add parmesan and Asiago cheeses; pulse just until blended. Set aside.

3. When the lamb is cool enough to handle, remove the meat from bones; discard the bones. Shred meat with 2 forks. Strain cooking juices, adding the vegetables to the shredded meat; skim fat. Return cooking juices and meat to slow cooker. Heat through. Serve on buns with pesto and feta.

1 slider: 339 cal., 22g fat (7g sat. fat), 56mg chol., 459mg sod., 16g carb. (2g sugars, 1g fiber), 18g pro.

Instant Pot Options

The modern complement to the slow cooker is the Instant Pot—because sometimes you want to cook dinner fast! These recipes are perfect for the newest must-have kitchen gadget, and allow you to have delicious, comforting meals on the table in record time.

PRESTO MEXICAN PEPPERS

These traditional stuffed peppers feature a southwestern twist! The filling also makes a delicious meat loaf that we even like cold as a sandwich with Mexican-blend or cheddar cheese, mayo and salsa.

—*Traci Wynne, Denver, PA*

Prep: 20 min. • **Cook:** 15 min. + releasing
Makes: 4 servings

- 4   medium green, sweet red, orange and/or yellow peppers
- 1   large egg, beaten
- 1   cup salsa
- 1½ cups crushed tortilla chips
- 1   medium onion, chopped
- ½   cup minced fresh cilantro
- 1   red chili pepper, seeded and finely chopped
- 3   garlic cloves, minced
- 2   tsp. ground cumin
- 1   lb. lean ground beef (90% lean)
- ½   cup shredded Mexican cheese blend
  Sour cream and additional salsa, optional

1. Place trivet insert and 1 cup of water in a 6-qt. electric pressure cooker.
2. Cut and discard tops from peppers; remove seeds. In a small bowl, combine egg, salsa, chips, onion, cilantro, chili pepper, garlic and cumin. Crumble beef over egg mixture and mix well; spoon into peppers. Set peppers on trivet.
3. Lock lid; close pressure-release valve. Adjust to pressure-cook on high for 12 minutes. Let pressure release naturally. Sprinkle peppers with cheese. If desired, serve with sour cream and additional salsa.
Note: Wear disposable gloves when cutting hot peppers; the oils can burn skin. Avoid touching your face.
1 stuffed pepper: 435 cal., 20g fat (8g sat. fat), 136mg chol., 518mg sod., 32g carb. (10g sugars, 5g fiber), 30g pro.

Contest Winner

PRESSURE-COOKER CAJUN CHICKEN ALFREDO

This recipe is a true comfort food! Cajun spice adds nice heat to the creamy Alfredo sauce. And nothing beats having to clean just one pot! Add more or less seasoning depending on your preferred spice level. This recipe would also be tasty with shrimp or smoked sausage.

—*Jennifer Stowell, Deep River, IA*

Prep: 20 min. • **Cook:** 10 min.
Makes: 6 servings

- 2   Tbsp. olive oil, divided
- 2   medium green peppers, chopped
- 2   boneless skinless chicken breasts (6 oz. each), cubed
- 2   Tbsp. Cajun seasoning, divided
- 1   pkg. (16 oz.) bow tie pasta
- 3   cups chicken stock
- 2   cups water
- 2   cups heavy whipping cream
- 1   cup shredded Parmesan cheese

1. Select saute setting on a 6-qt. electric pressure cooker and adjust for medium heat; add 1 Tbsp. oil. When oil is hot, cook and stir peppers until crisp-tender, 3-4 minutes. Remove and keep warm. Heat remaining 1 Tbsp. oil. Add chicken and 1 Tbsp. Cajun seasoning. Cook and stir until browned, 3-4 minutes. Press cancel.
2. Add pasta, stock and water (do not stir). Lock lid; close pressure-release valve. Adjust to pressure-cook on high for 6 minutes. Let pressure release naturally for 3 minutes; quick-release any remaining pressure.
3. Select the saute setting, and adjust for low heat. Stir in cream, Parmesan cheese, remaining 1 Tbsp. Cajun seasoning and cooked peppers. Cook until heated through (do not boil).
1⅔ cups: 717 cal., 40g fat (22g sat. fat), 131mg chol., 935mg sod., 60g carb. (6g sugars, 3g fiber), 31g pro.

PRESSURE-COOKER MUSHROOM PORK RAGOUT

Savory, quickly made pork is luscious served in a delightful tomato gravy over noodles. It's a nice change from regular pork roast. I serve it with broccoli or green beans on the side.
—*Connie McDowell, Greenwood, DE*

Prep: 20 min. • **Cook:** 10 min.
Makes: 2 servings

1	pork tenderloin (¾ lb.)
⅛	tsp. salt
⅛	tsp. pepper
1½	cups sliced fresh mushrooms
¾	cup canned crushed tomatoes
¾	cup reduced-sodium chicken broth, divided
⅓	cup sliced onion
1	Tbsp. chopped sun-dried tomatoes (not packed in oil)
1¼	tsp. dried savory
1	Tbsp. cornstarch
1½	cups hot cooked egg noodles

1. Rub pork with salt and pepper; cut in half. Place in a 6-qt. electric pressure cooker. Top with sliced mushrooms, tomatoes, ½ cup broth, the sliced onion, sun-dried tomatoes and savory.
2. Lock lid and close pressure-release valve. Adjust to pressure-cook on high for 6 minutes. Quick-release pressure. (A thermometer inserted in the pork should read at least 145°.) Remove pork; keep warm.
3. In a small bowl, mix cornstarch and the remaining broth until smooth; stir into the pressure cooker. Select the saute setting and adjust for low heat. Simmer, stirring constantly, until thickened, 1-2 minutes.

1 serving: 387 cal., 8g fat (2g sat. fat), 119mg chol., 613mg sod., 37g carb. (8g sugars, 4g fiber), 43g pro. **Diabetic exchanges:** 5 lean meat, 2 vegetable, 1 starch.

PRESSURE-COOKER AUTUMN APPLE CHICKEN

You can fill the whole house with the aroma of chicken with apples and barbecue sauce. This is a delicious meal you won't want to wait to dig into.
—*Caitlyn Hauser, Brookline, NH*

Prep: 25 min. • **20 min.**
Makes: 4 servings

4	bone-in chicken thighs (about 1½ lbs.), skin removed
¼	tsp. salt
¼	tsp. pepper
1	Tbsp. canola oil
½	cup apple cider or juice
1	medium onion, chopped
⅓	cup barbecue sauce
1	Tbsp. honey
1	garlic clove, minced
2	medium Fuji or Gala apples, coarsely chopped

1. Sprinkle chicken with salt and pepper. Select the saute or browning setting on a 6-qt. electric pressure cooker. Adjust for medium heat; add oil. When oil is hot, brown chicken; remove and keep warm.
2. Add cider, stirring to loosen browned bits from pan. Stir in onion, barbecue sauce, honey, garlic and chicken. Press cancel. Lock lid; close pressure-release valve. Adjust to pressure-cook on high for 10 minutes. Let pressure release naturally for 5 minutes; quick-release any remaining pressure. Press cancel. A thermometer inserted in the chicken should read at least 170°.
3. Remove chicken; keep warm. Select saute setting and adjust for low heat. Add apples; simmer, stirring constantly, until apples are tender, about 10 minutes. Serve with chicken.

1 chicken thigh with ½ cup apple mixture: 340 cal., 13g fat (3g sat. fat), 87mg chol., 458mg sod., 31g carb. (24g sugars, 3g fiber), 25g pro. **Diabetic exchanges:** 4 lean meat, 1½ starch, ½ fruit.

Cookies, Bars & Candies

From classic cookies to dressed-up delicacies, this chapter delivers a treasure trove of sweet treats. Bake sale goodies, after-school snacks, party pleasers and holiday indulgences—there's plenty to choose from. Plus, a special collection of recipes explores the possibilities of classic brownies!

FIVE-INGREDIENT FUDGE

You're moments away from a pan of creamy fudge. Just microwave, stir and spread. This easy homemade fudge recipe is the best.
—*Sue Tucker, Edgemoor, SC*

Prep: 10 min. + chilling
Makes: about 2⅓ lbs. (81 pieces)

1½ tsp. plus 1 Tbsp. butter, divided
2 cups semisweet chocolate chips
1 pkg. (11½ oz.) milk chocolate chips
1 can (14 oz.) sweetened condensed milk
1 tsp. vanilla extract

1. Line a 9-in. square pan with foil; grease foil with 1½ tsp. butter. Set aside.
2. In a large microwave-safe bowl, melt the chocolate chips and the remaining butter, stirring after 1 minute and every 30 seconds thereafter. Stir in milk and vanilla. Spread into the prepared pan. Refrigerate until firm.
3. Using foil, lift fudge out of pan. Remove foil; cut fudge into 1-in. squares. Store in an airtight container in the refrigerator.
1 piece: 59 cal., 3g fat (2g sat. fat), 3mg chol., 12mg sod., 8g carb. (7g sugars, 0 fiber), 1g pro.
Pie-Spice Sugar-Topped Fudge: Mix 1½ tsp. confectioners' sugar, ½ tsp. pumpkin pie spice and ¼ tsp. baking cocoa. Dust fudge with the sugar mixture just before serving.

LEMONY GINGERBREAD WHOOPIE PIES

These whoopie pies are spiced just right, combining two popular flavors in one treat. I roll the dough in sugar before baking for a bit of a crunch; skip that step for a softer cookie.
—*Jamie Jones, Madison, GA*

Prep: 25 min. + chilling
Bake: 10 min./batch + cooling
Makes: about 2 dozen

¾ cup butter, softened
¾ cup packed brown sugar
½ cup molasses
1 large egg, room temperature
3 cups all-purpose flour
2 tsp. ground ginger
1 tsp. ground cinnamon
1 tsp. baking soda
¼ tsp. salt
½ cup sugar
FILLING
¾ cup butter, softened
¾ cup marshmallow creme
1½ cups confectioners' sugar
¾ tsp. lemon extract

1. In a large bowl, cream butter and brown sugar until light and fluffy. Beat in molasses and egg. Combine flour, ginger, cinnamon, baking soda and salt; gradually add to creamed mixture and mix well. Cover and refrigerate for at least 3 hours.
2. Preheat oven to 350°. Shape dough into 1-in. balls; roll in sugar. Place 3 in. apart on ungreased baking sheets. Flatten to ½-in. thickness with a glass dipped in sugar. Bake 8-10 minutes or until set. Cool for 2 minutes before removing from pans to wire racks to cool completely.
3. For filling, in a small bowl, beat butter and marshmallow creme until light and fluffy. Gradually beat in the confectioners' sugar and extract.
4. Spread filling on the bottoms of half of the cookies, about 1 Tbsp. on each; top with the remaining cookies.
1 sandwich cookie: 286 cal., 13g fat (8g sat. fat), 42mg chol., 184mg sod., 41g carb. (26g sugars, 1g fiber), 2g pro.

THREE-CHIP ENGLISH TOFFEE

With its melt-in-your-mouth texture and scrumptiously rich flavor, this is the ultimate toffee! Layered on top are three kinds of melted chips plus a sprinkling of walnuts. When packaged in colorful tins, these pretty pieces make impressive gifts.

—Lana Petfield, Richmond, VA

Prep: 15 min. + chilling • **Cook:** 30 min.
Makes: 20 pieces (about 2½ lbs.)

- ½ tsp. plus 2 cups butter, divided
- 2 cups sugar
- 1 cup slivered almonds
- 1 cup milk chocolate chips
- 1 cup chopped walnuts
- ½ cup semisweet chocolate chips
- ½ cup white baking chips
- 1½ tsp. shortening

1. Butter a 15x10x1-in. pan with ½ tsp. butter. In a heavy saucepan over medium-low heat, bring sugar and the remaining butter to a boil, stirring constantly. Cover and cook for 2-3 minutes.

2. Uncover; add the almonds. Cook and stir with a clean spoon until a candy thermometer reads 300° (hard-crack stage) and the mixture is golden brown.

3. Pour into prepared pan (do not scrape the sides of the saucepan). Surface will be buttery. Cool for 1-2 minutes. Sprinkle with milk chocolate chips. Let stand for 1-2 minutes; spread chocolate over the top. Sprinkle with walnuts; press down gently with the back of a spoon. Chill for 10 minutes.

4. In a microwave, melt semisweet chips; stir until smooth. Drizzle over walnuts. Refrigerate for 10 minutes. Melt the vanilla chips and shortening; stir until smooth. Drizzle over walnuts. Cover and refrigerate for 1-2 hours. Break into pieces.

Note: We recommend you test your candy thermometer before each use by bringing water to a boil; the thermometer should read 212°. Adjust the recipe temperature up or down based on your test.

1 piece: 397 cal., 30g fat (15g sat. fat), 52mg chol., 197mg sod., 32g carb. (26g sugars, 1g fiber), 4g pro.

TROUBLESHOOTING TOFFEE

If the toffee separates during cooking, add ½ cup hot water and stir vigorously. Bring back up to 300°, and proceed as the recipe directs.

COCONUT JOYS

If you like coconut, you'll love these no-bake, no-fuss sweets. They make a rewarding treat to keep in the fridge during the holidays—and they're cute as can be.

—Flo Burtnett, Gage, OK

Prep: 20 min. + chilling • **Makes:** 1½ dozen

- 1½ cups sweetened shredded coconut
- 1 cup confectioners' sugar
- ¼ cup butter, melted
- 1 oz. milk chocolate, melted
- 2 Tbsp. chopped pecans

1. In a large bowl, combine the coconut, confectioners' sugar and butter. Form mixture into 1-in. balls.

2. Using the end of a wooden spoon handle, make an indentation in the center of each ball. Fill indentation with chocolate. Sprinkle with pecans. Place on a waxed paper-lined baking sheet. Chill until chocolate is firm. Store in the refrigerator.

1 piece: 101 cal., 6g fat (4g sat. fat), 7mg chol., 38mg sod., 11g carb. (10g sugars, 0 fiber), 0 pro. **Diabetic exchanges:** 1 starch, 1 fat.

Contest Winner

FROSTED CASHEW COOKIES

Some merry snacking is guaranteed when you pass out these cashew-packed goodies! I found the recipe in a flier promoting dairy products years ago. It's been this farm wife's standby ever since.

—June Lindquist, Hammond, WI

- -

Prep: 25 min. • **Bake:** 10 min./batch + cooling
Makes: about 5 dozen

- ½ cup butter, softened
- 1 cup packed brown sugar
- 1 large egg, room temperature
- ½ tsp. vanilla extract
- 2 cups all-purpose flour
- ¾ tsp. baking powder
- ¾ tsp. baking soda
- ¼ tsp. salt
- ⅓ cup sour cream
- 1¾ cups chopped cashews

FROSTING

- ½ cup butter, cubed
- 3 Tbsp. half-and-half cream
- ¼ tsp. vanilla extract
- 2 cups confectioners' sugar
  Cashew halves, optional

1. Preheat oven to 375°. In a bowl, cream butter and brown sugar. Beat in egg and vanilla. Combine the dry ingredients; add alternately with sour cream to the creamed mixture. Stir in cashews.

2. Drop dough by tablespoonfuls onto greased baking sheets. Bake 8-10 minutes or until lightly browned. Cool cookies on a wire rack.

3. For frosting, lightly brown butter in a small saucepan. Remove from the heat and cool slightly. Add cream and vanilla. Beat in confectioners' sugar until smooth and thick.

4. Frost cookies; if desired, top each with a cashew half.

1 cookie: 100 cal., 5g fat (3g sat. fat), 12mg chol., 85mg sod., 12g carb. (8g sugars, 0 fiber), 1g pro.

CHEWY ALMOND COOKIES

My children and grandchildren often request these old-fashioned cookies. I freeze the unbaked dough so I can whip up a batch whenever my family comes for a visit. They are a good unfrosted choice for a cookie plate, too.
—*Betty Speth, Vincennes, IN*

Prep: 15 min. + chilling • **Bake:** 10 min./batch
Makes: 4½ dozen

- 3   **Tbsp. butter**
- 1   **cup packed brown sugar**
- 1   **large egg, room temperature**
- ¼   **tsp. vanilla extract**
- ¼   **tsp. almond extract**
- 1½ **cups all-purpose flour**
- ¼   **tsp. baking soda**
- ¼   **tsp. ground cinnamon**
- ½   **cup sliced almonds**

1. Beat butter and brown sugar until crumbly. Beat in egg and extracts. Combine the flour, baking soda and cinnamon; gradually add to the butter mixture and mix well. Shape into two 6-in. rolls; wrap each in plastic. Refrigerate overnight.
2. Unwrap rolls; cut into ¼-in. slices. Place 2 in. apart on greased baking sheets. Sprinkle with almonds.
3. Bake at 350° for 7-10 minutes or until lightly browned. Cool 2-3 minutes before removing to wire racks.
2 cookies: 80 cal., 2g fat (1g sat. fat), 11mg chol., 30mg sod., 14g carb. (8g sugars, 0 fiber), 1g pro.

CARDAMOM CHEESECAKE BARS

Fans of cheesecake will love these bite-sized desserts. Crunchy and smooth, they're perfect for the holidays—or any other time!
—*Judi Oudekerk, Buffalo, MN*

Prep: 35 min. • **Bake:** 35 min. + chilling
Makes: 16 bars

- ¾   **cup graham cracker crumbs**
- 2   **Tbsp. butter, melted**
- 2   **pkg. (8 oz. each) cream cheese, softened**
- ½   **cup sugar**
- 2   **tsp. ground cardamom, divided**
- 1   **tsp. vanilla extract**
- 2   **eggs, room temperature, lightly beaten**
- ⅓   **cup all-purpose flour**
- ⅓   **cup quick-cooking oats**
- ⅓   **cup packed brown sugar**
- ¼   **cup cold butter**
- ⅓   **cup sliced almonds**

1. In a small bowl, combine graham cracker crumbs and melted butter. Press onto the bottom of a greased 9-in. square baking pan. In a large bowl, beat the cream cheese, sugar, 1 tsp. cardamom and vanilla until smooth. Add eggs; beat on low speed just until combined. Pour over crust.
2. In a small bowl, combine flour, oats, brown sugar and remaining cardamom. Cut in cold butter until crumbly. Stir in almonds. Sprinkle over top.
3. Bake at 350° for 35-40 minutes or until center is almost set and topping is golden brown. Cool on a wire rack for 1 hour. Cover and refrigerate for at least 2 hours before serving. Cut into 16 bars.
1 bar: 232 cal., 16g fat (9g sat. fat), 69mg chol., 149mg sod., 18g carb. (12g sugars, 1g fiber), 4g pro.

CHERRY CHOCOLATE CHUNK COOKIES

These rich, fudgy cookies are chewy and studded with tangy dried cherries. It's a good thing the recipe makes only a small batch, because we eat them all in one night!
—*Trisha Kruse, Eagle, ID*

- -

Prep: 15 min. • **Bake:** 15 min./batch
Makes: about 1½ dozen

- ½ cup butter, softened
- ¾ cup sugar
- 1 large egg, room temperature
- 2 Tbsp. 2% milk
- ½ tsp. vanilla extract
- 1 cup all-purpose flour
- 6 Tbsp. baking cocoa
- ¼ tsp. baking soda
- ¼ tsp. salt
- 1 cup semisweet chocolate chunks
- ½ cup dried cherries

1. Preheat oven to 350°. Cream butter and sugar until light and fluffy. Beat in egg, milk and vanilla. In a separate bowl, whisk flour, cocoa, baking soda and salt; gradually beat into creamed mixture. Stir in chocolate and cherries.

2. Drop by rounded tablespoonfuls 2 in. apart onto baking sheets lightly coated with cooking spray. Bake until firm, 12-14 minutes. Cool for 1 minute before removing to a wire rack.

1 cookie: 159 cal., 8g fat (5g sat. fat), 22mg chol., 88mg sod., 22g carb. (15g sugars, 1g fiber), 2g pro.

CHEWY GOOD OATMEAL COOKIES

Here's a classic oatmeal cookie with all my favorite extras—dried cherries, white chocolate chips and macadamia nuts.
—*Sandy Harz, Spring Lake, MI*

- -

Prep: 20 min. • **Bake:** 10 min./batch
Makes: 3½ dozen

- 1 cup butter, softened
- 1 cup packed brown sugar
- ½ cup sugar
- 2 large eggs, room temperature
- 1 Tbsp. honey
- 2 tsp. vanilla extract
- 2½ cups quick-cooking oats
- 1½ cups all-purpose flour
- 1 tsp. baking soda
- ½ tsp. salt
- ½ tsp. ground cinnamon
- 1⅓ cups dried cherries
- 1 cup white baking chips
- 1 cup (4 oz.) chopped macadamia nuts

1. Preheat oven to 350°. In a large bowl, cream butter and sugars until light and fluffy. Beat in the eggs, honey and vanilla.

2. In a second bowl, mix the oats, flour, baking soda, salt and cinnamon; gradually beat into the creamed mixture. Stir in the remaining ingredients.

3. Drop the dough by rounded tablespoonfuls 2 in. apart onto greased baking sheets. Bake for 10-12 minutes or until golden brown. Cool on pan 2 minutes; remove to wire racks to cool.

1 cookie: 161 cal., 8g fat (4g sat. fat), 22mg chol., 105mg sod., 20g carb. (13g sugars, 1g fiber), 2g pro.

Chewy Cranberry Oatmeal Cookies: Substitute dried cranberries for the dried cherries.

Chewy Oatmeal Chip Cookies: Omit the cinnamon, dried cherries and macadamia nuts. Add 1 cup each semisweet chocolate chips and butterscotch chips with the white baking chips.

STRAWBERRY RHUBARB CHEESECAKE BARS

These cheesecake bars layer a buttery pecan shortbread crust with a rich and creamy filling and sweet-tart strawberry rhubarb jam. For larger servings, cut the pan into nine bars instead of 16.
—*Amanda Scarlati, Sandy, UT*

- -

Prep: 30 min. + chilling
Bake: 15 min. + cooling • **Makes:** 16 servings

- 1 cup all-purpose flour
- ⅓ cup packed brown sugar
  Dash kosher salt
- ½ cup cold butter, cubed
- ⅓ cup finely chopped pecans

FILLING
- 1 pkg. (8 oz.) cream cheese, softened
- ¼ cup sugar
- 2 Tbsp. 2% milk
- 1 Tbsp. lemon juice
- ½ tsp. vanilla extract
  Dash kosher salt

- 1 large egg, room temperature, lightly beaten

JAM
- ½ cup sugar
- 2 Tbsp. cornstarch
- 1⅓ cups chopped fresh strawberries
- 1⅓ cups sliced fresh or frozen rhubarb
- 1 Tbsp. lemon juice

1. Preheat oven to 350°. Line an 8-in. square baking pan with parchment, letting the ends extend up the sides; set aside. In a small bowl, mix flour, brown sugar and salt; cut in butter until crumbly. Stir in pecans.

2. Press mixture into the bottom of the prepared pan. Bake until edges just begin to brown, 12-15 minutes. Cool completely on a wire rack.

3. In a large bowl, beat the cream cheese and sugar until smooth. Beat in milk, lemon juice, vanilla and salt. Add egg; beat on low speed just until blended. Pour over the crust.

4. Bake until filling is set, 15-20 minutes. Cool on a wire rack for 1 hour.

5. For the jam, in a small saucepan, mix sugar and cornstarch. Add strawberries, rhubarb and lemon juice. Bring to a boil. Reduce heat; simmer, uncovered, until mixture begins to thicken, 6-8 minutes. Cool completely. Spread over filling. Refrigerate until set, 8 hours or overnight.

6. Using parchment, carefully remove cheesecake from baking pan. Cut into bars for serving.

Note: If using frozen rhubarb, measure rhubarb while still frozen, then thaw completely. Drain in a colander, but do not press liquid out.

1 bar: 215 cal., 13g fat (7g sat. fat), 41mg chol., 113mg sod., 24g carb. (15g sugars, 1g fiber), 3g pro.

CINNAMON CHIP CHAI-SPICED SNICKERDOODLES

I love cinnamon chips, and this is an intriguing way to use them. In many areas, they're available only at the holidays, so be sure to stock up so you have plenty to last the year!
—*Marietta Slater, Justin, TX*

- -

Prep: 30 min. + chilling
Bake: 15 min./batch + cooling
Makes: about 6 dozen

- ½ cup sugar
- 2 tsp. ground cardamom
- 2 tsp. ground cinnamon
- ½ tsp. ground ginger
- ½ tsp. ground cloves
- ¼ tsp. ground nutmeg

DOUGH

- ½ cup butter, softened
- ½ cup shortening
- 1 cup sugar
- 2 large eggs, room temperature
- 1 tsp. vanilla extract
- 2¾ cups all-purpose flour
- 2 tsp. cream of tartar
- 1 tsp. baking soda
  Dash salt
- 1 pkg. (10 oz.) cinnamon baking chips

1. Preheat oven to 350°. Mix the first 6 ingredients.
2. In a large bowl, cream the butter, shortening, sugar and 2 Tbsp. of the spiced sugar mixture until light and fluffy. Beat in eggs and vanilla.
3. In another bowl, whisk together flour, cream of tartar, baking soda and salt; gradually beat into the creamed mixture. Stir in baking chips. Refrigerate, covered, until firm enough to shape, about 1 hour.
4. Shape dough into 1-in. balls; roll in remaining spiced sugar mixture. Place 2 in. apart on greased baking sheets.
5. Bake until set, 11-13 minutes. Remove from pans to wire racks to cool.
1 cookie: 81 cal., 4g fat (2g sat. fat), 9mg chol., 59mg sod., 10g carb. (7g sugars, 0 fiber), 1g pro.

═══════════════════════════

FREEZE YOUR DOUGH

Most types of cookie dough can be frozen for up to 3 months. Shape the dough into 2 or 3 logs, wrap them in several layers of plastic, then place in a freezer container. Thaw in the refrigerator overnight before baking.

LEMON POPPY SEED CUTOUTS

I love to package up these tart, tender cookies to share with friends! You could spread buttercream or cream cheese frosting on them to make sandwich cookies. And they'd be delicious dipped in white chocolate.
—*Ilana Pulda, Bellevue, WA*

- -

Prep: 30 min. + chilling • **Bake:** 10 min./batch
Makes: about 3 dozen

- 1 cup unsalted butter, softened
- ½ cup confectioners' sugar
- 1 Tbsp. sugar
- 1 Tbsp. grated lemon zest
- 4 tsp. lemon juice
- ½ tsp. vanilla extract
- 2 cups all-purpose flour
- 1 Tbsp. poppy seeds
- ¼ tsp. salt

1. Cream butter and sugars until light and fluffy. Beat in lemon zest, juice and vanilla. In another bowl, whisk flour, poppy seeds and salt; gradually beat into the creamed mixture. Shape into a disk; cover tightly. Refrigerate 4 hours or until firm enough to roll.
2. Preheat oven to 350°. Roll dough between 2 sheets of waxed paper to ¼-in. thickness. Cut with a floured 1½-in. cookie cutter; reroll scraps. Place 1 in. apart on parchment-lined baking sheets. Bake until the edges begin to brown, 10-12 minutes. Remove from pans to wire racks to cool.
1 cookie: 80 cal., 5g fat (3g sat. fat), 14mg chol., 17mg sod., 7g carb. (2g sugars, 0 fiber), 1g pro.

GRANDMA'S SCOTTISH SHORTBREAD

My Scottish grandmother was renowned for her baking, and one of the highlights whenever we visited was her bringing out the baking tin. Her shortbread was my favorite, and now, whenever I make it, I remember her. This is not a thin, crispy shortbread—it's a deep bar best served with a cup of tea.
—*Jane Kelly, Wayland, MA*

- -

Prep: 15 min. • **Bake:** 45 min. + cooling
Makes: 4 dozen

- 2 cups butter, softened
- 1¼ cups superfine sugar
- 3⅔ cups all-purpose flour
- 1⅓ cups white rice flour

1. Preheat oven to 300°. Cream butter and sugar until light and fluffy. Combine flours; gradually beat into the creamed mixture. Press dough into an ungreased 13x9-in. baking pan. Prick with a fork.
2. Bake until light brown, 45-50 minutes. Cut into 48 bars or triangles while warm. Remove to a wire rack to cool completely.
1 bar: 139 cal., 8g fat (5g sat. fat), 20mg chol., 61mg sod., 16g carb. (5g sugars, 0 fiber), 1g pro.

CHOCOLATE PECAN PIE BARS

These yummy pecan bars start with a homemade pastry crust and pile on lots of semisweet chocolate. They're perfect for a holiday bake sale or casual get-together.
—*Heather Biedler, Martinsburg, WV*

- -

Prep: 30 min. + chilling
Bake: 50 min. + cooling • **Makes:** 3 dozen

- 1¾ cups all-purpose flour
- ¼ tsp. salt
- ¾ cup cold butter
- ¼ to ½ cup ice water
- FILLING
- 4 large eggs
- 2 cups sugar
- ½ tsp. salt
- 1 cup all-purpose flour
- 1 cup butter, melted and cooled
- 4 tsp. vanilla extract
- 2⅔ cups semisweet chocolate chips
- 1⅓ cups chopped pecans

1. In a small bowl, mix flour and salt; cut in butter until crumbly. Gradually add ice water, tossing with a fork until dough holds together when pressed. Shape into a disk; wrap in plastic. Refrigerate 1 hour or overnight.
2. Preheat oven to 350°. On a lightly floured surface, roll dough to fit bottom of a 13x9-in. baking pan; press into pan. Refrigerate while preparing filling.
3. In a large bowl, beat eggs, sugar, and salt on high speed for 2 minutes. Stir in flour, melted butter and vanilla. Fold in chocolate chips. Pour over crust; sprinkle with pecans.
4. Cover loosely with foil. Place on a lower oven rack; bake 20 minutes. Bake, uncovered, 30 minutes longer or until the top is golden brown and a knife inserted in the center comes out clean.
5. Cool in pan on a wire rack. Cut into 36 bars. Refrigerate leftovers.
1 bar: 254 cal., 16g fat (8g sat. fat), 44mg chol., 130mg sod., 27g carb. (18g sugars, 1g fiber), 3g pro.

Contest Winner

FRUITCAKE COOKIES WITH RUM GLAZE

Like fruitcake—only better! You can leave out the rum if you wish, but if you do make these cookies nonalcoholic, you may want to increase the rum extract for flavor.
—*Sheila Joan Suhan, Scottdale, PA*

- -

Prep: 45 min. + cooling
Bake: 15 min./batch + cooling
Makes: about 4 dozen

- 1 cup golden raisins
- ¾ cup dried cherries
- ½ cup diced dried apricots
- ¾ cup water
- ¼ cup rum or additional water
- ¾ cup chopped pecans
- ⅓ cup diced crystallized ginger
- ⅓ cup diced candied orange peel
- 1 cup butter, softened
- 2 cups sugar, divided
- 2 large eggs, room temperature
- 1½ tsp. rum extract
- 3½ cups all-purpose flour
- 1 tsp. baking soda
- ½ tsp. salt

GLAZE
- 3 cups confectioners' sugar
- 3 to 5 Tbsp. 2% milk
- 3 Tbsp. rum or additional milk

1. Place the first 5 ingredients in a small saucepan; bring to a boil. Reduce heat; simmer, uncovered, until the liquid is almost absorbed, 12-15 minutes. Cool completely. Stir in pecans, ginger and orange peel.

2. Preheat oven to 350°. Cream butter and 1½ cups sugar until light and fluffy. Beat in eggs and extract. In another bowl, whisk together flour, baking soda and salt; gradually beat into the creamed mixture. Stir in the fruit mixture.

3. Place the remaining sugar in a shallow bowl. Shape into balls, using 2 tablespoonsful of dough for each; toss in sugar to coat lightly. Place 2 in. apart on parchment-lined baking sheets.

4. Bake until golden brown and just set, 11-13 minutes. Remove from pans to wire racks; cool completely.

5. Mix glaze ingredients. Drizzle over the cookies.

1 cookie: 176 cal., 5g fat (3g sat. fat), 18mg chol., 92mg sod., 31g carb. (21g sugars, 1g fiber), 2g pro.

CRANBERRY BOG BARS

These sweet and chewy bars combine the flavors of oats, cranberries, brown sugar and pecans. I sprinkle them with confectioners' sugar before serving.
—*Sally Wakefield, Gans, PA*

Prep: 25 min. • **Bake:** 25 min. + cooling
Makes: 2 dozen

1¼ cups butter, softened, divided
1½ cups packed brown sugar, divided
3½ cups old-fashioned oats, divided
1 cup all-purpose flour
1 can (14 oz.) whole-berry
    cranberry sauce
½ cup finely chopped pecans

1. In a large bowl, cream 1 cup butter and 1 cup brown sugar until light and fluffy. Combine 2½ cups oats and flour. Gradually add to creamed mixture until crumbly. Press into a greased 13x9-in. baking pan. Spread with cranberry sauce.
2. In a microwave-safe bowl, melt the remaining butter; stir in pecans and the remaining brown sugar and oats. Sprinkle over cranberry sauce. Bake at 375°. until lightly browned, 25-30 minutes. Cool on a wire rack. Cut into bars.
1 bar: 239 cal., 12g fat (6g sat. fat), 25mg chol., 88mg sod., 32g carb. (18g sugars, 2g fiber), 2g pro.

BUTTER PECAN FUDGE

Toasted pecans add a nutty crunch to creamy fudge. I've given this candy, with its wonderful caramel flavor, as Christmastime gifts—and people always rave about it!
—*Pam Smith, Alta Loma, CA*

Prep: 10 min. • **Cook:** 10 min. + cooling
Makes: about 1½ lbs. (64 pieces)

1 tsp. plus ½ cup butter, cubed
½ cup sugar
½ cup packed brown sugar
½ cup heavy whipping cream
⅛ tsp. salt
1 tsp. vanilla extract
2 cups sifted confectioners' sugar
1 cup coarsely chopped
    pecans, toasted

1. Line an 8-in. square pan with foil. Grease foil with 1 tsp. butter; set aside.
2. In a large heavy saucepan, combine remaining butter, the granulated and brown sugars, cream and salt. Bring to a rapid boil over medium heat, stirring constantly. Cook, without stirring, until a candy thermometer reads 234° (soft-ball stage). Remove from heat. Add vanilla to pan (do not stir).
3. Cool, without stirring, to 110°, about 30 minutes. Beat with a spoon until the fudge just begins to thicken. Gradually stir in confectioners' sugar until smooth; add nuts and continue stirring until the fudge becomes very thick and just begins to lose its sheen. Immediately spread into the prepared pan. Let cool completely.
4. Using foil, lift the fudge out of pan. Remove foil; cut fudge into 1-in. squares. Store between layers of waxed paper in an airtight container.
Note: To toast nuts, bake in a shallow pan in a 350° oven for 5-10 minutes or cook in a skillet over low heat until lightly browned, stirring occasionally.
1 piece: 59 cal., 3g fat (1g sat. fat), 7mg chol., 18mg sod., 7g carb. (7g sugars, 0 fiber), 0 pro.

BUTTERSCOTCH-RUM RAISIN TREATS

I love making rum raisin rice pudding—and those classic flavors inspired this confection. Crispy rice cereal adds crunch, but nuts, toasted coconut or candied pineapple could do the job, too.
—*Crystal Schlueter, Northglenn, CO*

Takes: 20 min. • **Makes:** about 4½ dozen

- 1 pkg. (10 to 11 oz.) butterscotch chips
- 1 pkg. (10 to 12 oz.) white baking chips
- ½ tsp. rum extract
- 3 cups Rice Krispies
- 1 cup raisins

1. Line 56 mini muffin cups with paper liners. In a large bowl, combine butterscotch and white chips. Microwave, uncovered, on high for 30 seconds; stir. Microwave in additional 30-second intervals, stirring until smooth.
2. Stir in rum extract, Rice Krispies and raisins. Drop by rounded tablespoonfuls into prepared mini muffin cups. Chill until set.
Freeze option: Freeze treats in freezer containers, separating layers with waxed paper. Thaw before serving.
1 treat: 76 cal., 4g fat (3g sat. fat), 1mg chol., 21mg sod., 11g carb. (9g sugars, 0 fiber), 0 pro.

RASPBERRY COCONUT COOKIES

My mother gave me the recipe for these rich, buttery cookies. Raspberry preserves and a cream filling make them doubly delicious.
—*June Brown, Veneta, OR*

Prep: 20 min. • **Bake:** 15 min./batch + cooling
Makes: 2½ dozen

- ¾ cup butter, softened
- ½ cup sugar
- 1 large egg, room temperature
- 1 tsp. vanilla extract
- 2 cups all-purpose flour
- ½ cup sweetened shredded coconut
- 1½ tsp. baking powder
- ¼ tsp. salt

FILLING

- ¼ cup butter, softened
- ¾ cup confectioners' sugar
- 2 tsp. 2% milk
- ½ tsp. vanilla extract
- ½ cup raspberry preserves

1. Preheat oven to 350°. In a large bowl, cream butter and sugar until light and fluffy. Beat in egg and vanilla. Combine flour, coconut, baking powder and salt; gradually add to the creamed mixture and mix well.
2. Shape dough into 1-in. balls. Place 1½ in. apart on ungreased baking sheets; flatten with a glass dipped in flour.
3. Bake for 12-14 minutes or until edges begin to brown. Cool on wire racks.
4. In a small bowl, beat the butter, confectioners' sugar, milk and vanilla until smooth. Place ½ tsp. preserves and a scant teaspoonful of filling on the bottoms of half of the cookies; top with remaining cookies. Store in an airtight container in the refrigerator.
1 sandwich cookie: 133 cal., 7g fat (4g sat. fat), 23mg chol., 108mg sod., 17g carb. (10g sugars, 0 fiber), 1g pro.

HONEY CINNAMON BARS

My Aunt Ellie gave us the recipe for these sweet bar cookies with cinnamon and walnuts. Drizzle with icing, and serve with coffee or tea.

—*Diane Myers, Star, ID*

Prep: 25 min. • **Bake:** 10 min. + cooling
Makes: 2 dozen

- 1 cup sugar
- ¾ cup canola oil
- ¼ cup honey
- 1 large egg
- 2 cups all-purpose flour
- 1 tsp. baking soda
- 1 tsp. ground cinnamon
- ¼ tsp. salt
- 1 cup chopped walnuts, toasted

GLAZE

- 1 cup confectioners' sugar
- 2 Tbsp. mayonnaise
- 1 tsp. vanilla extract
- 1 to 2 Tbsp. water
  Additional toasted chopped walnuts, optional

1. Preheat oven to 350°. In a large bowl, beat sugar, oil, honey and egg until well blended. In another bowl, whisk flour, baking soda, cinnamon and salt; gradually beat into the sugar mixture. Stir in 1 cup chopped walnuts.

2. Spread into a greased 15x10x1-in. baking pan. Bake until golden brown (edges will puff up), 10-12 minutes. Cool completely on a wire rack.

3. For glaze, in a small bowl, mix the confectioners' sugar, mayonnaise, vanilla and enough water to reach the desired consistency; spread over top. If desired, sprinkle with additional walnuts. Let stand until set. Cut into bars. Refrigerate leftovers.

Note: To toast nuts, bake in a shallow pan in a 350° oven for 5-10 minutes or cook in a skillet over low heat until lightly browned, stirring occasionally.

1 bar: 206 cal., 11g fat (1g sat. fat), 8mg chol., 86mg sod., 25g carb. (16g sugars, 1g fiber), 2g pro.

SALTED PECAN SHORTBREAD SQUARES

My shortbread squares are the ultimate go-to for cookie trays and gift-giving. The buttery caramel and toasted nuts make it tough to eat just one.

—Diana Ashcraft, Monmouth, OR

- -

Prep: 25 min. • **Bake:** 25 min. + cooling
Makes: 4 dozen

1½ cups all-purpose flour
1 cup confectioners' sugar
½ cup cornstarch
1 tsp. sea salt
1 cup cold unsalted butter, cubed

FILLING

¾ cup unsalted butter, cubed
1½ cups packed brown sugar
½ cup dark corn syrup
½ tsp. sea salt
½ cup milk chocolate chips
¼ cup heavy whipping cream
1 tsp. vanilla extract
4 cups coarsely chopped pecans, toasted

1. Preheat the oven to 350°. Line two 13x9-in. baking pans with foil, letting the ends extend up sides of pan.
2. Place flour, confectioners' sugar, cornstarch and salt in a food processor; pulse until blended. Add butter; pulse until butter is the size of peas. Divide mixture between prepared pans; press onto bottom of pans. Bake 10-12 minutes or until light brown. Cool on a wire rack.
3. For filling, melt butter in a large saucepan. Stir in brown sugar, corn syrup and salt; bring to a boil. Reduce heat to medium; cook and stir until sugar is completely dissolved, about 3 minutes. Remove from heat; stir in chocolate chips, cream and vanilla until smooth. Stir in pecans. Spread over crusts.
4. Bake 12-15 minutes or until filling is bubbly. Cool completely in pans on racks. Using foil, lift shortbread out of pans. Gently peel off foil; cut each shortbread into 24 bars. Store in an airtight container.
Note: To toast nuts, bake in a shallow pan in a 350° oven for 5-10 minutes or cook in a skillet over low heat until lightly browned, stirring occasionally.
1 bar: 201 cal., 14g fat (5g sat. fat), 20mg chol., 70mg sod., 18g carb. (13g sugars, 1g fiber), 1g pro.

BLUEBERRY LATTICE BARS

My daughters and I are always looking for new berry recipes to enter in the cooking contest in the local annual blueberry festival. These lovely, yummy bars won a blue ribbon one year.

—*Debbie Ayers, Baileyville, ME*

Prep: 25 min. + chilling
Bake: 30 min. + cooling
Makes: 2 dozen

- 1⅓ cups butter, softened
- ⅔ cup sugar
- ¼ tsp. salt
- 1 large egg, room temperature
- ½ tsp. vanilla extract
- 3¾ cups all-purpose flour

FILLING
- 3 cups fresh or frozen blueberries
- 1 cup sugar
- 3 Tbsp. cornstarch

1. Cream butter, sugar and salt until light and fluffy; beat in egg and vanilla. Gradually beat in flour. Divide dough in half; shape each half into a 1-in.-thick rectangle. Wrap and refrigerate 2 hours or overnight.

2. Preheat oven to 375°. Place the blueberries, sugar and cornstarch in a small saucepan. Bring to a boil over medium heat, stirring frequently; cook and stir until thickened, about 2 minutes. Cool slightly.

3. Roll each portion of dough between 2 sheets of plastic wrap into a 14x10-in. rectangle. Place each rectangle on a separate baking sheet; freeze until firm, 5-10 minutes. Place 1 rectangle in a greased 13x9-in. baking pan, pressing onto bottom and about ½ in. up the sides. Add filling.

4. Cut the remaining rectangle into ½-in. strips; freeze 5-10 minutes to firm. Arrange strips over filling in crisscross fashion. If desired, press the edges with a fork to seal strips. Bake until the top crust is golden brown, 30-35 minutes. Cool on a wire rack. Cut into bars.

1 bar: 233 cal., 11g fat (7g sat. fat), 35mg chol., 109mg sod., 32g carb. (16g sugars, 1g fiber), 3g pro.

HOMEMADE PEANUT BUTTER CUPS

I make these for holidays all year round—the irresistible candies with gooey peanut butter centers are so easy to stir up and assemble!

—*LaVonne Hegland, St. Michael, MN*

Takes: 20 min. + chilling • **Makes:** 3 dozen

- 1 cup creamy peanut butter, divided
- ½ cup confectioners' sugar
- 4½ tsp. butter, softened
- ½ tsp. salt
- 2 cups semisweet chocolate chips
- 4 milk chocolate candy bars (1.55 oz. each), coarsely chopped
  Colored sprinkles, optional

1. Combine ½ cup peanut butter, confectioners' sugar, butter and salt until smooth.

2. In a microwave, melt chocolate chips, candy bars and the remaining peanut butter; stir until smooth.

3. Drop teaspoonfuls of the chocolate mixture into paper-lined mini muffin cups. Drop a scant teaspoonful of the peanut butter mixture into each cup; top with another teaspoonful of the chocolate mixture. If desired, decorate with sprinkles. Refrigerate until set. Store in an airtight container.

1 piece: 123 cal., 8g fat (4g sat. fat), 2mg chol., 76mg sod., 12g carb. (10g sugars, 1g fiber), 3g pro.

CHOOSE YOUR HOLIDAY

You can make these candies for any holiday—just use different patterns of muffin liners and different colors of sprinkles to suit the day. Try red and green for Christmas; pastels for Easter; or red, white and blue for July Fourth. You'll find endless possibilities!

Fresh Takes on Brownies

The classic all-American favorite is the foundation for this collection of recipes, which take the basic brownie several steps further. With different flavors added, swirled with cream cheese or as a base for fresh fruit, these brownies are something else!

PEPPERMINT BROWNIES

My grandmother encouraged me to enter these mint brownies in the county fair some years ago, and they earned top honors! They're a delicious treat to serve during the holiday, but why wait until then?
—*Marcy Greenblatt, Redding, CA*

- -

Prep: 15 min. • **Bake:** 35 min. + cooling.
Makes: 2 dozen

- 1⅓ cups all-purpose flour
- 1 cup baking cocoa
- 1 tsp. salt
- 1 tsp. baking powder
- ¾ cup canola oil
- 2 cups sugar
- 2 tsp. vanilla extract
- 4 large eggs, room temperature
- ⅔ cup crushed peppermint candies

GLAZE
- 1 cup semisweet chocolate chips
- 1 Tbsp. shortening
- 2 Tbsp. crushed peppermint candies

1. Preheat oven to 350°. Line a 13x9-in. baking pan with foil; grease foil.
2. In a bowl, whisk together the first 4 ingredients. In a large bowl, beat oil and sugar until blended. Beat in vanilla and 1 egg at a time, beating well after each addition. Gradually add the flour mixture; stir in peppermint candies. Spread into the prepared pan.
3. Bake until a toothpick inserted in center comes out clean, 35-40 minutes. Cool in pan on a wire rack.
4. In a microwave, melt chocolate chips and shortening; stir until smooth. Spread over brownies; sprinkle with candies.
1 brownie: 222 cal., 11g fat (3g sat. fat), 35mg chol., 128mg sod., 31g carb. (22g sugars, 1g fiber), 3g pro.

BERRY-PATCH BROWNIE PIZZA

I just love the combination of fruit, almonds and chocolate that makes this brownie so distinctive. The fruit lightens the chocolate and works a bit of magic—it makes it feel as though you're eating something that's both decadent and healthy!
—*Sue Kauffman, Columbia City, IN*

- -

Prep: 20 min. + chilling
Bake: 15 min. + cooling • **Makes:** 12 servings

- 1 pkg. fudge brownie mix (13x9-in. pan size)
- ⅓ cup chopped unblanched almonds
- 1 tsp. almond extract

TOPPING
- 1 pkg. (8 oz.) cream cheese, softened
- 1 Tbsp. sugar
- 1 tsp. vanilla extract
- ½ tsp. grated lemon zest
- 2 cups whipped topping

- Assorted fresh berries
- Fresh mint leaves and coarse sugar, optional

1. Preheat oven to 375°. Prepare brownie batter according to package directions for fudgelike brownies, adding almonds and almond extract. Spread into a greased 14-in. pizza pan.
2. Bake until a toothpick inserted in the center comes out clean, 15-18 minutes. Cool completely on a wire rack.
3. Beat the first 4 topping ingredients until smooth; fold in whipped topping. Spread over crust to within ½ in. of edges; refrigerate, loosely covered, 2 hours.
4. To serve, cut into 12 slices; top with berries of choice. If desired, top with mint and sprinkle with coarse sugar.
1 slice: 404 cal., 26g fat (8g sat. fat), 51mg chol., 240mg sod., 39g carb. (26g sugars, 2g fiber), 5g pro.

CREAM CHEESE SWIRL BROWNIES

I'm a chocolate lover, and this treat has satisfied my cravings many times. No one guesses the brownies are light because their chewy texture and rich chocolate taste can't be beat. My family requests them often, and I'm always happy to oblige!

—*Heidi Johnson, Worland, WY*

- -

Prep: 20 min. • **Bake:** 25 min. • **Makes:** 1 dozen

- 3 large eggs, divided use
- 6 Tbsp. reduced-fat butter, softened
- 1 cup sugar, divided
- 3 tsp. vanilla extract
- ½ cup all-purpose flour
- ¼ cup baking cocoa
- 1 pkg. (8 oz.) reduced-fat cream cheese

1. Preheat oven to 350°. Separate 2 eggs, putting each white in a separate bowl; set aside (discard yolks or save for later use). In a small bowl, beat butter and ¾ cup sugar until crumbly. Beat in the remaining whole egg, 1 egg white and vanilla until well combined. Combine flour and cocoa; gradually add to the egg mixture until blended. Pour into a 9-in. square baking pan coated with cooking spray; set aside.
2. In a small bowl, beat cream cheese and the remaining sugar until smooth. Beat in the second egg white. Drop by rounded tablespoonfuls over the batter; cut through batter with a knife to swirl.
3. Bake for 25-30 minutes or until center is set and the edges pull away from sides of pan. Cool on a wire rack.

1 brownie: 172 cal., 8g fat (5g sat. fat), 36mg chol., 145mg sod., 23g carb. (18g sugars, 0 fiber), 4g pro. **Diabetic exchanges:** 1½ starch, 1½ fat.

S'MORES BROWNIES

Our family simply adores our daughter's fudgy s'mores brownies. The cinnamon graham cracker crust and dark chocolate brownies bring our passion for s'mores to a whole new level!

—*Jennifer Gilbert, Brighton, MI*

- -

Prep: 20 min. • **Bake:** 30 min. • **Makes:** 2 dozen

- 1½ cups graham cracker crumbs (about 10 whole crackers)
- ¼ cup sugar
- 1 tsp. ground cinnamon
- ½ cup butter, melted

BROWNIES
- 1 oz. unsweetened baking chocolate
- ½ cup butter, softened
- 1¼ cups sugar
- 3 large eggs, room temperature
- 1 tsp. vanilla extract
- 1¼ cups all-purpose flour
- ⅓ cup dark baking cocoa
- ½ tsp. baking powder
- ¼ tsp. salt
- 1 cup miniature marshmallows

TOPPING
- 1 cup miniature marshmallows
- 5 whole graham crackers, broken into bite-size pieces

1. Preheat oven to 350°. Combine cracker crumbs, sugar and cinnamon. Stir in melted butter. Press mixture onto the bottom of an ungreased 13x9-in. baking pan. Bake until lightly browned, 7-9 minutes. Cool on a wire rack.
2. Melt unsweetened chocolate on high in a microwave, stirring every 30 seconds. Cool slightly. Cream butter and sugar on medium speed until light and fluffy. Add eggs and beat well; beat in the melted chocolate and vanilla. In another bowl, whisk together flour, cocoa, baking powder and salt; stir into the creamed mixture. Fold in 1 cup of miniature marshmallows.
3. Spread the batter over the graham cracker crust. Top with the remaining marshmallows and the broken graham crackers. Bake until center is set, 18-22 minutes (do not overbake).

1 brownie: 215 cal., 10g fat (6g sat. fat), 44mg chol., 157mg sod., 30g carb. (17g sugars, 1g fiber), 3g pro.

Dazzling Desserts

Dinner without dessert is simply incomplete. Cap off your family meal with one of these luscious sweets—cakes and cheesecakes, pies, cobblers and more! From frosty summer treats to rich, elegant cakes perfect for a holiday feast, these indulgent recipes are just what's needed to finish your meal in style.

FAVORITE PUMPKIN CAKE ROLL

Keep this cake roll in the freezer for a quick dessert for family or unexpected guests, to take to a gathering or to give as a yummy gift.
—*Erica Berchtold, Freeport, IL*

Prep: 30 min. • **Bake:** 15 min. + freezing
Makes: 10 servings

- 3 **large eggs, separated, room temperature**
- 1 **cup sugar, divided**
- ⅔ **cup canned pumpkin**
- ¾ **cup all-purpose flour**
- 1 **tsp. baking soda**
- ½ **tsp. ground cinnamon**
- ⅛ **tsp. salt**

FILLING
- 8 **oz. cream cheese, softened**
- 2 **Tbsp. butter, softened**
- 1 **cup confectioners' sugar**
- ¾ **tsp. vanilla extract**
   Additional confectioners' sugar

1. Line a 15x10x1-in. baking pan with waxed paper; grease paper and set aside. Beat egg yolks on high speed until thick and lemon-colored. Gradually add ½ cup sugar and pumpkin, beating on high until sugar is almost dissolved.

2. In a small bowl, beat egg whites until soft peaks form. Gradually add remaining sugar, beating until stiff peaks form. Fold into egg yolk mixture. Combine the flour, baking soda, cinnamon and salt; gently fold into pumpkin mixture. Spread into prepared pan.

3. Bake at 375° until cake springs back when lightly touched, 12-15 minutes. Cool for 5 minutes. Turn onto a kitchen towel dusted with confectioners' sugar. Gently peel off waxed paper. Roll up cake in the towel jelly-roll style, starting with a short side. Cool completely on a wire rack.

4. In a small bowl, beat the cream cheese, butter, confectioners' sugar and vanilla until smooth. Unroll cake; spread filling evenly to within ½ in. of edges. Roll up again, without towel. Cover and freeze until firm. Remove from the freezer 15 minutes before cutting. Dust with confectioners' sugar.

1 slice: 285 cal., 12g fat (7g sat. fat), 94mg chol., 261mg sod., 41g carb. (32g sugars, 1g fiber), 5g pro.

BUTTERMILK PEACH ICE CREAM

My mother's family owned peach orchards in Missouri. Now I live in Tennessee, a top consumer of buttermilk. This summery ice cream combines my past and present.
—*Kim Higginbotham, Knoxville, TN*

Prep: 15 min. + chilling
Process: 30 min./batch + freezing
Makes: 2 qt.

- 2 lbs. ripe peaches (about 7 medium), peeled and quartered
- ½ cup sugar
- ½ cup packed brown sugar
- 1 Tbsp. lemon juice
- 1 tsp. vanilla extract
  Pinch salt
- 2 cups buttermilk
- 1 cup heavy whipping cream

1. Place peaches in a food processor; process until smooth. Add the sugars, lemon juice, vanilla and salt; process until blended.
2. In a large bowl, mix buttermilk and cream. Stir in peach mixture. Refrigerate, covered, 1 hour or until cold.
3. Fill cylinder of ice cream maker no more than two-thirds full. Freeze according to manufacturer's directions, refrigerating any remaining mixture to process later. Transfer ice cream to freezer containers, allowing headspace for expansion. Freeze 2-4 hours or until firm. Let ice cream stand at room temperature 10 minutes before serving.
½ cup: 137 cal., 6g fat (4g sat. fat), 22mg chol., 75mg sod., 20g carb. (19g sugars, 1g fiber), 2g pro. **Diabetic exchanges:** 1 starch, 1 fat.

MOCHA TRUFFLE CHEESECAKE

I went through a phase when I couldn't get enough cheesecake or coffee, so I created this rich dessert to get more of both. Its brownie-like crust and creamy mocha layer really hit the spot. It's ideal for get-togethers.
—*Shannon Dormady, Great Falls, MT*

Prep: 20 min. • **Bake:** 50 min. + chilling
Makes: 16 servings

- 1 pkg. devil's food cake mix (regular size)
- 6 Tbsp. butter, melted
- 1 large egg, room temperature
- 1 to 3 Tbsp. instant coffee granules

FILLING/TOPPING
- 2 pkg. (8 oz. each) cream cheese, softened
- 1 can (14 oz.) sweetened condensed milk
- 2 cups semisweet chocolate chips, melted and cooled
- 3 to 6 Tbsp. instant coffee granules
- ¼ cup hot water
- 3 large eggs, room temperature, lightly beaten
- 1 cup heavy whipping cream
- ¼ cup confectioners' sugar
- ½ tsp. almond extract
- 1 Tbsp. baking cocoa, optional

1. Preheat oven to 325°. In a large bowl, combine the cake mix, butter, egg and coffee granules until well blended. Press mixture onto the bottom and 2 in. up the sides of a greased 10-in. springform pan.
2. In another large bowl, beat the cream cheese until smooth. Beat in milk and melted chips. Dissolve coffee granules in water; add to the cream cheese mixture. Add eggs; beat on low speed just until combined. Pour into crust. Place pan on a baking sheet.
3. Bake until the center is almost set, 50-55 minutes. Cool on a wire rack for 10 minutes. Carefully run a knife around edge of pan to loosen; cool 1 hour longer. Chill overnight.
4. Just before serving, in a large bowl, beat cream until soft peaks form. Beat in sugar and extract until stiff peaks form. Spread over the top of the cheesecake. Sprinkle with cocoa if desired. Refrigerate any leftovers.
1 slice: 484 cal., 28g fat (16g sat. fat), 109mg chol., 389mg sod., 55g carb. (41g sugars, 2g fiber), 7g pro.

SOUTHERN LANE CAKE

I just love this impressive, old-fashioned cake, and so do my dinner guests. With the fruit filling and topping it's reminiscent of a fruit cake—but so much more delicious!
—*Mabel Parvi, Ridgefield, WA*

- -

Prep: 40 min. • **Bake:** 20 min. + cooling
Makes: 12 servings

- 6 **large egg whites**
- ¾ **cup butter, softened**
- 1½ **cups sugar**
- 1 **tsp. vanilla extract**
- 2¼ **cups all-purpose flour**
- 2½ **tsp. baking powder**
- ½ **tsp. salt**
- ¾ **cup 2% milk**

FILLING
- 6 **large egg yolks**
- 1 **cup sugar**
- ½ **cup butter, cubed**
- ¼ **cup bourbon**
- 1 **Tbsp. grated orange zest**
- ¼ **tsp. salt**
- ¾ **cup raisins**
- ¾ **cup sweetened shredded coconut**
- ¾ **cup chopped pecans**
- ¾ **cup coarsely chopped red candied cherries**
- 1 **cup heavy whipping cream, whipped and sweetened**

1. Line the bottoms of 3 greased 9-in. round baking pans with parchment. Grease parchment; set aside. Place egg whites in a large bowl; let stand at room temperature for 30 minutes.

2. Preheat oven to 325°. In a large bowl, cream the butter and sugar until light and fluffy. Beat in vanilla. In another bowl, whisk the flour, baking powder and salt; add to the creamed mixture alternately with milk, beating well after each addition.

3. Beat the egg whites until stiff peaks form; fold into the batter. Transfer batter to the prepared pans.

4. Bake until a toothpick inserted in the center comes out clean, 20-25 minutes. Cool for 10 minutes before removing from pans to wire racks; remove parchment. Cool completely.

5. For the filling, combine egg yolks and sugar in a large saucepan. Add butter; cook and stir over medium-low heat until the sugar is dissolved and the mixture thickens (do not boil). Remove from heat. Stir in bourbon, orange zest and salt. Fold in raisins, coconut, pecans and cherries. Cool.

6. Place 1 cake layer on a serving plate; spread with a third of the filling. Repeat layers twice. Frost the sides of the cake with whipped cream. Refrigerate until ready to serve.

To make ahead: Cake can be made a day in advance. Cover and refrigerate. Remove from the refrigerator 30 minutes before serving.

1 piece: 677 cal., 36g fat (20g sat. fat), 167mg chol., 469mg sod., 81g carb. (58g sugars, 2g fiber), 8g pro.

RHUBARB UPSIDE-DOWN CAKE

I've baked this cake every spring for many years—my family loves it! Use your own fresh rhubarb, hit up a farmers market or find a neighbor who will trade stalks for the recipe.
—*Helen Breman, Mattydale, NY*

Prep: 20 min. • **Bake:** 35 min.
Makes: 10 servings

- 3 cups sliced fresh or frozen rhubarb
- 1 cup sugar
- 2 Tbsp. all-purpose flour
- ¼ tsp. ground nutmeg
- ¼ cup butter, melted

BATTER
- ¼ cup butter, melted
- ¾ cup sugar
- 1 large egg, room temperature
- 1½ cups all-purpose flour
- 2 tsp. baking powder
- ½ tsp. ground nutmeg
- ¼ tsp. salt
- ⅔ cup 2% milk
  Sweetened whipped cream, optional

1. Preheat oven to 350°. Place rhubarb in a greased 10-in. cast-iron or other heavy ovenproof skillet. Combine sugar, flour and nutmeg; sprinkle over rhubarb. Drizzle with butter; set aside.

2. For batter, in a large bowl, beat the butter and sugar until blended. Beat in egg. Combine flour, baking powder, nutmeg and salt. Gradually add to the egg mixture alternately with milk, beating well after each addition.

3. Spread batter over rhubarb mixture. Bake until a toothpick inserted in center comes out clean, about 35 minutes. Run a knife around the edge of the cake immediately; invert onto a serving dish. Serve warm. If desired, serve with whipped cream.

1 piece: 316 cal., 10g fat (6g sat. fat), 48mg chol., 248mg sod., 53g carb. (36g sugars, 1g fiber), 4g pro.

GINGER-LIME PEAR COBBLER

We have a huge pear tree in our yard, which is why I came up with this recipe. The tart lime, sweet pears and tangy ginger are a winning combination.
—*Heather Naas, Lompoc, CA*

Prep: 25 min. • **Bake:** 50 min. + cooling
Makes: 10 servings

- ¾ cup sugar
- ⅛ tsp. ground ginger
- 5 cups sliced peeled fresh pears
- 2 Tbsp. finely chopped crystallized ginger
- 2 Tbsp. lime juice
- ½ cup butter, melted

BATTER
- ¾ cup all-purpose flour
- ½ cup sugar
- 2 tsp. baking powder
- 1 tsp. grated lime zest
- ⅛ tsp. salt
  Pinch ground ginger
- ¾ cup 2% milk

1. Preheat oven to 350°. In a large bowl, combine sugar and ground ginger. Stir in the pears, crystallized ginger and lime juice; set aside.

2. Pour butter into an ungreased 11x7-in. baking dish. For the batter, combine the flour, sugar, baking powder, lime zest, salt and ginger. Stir in milk. Pour over the butter (do not stir). Spoon the pear mixture over the top.

3. Bake 50-55 minutes or until bubbly and golden brown. Cool for 10 minutes before serving.

1 serving: 281 cal., 10g fat (6g sat. fat), 26mg chol., 184mg sod., 49g carb. (35g sugars, 3g fiber), 2g pro.

PEANUT BUTTER ICEBOX DESSERT

Leftover crushed cookies create the yummy crust for this crowd-pleasing dessert. It's covered with a smooth cream cheese mixture, chocolate pudding and whipped topping for a lovely layered look.

—Nancy Mueller, Highlands Ranch, CO

- -

Prep: 20 min. + chilling • **Makes:** 15 servings

- 16 Nutter Butter cookies, crushed (about 2 cups), divided
- ¼ cup sugar
- ¼ cup butter, melted
- 1 pkg. (8 oz.) cream cheese, softened
- 1⅓ cups confectioners' sugar
- 1 carton (8 oz.) frozen whipped topping, thawed, divided
- 2½ cups cold 2% milk
- 2 pkg. (3.9 oz. each) instant chocolate pudding mix

1. Preheat oven to 350°. In a large bowl, combine 1¾ cups crushed cookies, the sugar and butter; press into an ungreased 13x9-in. baking dish. Bake until golden brown, 6-8 minutes; cool on a wire rack.
2. In a large bowl, beat cream cheese and confectioners' sugar until smooth; fold in 1½ cups whipped topping. Spread over the cooled crust.
3. In another large bowl, beat milk and pudding mix on low speed until thickened, about 2 minutes. Spread over the cream cheese layer. Top with remaining whipped topping; sprinkle with remaining ¼ cup crushed cookies. Cover and refrigerate for at least 1 hour before serving.

1 piece: 323 cal., 15g fat (9g sat. fat), 27mg chol., 217mg sod., 43g carb. (31g sugars, 1g fiber), 4g pro.

RUSTIC CARAMEL APPLE TART

Like an apple pie without the pan, this most scrumptious tart has a crispy crust that cuts nicely and a delectable caramel topping.

—Betty Fulks, Onia, AR

- -

Prep: 20 min. + chilling • **Bake:** 25 min.
Makes: 4 servings

- ⅔ cup all-purpose flour
- 1 Tbsp. sugar
- ⅛ tsp. salt
- ¼ cup cold butter, cubed
- 6½ tsp. cold water
- ⅛ tsp. vanilla extract
FILLING
- 1½ cups chopped peeled tart apples
- 3 Tbsp. sugar
- 1 Tbsp. all-purpose flour
TOPPING
- 1 tsp. sugar
- ¼ tsp. ground cinnamon
- 1 large egg
- 1 Tbsp. water
- 2 Tbsp. caramel ice cream topping, warmed

1. In a large bowl, combine flour, sugar and salt; cut in butter until crumbly. Gradually add water and vanilla, tossing with a fork until dough forms a ball. Cover and refrigerate 30 minutes or until easy to handle.
2. Preheat oven to 400°. On a lightly floured surface, roll the dough into a 10-in. circle. Transfer to a parchment-lined baking sheet. Combine the filling ingredients; spoon over the crust to within 2 in. of edges. Fold up edges of the crust over filling, leaving the center uncovered. Combine the sugar and cinnamon; sprinkle over filling. Whisk egg and water; brush over crust.
3. Bake for 25-30 minutes or until the crust is golden and the filling is bubbly. Using parchment, slide the tart onto a wire rack. Drizzle with caramel topping. Serve warm.

1 slice: 298 cal., 13g fat (8g sat. fat), 77mg chol., 218mg sod., 42g carb. (24g sugars, 1g fiber), 4g pro.

7UP POUND CAKE

My grandmother gave me my first cake recipe—a pound cake using 7UP—and her grandmother had given it to her. On top of being delicious, this cake represents family tradition, connection and love.

—*Marsha Adele Davis, Desert Hot Springs, CA*

- -

Prep: 25 min. • **Bake:** 65 min. + cooling
Makes: 16 servings

1½ cups butter, softened
3 cups sugar
5 large eggs, room temperature
2 Tbsp. lemon juice
1 tsp. vanilla extract
3 cups all-purpose flour
¾ cup 7UP soda
GLAZE
1½ cups confectioners' sugar
1 Tbsp. lemon or lime juice
1 to 2 Tbsp. 7UP soda
½ tsp. grated lemon or
   lime zest, optional

1. Preheat oven to 350°. Grease and flour a 10-in. fluted or plain tube pan.
2. In a large bowl, cream butter and sugar until light and fluffy. Add 1 egg at a time, beating well after each addition. Beat in lemon juice and vanilla. Add flour alternately with 7UP, beating well after each addition.
3. Transfer batter to prepared pan. Bake until a toothpick inserted in center comes out clean, 65-75 minutes. Cool in pan for 20 minutes before removing to a wire rack to cool completely.
4. For glaze, in a small bowl, mix confectioners' sugar, lemon juice and enough 7UP to reach desired consistency. If desired, stir in zest. Drizzle over cake.
1 slice: 457 cal., 19g fat (11g sat. fat), 104mg chol., 177mg sod., 69g carb. (50g sugars, 1g fiber), 5g pro.

COOL-DOWN TIME

*It's important to let this cake cool in the pan for 20 minutes after baking; as it cools, it will set up and become more sturdy, preventing it from breaking when you remove it from the pan.
To prevent sticking, use solid shortening to grease plain and fluted tube pans.*

SOUR CREAM-LEMON PIE

I first tasted this pie at a local restaurant and hunted around until I found a similar recipe. Now it's my husband's favorite.
—*Martha Sorensen, Fallon, NV*

Takes: 20 min. + chilling • **Makes:** 8 servings

    Pastry for single-crust pie
1   **cup sugar**
3   **Tbsp. plus 1½ tsp. cornstarch**
1   **cup whole milk**
½   **cup lemon juice**
3   **large egg yolks, lightly beaten**
¼   **cup butter, cubed**
1   **Tbsp. grated lemon zest**
1   **cup sour cream**
1   **cup heavy whipping cream, whipped**

1. Preheat oven to 450°. On a lightly floured surface, roll dough to a ⅛-in.-thick circle; transfer to a 9-in. pie plate. Trim the crust to ½ in. beyond rim of plate; flute edge.
2. Line unpricked crust with a double thickness of foil. Fill with pie weights, dried beans or uncooked rice. Bake until the bottom is lightly browned, 8 minutes. Remove foil and weights; bake until golden brown, 5-7 minutes longer. Cool on a wire rack.
3. In a large heavy saucepan, mix sugar and cornstarch. Whisk in milk and lemon juice until smooth. Cook and stir over medium-high heat until thickened and bubbly. Reduce heat to low; cook and stir 2 minutes longer. Remove from heat.
4. In a small bowl, whisk a small amount of the hot mixture into egg yolks; return all to the pan, whisking constantly. Bring to a gentle boil; cook and stir 2 minutes. Remove from heat. Stir in butter and lemon zest. Cool without stirring.
5. Stir in sour cream. Add filling to crust. Top with whipped cream. Store in the refrigerator.
1 piece: 437 cal., 26g fat (15g sat. fat), 145mg chol., 197mg sod., 46g carb. (29g sugars, 0 fiber), 4g pro.

BEST STRAWBERRY SHORTCAKE

For a dazzling summer dessert, you can't beat juicy strawberries and fresh whipped cream over homemade shortcake. My father added even more indulgence to this recipe by buttering the shortcake.
—*Shirley Joan Helfenbein, Lapeer, MI*

Prep: 15 min. • **Bake:** 15 min. + cooling
Makes: 4 servings

1   **cup all-purpose flour**
1   **Tbsp. sugar**
1½   **tsp. baking powder**
¼   **tsp. salt**
¼   **cup butter, cold**
1   **large egg, room temperature**
⅓   **cup half-and-half cream**
½   **cup heavy whipping cream**
1   **Tbsp. confectioners' sugar**
⅛   **tsp. vanilla extract**
2   **tsp. butter, softened**
2   **cups fresh strawberries, sliced**

1. Preheat oven to 450°. In a small bowl, combine the flour, sugar, baking powder and salt. Cut in ¼ cup butter until the mixture resembles coarse crumbs. In a small bowl, combine egg and half-and-half; stir into crumb mixture just until moistened.
2. Spread batter into a 6-in. round baking pan coated with cooking spray, slightly building up the edges. Bake 13-15 minutes or until golden. Cool 10 minutes before removing from pan to a wire rack.
3. In a small bowl, beat whipping cream, confectioners' sugar and vanilla until soft peaks form. Cut cake horizontally into 2 layers. Place bottom layer on a serving plate; spread with softened butter. Top with half each of the strawberries and cream mixture. Add second layer of cake; top with the remaining cream mixture and strawberries.
1 piece: 420 cal., 28g fat (17g sat. fat), 140mg chol., 471mg sod., 36g carb. (10g sugars, 2g fiber), 7g pro.

HUMMINGBIRD CAKE

This impressive cake is my dad's favorite, so I always make it for his birthday. The beautiful, old-fashioned layered delight makes a memorable celebration dessert any time of year.

—Nancy Zimmerman,
Cape May Court House, NJ

Prep: 40 min. • **Bake:** 25 min. + cooling
Makes: 14 servings

- 2 cups mashed ripe bananas
- 1½ cups canola oil
- 3 large eggs, room temperature
- 1 can (8 oz.) unsweetened crushed pineapple, undrained
- 1½ tsp. vanilla extract
- 3 cups all-purpose flour
- 2 cups sugar
- 1 tsp. salt
- 1 tsp. baking soda
- 1 tsp. ground cinnamon
- 1 cup chopped walnuts

PINEAPPLE FROSTING
- ¼ cup shortening
- 2 Tbsp. butter, softened
- 1 tsp. grated lemon zest
- ¼ tsp. salt
- 6 cups confectioners' sugar
- ½ cup unsweetened pineapple juice
- 2 tsp. half-and-half cream
  Chopped walnuts, optional

1. Preheat oven to 350°. In a large bowl, beat bananas, oil, eggs, pineapple and vanilla until well blended. In another bowl, combine the flour, sugar, salt, baking soda and cinnamon; gradually beat into the banana mixture until blended. Stir in walnuts.

2. Pour into 3 greased and floured 9-in. round baking pans. Bake until a toothpick inserted in the center comes out clean, 25-30 minutes. Cool for 10 minutes before removing from pans to wire racks to cool completely.

3. For frosting, in a large bowl, beat the shortening, butter, lemon zest and salt until fluffy. Add confectioners' sugar alternately with pineapple juice. Beat in cream. Spread between layers and over top and sides of cake. If desired, sprinkle with chopped walnuts.

1 slice: 777 cal., 35g fat (6g sat. fat), 50mg chol., 333mg sod., 113g carb. (85g sugars, 2g fiber), 7g pro.

AMARETTO RICOTTA CHEESECAKE

There's a good reason why this cherished recipe was handed down to me by a relative—it's a keeper! The amaretto and ricotta make for a truly memorable dessert.
—*Isabel Neuman, Surprise, AZ*

- -

Prep: 35 min. + chilling
Bake: 1 hour + chilling • **Makes:** 16 servings

2¾ cups whole-milk ricotta cheese
⅓ cup cornstarch
¼ cup amaretto
2 pkg. (8 oz. each) cream cheese, softened
1½ cups sugar
1 cup sour cream
5 large eggs, room temperature, lightly beaten

TOPPING
1 cup sour cream
2 Tbsp. sugar
2 Tbsp. amaretto

GARNISH
1 Tbsp. light corn syrup
1 cup fresh cranberries
⅓ cup sugar
½ cup sliced almonds, toasted

1. Line a strainer or colander with 4 layers of cheesecloth or 1 coffee filter; place over a bowl. Place ricotta in the prepared strainer; cover the ricotta with the sides of the cheesecloth. Refrigerate for at least 8 hours or overnight. Remove ricotta from cheesecloth; discard the liquid in the bowl.

2. Preheat oven to 350°. In a small bowl, mix cornstarch and amaretto. In a large bowl, beat cream cheese, sugar, sour cream and drained ricotta until smooth. Beat in the amaretto mixture. Add eggs; beat on low speed just until blended.

3. Pour into a greased 10-in. springform pan. Place on a baking sheet. Bake until center is almost set, 1-1¼ hours. Let stand 5 minutes on a wire rack.

4. In a small bowl, mix the topping ingredients; spread over the top of cheesecake. Bake 5 minutes longer.

5. Cool on a wire rack for 10 minutes. Use a knife to loosen the sides of the cake from the pan. Cool 1 hour longer. Refrigerate overnight; cover when completely cooled. Remove rim from pan.

6. For garnish, place corn syrup in a small microwave-safe bowl. Microwave, uncovered, until warm, about 10 seconds. Add cranberries; toss to coat. Place sugar in a small bowl; add cranberries and toss to coat. Place on waxed paper and let stand until set, about 1 hour. Top cheesecake with almonds and the sugared cranberries.

Note: To toast nuts, bake in a shallow pan in a 350° oven for 5-10 minutes or cook in a skillet over low heat until lightly browned, stirring occasionally.

1 slice: 351 cal., 21g fat (13g sat. fat), 134mg chol., 168mg sod., 29g carb. (26g sugars, 0 fiber), 10g pro.

PEPPERMINT CREAM POUND CAKE

I came up with this recipe when I was looking for a new twist on a tried-and-true pound cake. I really like the look and flavor of peppermint, especially around Christmas, and this was the result. Everyone at work loved it, and my family did, too.
—*Carolyn Webster, Winston-Salem, NC*

Prep: 35 min. • **Bake:** 1 hour + cooling
Makes: 12 servings

- 1 cup unsalted butter, softened
- ½ cup butter-flavored shortening
- 2 cups sugar
- 6 large eggs, room temperature
- 1 tsp. vanilla extract
- ½ tsp. peppermint extract
- 3 cups all-purpose flour
- 1 tsp. baking powder
- 1 cup heavy whipping cream
- ½ cup finely crushed peppermint candies

GLAZE
- 1½ cups confectioners' sugar
- 1 tsp. unsalted butter, melted
- ¼ tsp. vanilla extract
- ⅛ tsp. salt
- 4 to 5 Tbsp. heavy whipping cream
  Additional crushed peppermint candies

Contest Winner

1. Preheat oven to 325°. Generously grease and flour a 10-in. fluted tube pan; set aside. In a large bowl, cream the butter, shortening and sugar until light and fluffy. Add 1 egg at a time, beating well after each addition. Beat in extracts. Combine flour and baking powder; add to the creamed mixture alternately with whipping cream. Fold in candies.
2. Transfer to prepared tube pan. Bake until a toothpick inserted in the center comes out clean, 1-1¼ hours. Cool for 10 minutes before removing from pan to a wire rack to cool completely.
3. In a small bowl, combine confectioners' sugar, butter, vanilla and salt. Stir in enough cream to achieve a drizzling consistency. Drizzle over the cake. Sprinkle with additional candies. Refrigerate any leftovers.
1 slice: 649 cal., 35g fat (18g sat. fat), 181mg chol., 107mg sod., 77g carb. (50g sugars, 1g fiber), 7g pro.

DOWN EAST BLUEBERRY BUCKLE

This buckle won a baking contest at my daughter's college. As the prize, they shipped us four lobsters, but the real reward was seeing the smile on our daughter's face!
—*Dianne van der Veen, Plymouth, MA*

Prep: 15 min. • **Bake:** 30 min.
Makes: 9 servings

- 2 cups all-purpose flour
- ¾ cup sugar
- 2½ tsp. baking powder
- ¼ tsp. salt
- 1 large egg, room temperature
- ¾ cup 2% milk
- ¼ cup butter, melted
- 2 cups fresh or frozen blueberries

TOPPING
- ½ cup sugar
- ⅓ cup all-purpose flour
- ½ tsp. ground cinnamon
- ¼ cup butter, softened

1. Preheat oven to 375°. In a large bowl, whisk flour, sugar, baking powder and salt. In another bowl, whisk egg, milk and melted butter until blended. Add to the flour mixture; stir just until moistened. Fold in blueberries. Transfer to a greased 9-in. square baking pan.
2. For topping, in a small bowl, mix sugar, flour and cinnamon. Using a fork, stir in softened butter until mixture is crumbly. Sprinkle over the batter.
3. Bake for 30-35 minutes or until a toothpick inserted in the center comes out clean (do not overbake). Cool in pan on a wire rack. Serve warm or at room temperature.
Note: If using frozen blueberries, use without thawing to avoid discoloring the batter.
1 piece: 354 cal., 12g fat (7g sat. fat), 49mg chol., 277mg sod., 59g carb. (32g sugars, 2g fiber), 5g pro.

CHERRY UPSIDE-DOWN BREAD PUDDING

I've always loved bread pudding, and I enjoy fixing this for my family on a chilly day. To create a completely different dessert, use another flavor of pie filling and omit the chocolate chips.
—*Ronna Farley, Rockville, MD*

Prep: 20 min. + cooling • **Cook:** 2¾ hours
Makes: 12 servings

- 1 loaf (16 oz.) sliced white bread
- 1 can (21 oz.) cherry pie filling
- ½ cup butter, softened
- 1 cup sugar
- 5 large eggs, room temperature
- 2 cups 2% milk
- 1 tsp. ground cinnamon
- 1 tsp. vanilla extract
- ¾ cup semisweet chocolate chips
  Sweetened whipped cream, optional

1. Place bread slices on ungreased baking sheets. Broil 3-4 in. from heat until bread is golden brown, 1-2 minutes on each side; let cool. Cut bread into 1-in. pieces; set aside. Spoon pie filling into a greased 5- or 6-qt. slow cooker.

2. In a large bowl, cream butter and sugar until crumbly. Add 1 egg at a time, beating well after each addition. Beat in milk, cinnamon and vanilla (mixture may appear curdled). Gently stir in chocolate chips and bread cubes; let stand until the bread is softened, about 10 minutes. Transfer to slow cooker.

3. Cook, covered, on low until set and a knife inserted in the center comes out clean, 2¾-3¼ hours. Serve warm, with whipped cream if desired.

¾ cup: 393 cal., 15g fat (8g sat. fat), 101mg chol., 305mg sod., 58g carb. (27g sugars, 2g fiber), 8g pro.

LEMON RHUBARB TUBE CAKE

For a true taste of summer, try this dessert! The cake's fresh lemon flavor and tart rhubarb topping are so refreshing.
—*Courtney Stultz, Weir, KS*

Prep: 35 min. • **Bake:** 50 min. + cooling
Makes: 12 servings

- 3 medium lemons
- 1 cup butter, softened
- 2 cups sugar
- 3 large eggs, room temperature
- 3 cups all-purpose flour
- 1 tsp. baking powder
- ½ tsp. baking soda
- ½ tsp. salt
- 1 cup buttermilk

RHUBARB TOPPING

- 1 cup sugar
- 1 cup sliced fresh or frozen rhubarb
- 1 cup halved fresh strawberries
  Confectioners' sugar, optional

1. Preheat oven to 350°. Grease and flour a 10-in. fluted tube pan. Finely grate enough zest from lemons to measure 2 Tbsp. Cut lemons crosswise in half; squeeze juice from the lemons to measure ¼ cup. (Save remaining juice for future use.)

2. In a large bowl, cream butter and sugar until light and fluffy. Add 1 egg at a time; beat well after each addition. Beat in lemon juice and zest. In another bowl, whisk flour, baking powder, baking soda and salt; add to the creamed mixture alternately with buttermilk, beating well after each addition.

3. Transfer batter to prepared pan. Bake until a toothpick inserted in the center comes out clean, 50-60 minutes. Cool in pan 10 minutes before removing to a wire rack to cool.

4. Meanwhile, for topping, combine sugar and rhubarb in a small saucepan. Bring to a boil; reduce heat. Simmer until rhubarb is almost tender, 8-10 minutes. Add halved strawberries; cook until strawberries and rhubarb are softened. Serve with cake. If desired, dust with confectioners' sugar.

1 slice with ¼ cup sauce: 481 cal., 17g fat (10g sat. fat), 88mg chol., 371mg sod., 78g carb. (53g sugars, 2g fiber), 6g pro.

BLUEBERRY ZUCCHINI SQUARES

I saw a bar recipe on a muffin mix box using apple and lemon zest. I tried it from scratch with shredded zucchini and fresh blueberries instead. It's a nifty combo!
—*Shelly Bevington, Hermiston, OR*

Prep: 30 min. • **Bake:** 30 min. + cooling
Makes: 2 dozen

- 2 cups shredded zucchini (do not pack)
- ½ cup buttermilk
- 1 Tbsp. grated lemon zest
- 3 Tbsp. lemon juice
- 1 cup butter, softened
- 2½ cups sugar
- 2 large eggs, room temperature
- 3¼ cups plus 2 Tbsp. all-purpose flour, divided
- 1 tsp. baking soda
- ½ tsp. salt
- 2 cups fresh or frozen blueberries

GLAZE

- 2 cups confectioners' sugar
- ¼ cup buttermilk
- 1 Tbsp. grated lemon zest
- 2 tsp. lemon juice
- ⅛ tsp. salt

1. Preheat oven to 350°. Grease a 15x10x1-in. baking pan; set aside.

2. In a small bowl, combine zucchini, buttermilk, lemon zest and lemon juice; toss to combine. In a large bowl, cream butter and sugar until light and fluffy. Beat in 1 egg at a time. In another bowl, whisk 3¼ cups flour, baking soda and salt; gradually add to the creamed mixture alternately with zucchini mixture, mixing well after each addition. Toss blueberries with the remaining flour; fold into batter.

3. Transfer batter to prepared pan, spreading evenly (pan will be full). Bake 30-35 minutes or until light golden brown and a toothpick inserted in center comes out clean. Cool completely in pan on a wire rack.

4. In a small bowl, mix the glaze ingredients until smooth; spread over top. Let stand until set.

Note: If using frozen blueberries, use without thawing to avoid discoloring the batter.

1 piece: 270 cal., 8g fat (5g sat. fat), 36mg chol., 197mg sod., 47g carb. (33g sugars, 1g fiber), 3g pro.

Contest Winner

BROWN SUGAR POUND CAKE

This tender pound cake is the first one I mastered when I was learning to bake. You'll want to eat the browned butter icing by the spoonful—it tastes like pralines!

—Shawn Barto, Winter Garden, FL

- -

Prep: 20 min. • **Bake:** 55 min. + cooling
Makes: 16 servings

1½	cups unsalted butter, softened
2¼	cups packed brown sugar
5	large eggs, room temperature
2	tsp. vanilla extract
3	cups all-purpose flour
1	tsp. baking powder
¼	tsp. salt
1	cup sour cream

GLAZE

3	Tbsp. unsalted butter
¼	cup chopped pecans
1	cup confectioners' sugar
¼	tsp. vanilla extract
	Dash salt
2	to 3 Tbsp. half-and-half cream

1. Preheat oven to 350°. Grease and flour a 10-in. fluted tube pan; set aside.
2. Cream butter and brown sugar until light and fluffy. Add 1 egg at a time, beating well after each addition. Beat in vanilla. In another bowl, whisk flour, baking powder and salt; add to the creamed mixture alternately with sour cream, beating after each addition just until combined.
3. Transfer batter to prepared pan. Bake until a toothpick inserted in center comes out clean, 55-65 minutes. Cool in pan 10 minutes before removing to a wire rack to cool completely.
4. For glaze, combine butter and pecans in a small saucepan over medium heat, stirring constantly, until butter is light golden brown, 4-5 minutes. Stir into the confectioners' sugar. Add vanilla, salt and enough cream to reach a drizzling consistency. Drizzle glaze over cake, allowing some to drip down sides. Let stand until set.

1 slice: 473 cal., 25g fat (15g sat. fat), 121mg chol., 193mg sod., 57g carb. (38g sugars, 1g fiber), 5g pro.

MISSISSIPPI MUD CAKE

This cake features a fudgy, brownie-like base topped with marshmallow creme and a nutty frosting. Serve up big slices with glasses of cold milk or steaming mugs of coffee.

—Tammi Simpson, Greensburg, KY

- -

Prep: 20 min. • **Bake:** 35 min. + cooling
Makes: 20 servings

1	cup butter, softened
2	cups sugar
4	large eggs, room temperature
1½	cups self-rising flour
½	cup baking cocoa
1	cup chopped pecans
1	jar (7 oz.) marshmallow creme

FROSTING

½	cup butter, softened
3¾	cups confectioners' sugar
3	Tbsp. baking cocoa
1	Tbsp. vanilla extract
4	to 5 Tbsp. 2% milk
1	cup chopped pecans

1. Preheat oven to 350°. In a large bowl, cream butter and sugar until light and fluffy. Add 1 egg at a time, beating well after each addition. Combine flour and cocoa; gradually add to the creamed mixture until blended. Fold in the pecans.
2. Transfer to a greased 13x9-in. baking pan. Bake until a toothpick inserted in the center comes out clean, 35-40 minutes. Cool for 3 minutes (cake will fall in the center). Spoon the marshmallow creme over cake; carefully spread to cover top. Cool completely.
3. For frosting, in a small bowl, cream butter and confectioners' sugar until light and fluffy. Beat in the cocoa, vanilla and enough milk to achieve frosting consistency. Fold in pecans. Spread over the marshmallow creme layer. Store in the refrigerator.

Note: As a substitute for 1½ cups self-rising flour, place 2¼ tsp. baking powder and ¾ tsp. salt in a measuring cup. Add all-purpose flour to measure 1 cup. Combine with an additional ½ cup all-purpose flour.

1 piece: 457 cal., 24g fat (10g sat. fat), 80mg chol., 270mg sod., 61g carb. (48g sugars, 2g fiber), 4g pro.

THOMAS JEFFERSON'S VANILLA ICE CREAM

The third U.S. president is credited with jotting down the first American recipe for this treat. No vanilla bean on hand? Substitute 1 tablespoon vanilla extract for the vanilla bean. Just stir the extract into the cream mixture after the ice-water bath.
—Taste of Home *Test Kitchen*

- -

Prep: 15 min. + chilling
Process: 20 min./batch + freezing
Makes: 2¼ qt.

- 2 **qt. heavy whipping cream**
- 1 **cup sugar**
- 1 **vanilla bean**
- 6 **large egg yolks**

1. In a large heavy saucepan, combine cream and sugar. Split vanilla bean in half lengthwise. With a sharp knife, scrape the seeds into the pan; add the bean pod. Heat cream mixture over medium heat until bubbles form around the sides of pan, stirring to dissolve sugar.
2. In a small bowl, whisk a small amount of the hot mixture into the egg yolks; return all to the pan, whisking constantly.
3. Cook over low heat until the mixture is just thick enough to coat a metal spoon and the temperature reaches 160°, stirring constantly. Do not allow to boil. Immediately transfer to a bowl.
4. Place bowl in a pan of ice water. Stir gently and occasionally for 2 minutes; discard the vanilla bean pod. Press waxed paper onto the surface of the custard. Refrigerate several hours or overnight.
5. Fill cylinder of ice cream freezer two-thirds full; freeze according to the manufacturer's directions. (Refrigerate the remaining mixture until ready to freeze.) Transfer ice cream to a freezer container; freeze for 4-6 hours or until firm. Repeat with remaining mixture.
½ cup: 424 cal., 40g fat (25g sat. fat), 182mg chol., 32mg sod., 14g carb. (14g sugars, 0 fiber), 4g pro.

Heavenly Angel Food Cakes

Light and airy angel food cake is the ultimate in sweet sophistication. If the delicate texture seems intimidating, start with a mix—then move on to beating egg whites into a frothy delight to create a homemade masterpiece.

APPLE-SPICE ANGEL FOOD CAKE

Angel food cake mix takes the worry out of making a chiffon cake and is lower in fat and calories than regular cake mix. Apple pie spice and toasted nuts add a festive fall flavor.
—*Joan Buehnerkemper, Teutopolis, IL*

- -

Prep: 10 min. • **Bake:** 35 min. + cooling
Makes: 16 servings

- 1   pkg. (16 oz.) angel food cake mix
- 1   cup water
- ⅔   cup unsweetened applesauce
- ½   cup finely chopped pecans, toasted
- 1   tsp. apple pie spice
   Optional: Reduced-fat whipped topping and apple slices

1. Preheat oven to 350°. In a large bowl, combine cake mix and water. Beat on low speed for 30 seconds. Beat on medium speed for 1 minute. Fold in applesauce, pecans and pie spice.
2. Gently spoon into an ungreased 10-in. tube pan. Cut through batter with a knife to remove air pockets. Bake on the lowest oven rack for 35-45 minutes or until lightly browned and the entire top appears dry. Immediately invert pan; cool completely without removing pan, about 1 hour.
3. Run a knife around sides and center tube of pan. Remove cake to a serving plate. Garnish with whipped topping or apple slices if desired.

1 slice: 136 cal., 3g fat (0 sat. fat), 0 chol., 209mg sod., 26g carb. (14g sugars, 1g fiber), 3g pro. **Diabetic exchanges:** 1½ starch, ½ fat.

GLAZED CHOCOLATE ANGEL FOOD CAKE

Light as air and loaded with big chocolate flavor, this low-fat dessert will become a standby at all your gatherings. Add fresh strawberries or raspberries and a dollop of sweetened whipped cream if desired.
—*Mary Relyea, Canastota, NY*

- -

Prep: 20 min. • **Bake:** 40 min. + cooling
Makes: 12 servings

- 1½   cups egg whites (about 10 large)
- 1   cup cake flour
- 2   cups sugar, divided
- ½   cup baking cocoa
- 1   tsp. cream of tartar
- 1   tsp. vanilla extract
- ¼   tsp. salt

GLAZE
- ½   cup semisweet chocolate chips
- 3   Tbsp. half-and-half cream

1. Place egg whites in a large bowl; let stand at room temperature 30 minutes.
2. Preheat oven to 350°. Sift flour, 1 cup sugar and cocoa together twice.
3. Add cream of tartar, vanilla and salt to the egg whites; beat on medium speed until soft peaks form. Gradually add the remaining sugar, 2 Tbsp. at a time, beating on high after each addition until sugar is dissolved. Continue beating until stiff glossy peaks form. Gradually fold in the flour mixture, about ½ cup at a time.
4. Gently transfer batter to an ungreased 10-in. tube pan. Cut through batter with a knife to remove air pockets. Bake on lowest oven rack until top springs back when lightly touched and cracks feel dry, 40-50 minutes. Immediately invert pan; cool completely in pan, about 1 hour.
5. Run a knife around sides and center tube of pan. Remove cake to a serving plate. For glaze, in a microwave, melt chocolate chips with cream; stir until smooth. Drizzle over cake.

1 slice: 235 cal., 3g fat (2g sat. fat), 2mg chol., 102mg sod., 49g carb. (37g sugars, 1g fiber), 5g pro.

LEMON MERINGUE ANGEL CAKE

I've been told that this dessert tastes exactly like a lemon meringue pie and that it's the best angel food cake anyone could ask for. It's delightful to serve and virtually fat free.
—Sharon Kurtz, Emmaus, PA

- -

Prep: 40 min. + standing
Bake: 50 min. + cooling • **Makes:** 14 servings

- 12 large egg whites
- 1½ cups sugar, divided
- 1 cup cake flour
- 2 tsp. cream of tartar
- 1½ tsp. vanilla extract
- ¼ tsp. salt
- 1 jar (10 oz.) lemon curd

MERINGUE

- 4 large egg whites, room temperature
- ¾ tsp. cream of tartar
- ½ cup sugar

1. Place 12 egg whites in a large bowl; let stand at room temperature 30 minutes.
2. Preheat oven to 350°. Sift ½ cup sugar and flour together twice; set aside.
3. Add cream of tartar, vanilla and salt to egg whites; beat on medium speed until foamy. Gradually beat in remaining sugar, 2 Tbsp. at a time, on high until stiff glossy peaks form and the sugar is dissolved. Gradually fold in the flour mixture, about ½ cup at a time.
4. Gently spoon the batter into an ungreased 10-in. tube pan. Cut through batter with a knife to remove air pockets. Bake on lowest oven rack until golden brown and the entire top appears dry, 35-40 minutes. Immediately invert pan; cool completely in pan, about 1 hour.
5. Run a knife around sides and center tube of pan. Remove cake; split into 2 layers. Place the bottom on a parchment-lined baking sheet. Spread with lemon curd; replace the cake top.
6. In a small bowl, beat egg whites and cream of tartar on medium until soft peaks form. Gradually beat in the sugar, 1 Tbsp. at a time, on high until stiff glossy peaks form and sugar is dissolved. Spread over top and sides of cake.
7. Bake at 350° until golden brown, 15-18 minutes. Transfer to a serving plate. Refrigerate any leftovers.
1 piece: 238 cal., 1g fat (1g sat. fat), 15mg chol., 121mg sod., 51g carb. (41g sugars, 0 fiber), 5g pro.

MOCHA-HAZELNUT GLAZED ANGEL FOOD CAKE

I love this recipe because it combines three of my favorite flavors: coffee, hazelnuts and cherries. It's amazing how the rich, earthy flavors pair perfectly with the light, airy cake.
—Joan Pecsek, Chesapeake, VA

- -

Prep: 25 min. • **Bake:** 30 min. + cooling
Makes: 16 servings

- 12 large egg whites (about 1⅔ cups)
- 1 cup cake flour
- ¼ tsp. instant coffee granules
- 1 tsp. cream of tartar
- 1 tsp. almond extract
- ½ tsp. salt
- 1¼ cups sugar

GLAZE

- 1 cup Nutella
- ½ cup confectioners' sugar
- ⅓ cup brewed coffee
- ¼ cup chopped hazelnuts
- 16 maraschino cherries with stems

1. Place egg whites in a large bowl; let stand at room temperature 30 minutes.
2. Preheat oven to 350°. In a small bowl, mix flour and coffee granules until blended.
3. Add cream of tartar, extract and salt to egg whites; beat on medium speed until soft peaks form. Gradually add sugar, 1 Tbsp. at a time, beating on high after each addition until sugar is dissolved. Continue beating until soft glossy peaks form. Gradually fold in flour mixture, about ½ cup at a time.
4. Gently transfer to an ungreased 10-in. tube pan. Cut through batter with a knife to remove air pockets. Bake on lowest oven rack 30-40 minutes or until top springs back when lightly touched. Immediately invert pan; cool cake in pan, about 1½ hours.
5. Run a knife around sides and center tube of pan. Remove cake to a serving plate. In a small bowl, whisk Nutella, confectioners' sugar and coffee until smooth. Drizzle over cake; sprinkle with hazelnuts. Serve with cherries.
1 slice: 234 cal., 7g fat (1g sat. fat), 0 chol., 123mg sod., 41g carb. (33g sugars, 1g fiber), 5g pro.

Substitutions & Equivalents

EQUIVALENT MEASURES

3 teaspoons = 1 tablespoon	**16 tablespoons** = 1 cup
4 tablespoons = ¼ cup	**2 cups** = 1 pint
5⅓ tablespoons = ⅓ cup	**4 cups** = 1 quart
8 tablespoons = ½ cup	**4 quarts** = 1 gallon

FOOD EQUIVALENTS

Macaroni	1 cup (3½ ounces) uncooked = 2½ cups cooked
Noodles, Medium	3 cups (4 ounces) uncooked = 4 cups cooked
Popcorn	⅓-½ cup unpopped = 8 cups popped
Rice, Long Grain	1 cup uncooked = 3 cups cooked
Rice, Quick-Cooking	1 cup uncooked = 2 cups cooked
Spaghetti	8 ounces uncooked = 4 cups cooked

Bread	1 slice = ¾ cup soft crumbs or ¼ cup fine dry crumbs
Graham Crackers	7 squares = ½ cup finely crushed
Buttery Round Crackers	12 crackers = ½ cup finely crushed
Saltine Crackers	14 crackers = ½ cup finely crushed

Bananas	1 medium = ⅓ cup mashed
Lemons	1 medium = 3 tablespoons juice + 2 teaspoons grated zest
Limes	1 medium = 2 tablespoons juice + 1½ teaspoons grated zest
Oranges	1 medium = ¼-⅓ cup juice + 4 teaspoons grated zest

Cabbage	1 head = 5 cups shredded	**Green Pepper**	1 large = 1 cup chopped
Carrots	1 pound = 3 cups shredded	**Mushrooms**	½ pound = 3 cups sliced
Celery	1 rib = ½ cup chopped	**Onions**	1 medium = ½ cup chopped
Corn	1 ear fresh = ⅔ cup kernels	**Potatoes**	3 medium = 2 cups cubed

Almonds	1 pound = 3 cups chopped	**Pecan Halves**	1 pound = 4½ cups chopped
Ground Nuts	3¾ ounces = 1 cup	**Walnuts**	1 pound = 3¾ cups chopped

EASY SUBSTITUTIONS

WHEN YOU NEED...		USE...
Baking Powder	1 teaspoon	½ teaspoon cream of tartar + ¼ teaspoon baking soda
Buttermilk	1 cup	1 tablespoon lemon juice or vinegar + enough milk to measure 1 cup (let stand 5 minutes before using)
Cornstarch	1 tablespoon	2 tablespoons all-purpose flour
Honey	1 cup	1¼ cups sugar + ¼ cup water
Half-and-Half Cream	1 cup	1 tablespoon melted butter + enough whole milk to measure 1 cup
Onion	1 small, chopped (⅓ cup)	1 teaspoon onion powder or 1 tablespoon dried minced onion
Tomato Juice	1 cup	½ cup tomato sauce + ½ cup water
Tomato Sauce	2 cups	¾ cup tomato paste + 1 cup water
Unsweetened Chocolate	1 square (1 ounce)	3 tablespoons baking cocoa + 1 tablespoon shortening or oil
Whole Milk	1 cup	½ cup evaporated milk + ½ cup water

Cooking Terms

Here's a quick reference for some of the most common cooking terms used in recipes:

BASTE To moisten food with melted butter, pan drippings, marinades or other liquid to add more flavor and juiciness.

BEAT A rapid movement to combine ingredients using a fork, spoon, wire whisk or electric mixer.

BLEND To combine ingredients until just mixed.

BOIL To heat liquids until bubbles form that cannot be stirred down. In the case of water, the temperature will reach 212°.

BONE To remove all meat from the bone before cooking.

CREAM To beat ingredients together to a smooth consistency, usually in the case of butter and sugar for baking.

DASH A small amount of seasoning, less than ⅛ teaspoon. If using a shaker, a dash would be a quick flick of the container.

DREDGE To coat foods with flour or other dry ingredients. Most often done with pot roasts and stew meat before browning.

FOLD To incorporate several ingredients by careful and gentle turning with a spatula. Often used with beaten egg whites or whipped cream when mixing into the rest of the ingredients to keep the batter light.

JULIENNE To cut foods into long thin strips much like matchsticks. Used most often for salads and stir-fry dishes.

MINCE To cut into very fine pieces. Used often for garlic or fresh herbs.

PARBOIL To cook partially. Usually used in the case of chicken, sausages and vegetables.

PARTIALLY SET Describes the consistency of gelatin after it has been chilled for a short amount of time. Mixture should resemble the consistency of egg whites.

PUREE To process foods to a smooth mixture. Can be prepared in an electric blender, food processor, food mill or sieve.

SAUTE To fry quickly in a small amount of fat, stirring almost constantly. Most often done with onions, mushrooms and other chopped vegetables.

SCORE To cut slits partway through the outer surface of foods. Often used with ham or flank steak.

STIR-FRY To cook meats and/or vegetables with a constant stirring motion in a small amount of oil in a wok or skillet over high heat.

Alphabetical Index